MODERNIZATION

BY

PURVI NISHAD

LIST OF FIGURES

LIST OF TABLES

CONTENTS

MODERNIZATION STRESS DUE TO ATTITUDE AMONG COLLEGE STUDENTS

ABSTRACT

The present study aimed at determines the impact of attitude towards modernization on stress among college students: an interventional approach. Modernization improves the lives of people in many tangible ways wherein higher standards of life, freedom, security and social justice are accepted goals of modernization. Modernization has its good and bad effects on people. It leads to many problems such as stress, anxiety, crime and break up of family groups. The onset of modernization has caused a significant amount of burgeoning rise in anxiety and stress among people. Stress is usually been researched focusing on major life events that produce change. Modernization and globalization have brought significant changes in the Indian society. Thus, the present study was planned to asses and find out the attitude of college students towards modernization across gender, socio economic groups and socio cultural settings; to assess and find out the level and type of stress among college students across gender, socio economic groups and socio cultural settings; to evaluate the impact of modernization on stress among the selected sample; to implement the prepared intervention package to reduce stress among the selected sample and to assess the efficacy of the intervention package in combating stress among the selected sample in the age group of 17 to 21 year. Exploratory research design was adopted for the present study and survey method was used to collect the data from college students. A sample of 300 respondents from which 150 urban students and 150 rural students, wherein 75 boys (25 each from lower, middle and upper socio economic groups) and 75 girls (25 each from lower, middle and upper socio economic groups) were selected through stratified random sampling technique. The socio economic status (SES) of the sample was ascertained using Kuppuswamy (1962) revised version of (2014) by Gururaj and Maheshwaran, Student Stress Scale (Agrawal 2012) and Comprehensive Modernization Inventory (Ahluwalia and Kalia 1985). The result revealed that maximum percentage of respondents irrespective of their socio economic status and socio cultural setting possessed average to high level of modernization. Highly significant gender differences as well as socio cultural differences were noticed among respondents belonging to different socio cultural background and socio economic

status with regard to attitude towards modernization wherein girls were found to be more modern in their attitude as compared to their male counterparts and urban respondents possessed more modern attitude in comparison to the rural respondents. Majority of respondents showed higher level of stress. Significant socio cultural variance and socio economic differences were observed in almost all the dimensions of stress under study. Significantly positive correlation was seen between modernization and all aspects of stress. The developed intervention programe had a significant impact in reducing all types of stress experienced by the selected sample which proved the efficacy of the intervention.

Keywords: Socio economic status, stress, modernization, rural and urban.

Chapter-I

INTRODUCTION

Adolescence is a critical period when young people prepare themselves for their future lives as adults. In modern and developing countries there are huge investment in the cognitive training of adolescents, imparting knowledge and skills that are believed to be necessary to acquire. College is a time when adolescents encounter extreme stress due to societal and parental pressures. College students have to live up to the expectations laid down by the parents which might be the source of stress. Modernization has been identified as one of the reason for stress as one has to adopt an outlook befitting the modern era which at times might prove to be difficult to adopt.

Modernization is change which might involve positive aspects as well as negative aspects. Modernization is a process of socio-cultural revolution. Modernization is a transformational model of transforming traditional society to a modern society. The scientific and secular education act as an important means of modernization. It helps in the dispersal of modern values of equality, freedom and humanism. There is a difference between westernization and modernization. Westernization is personal, optional and outward and it has its influence on middle class and higher class people whereas modernization changes people's concepts, ideas, thoughts, social norms and values.

With the fast increasing execution of science and technology the traditional thinking and the old landmarks are being radically replaced by the new model with regard to political, social and economic ideologies and cultural aspirations among the different nations of the world. These new changes in society are known as modernization. People are not born modern but are made so by their life experiences. The word modernization does not imply any ideology or manoeuvre, but only emphasises a process of transition. In fact modernization is understood as a procedure which indicates the adoption of modern ways of life and values. Modernization is similar to any other social occurrence because it too has its effect and side effects. Modernization is a framework of our development and human achievement from where we started.

"Modernization is the evolution of a total society from a relatively rural way of life based on, limited technology, animate power, parochial and traditional outlook, relatively undifferentiated institutions and values, towards a preponderantly urban way of life based on inanimate source of power, highly differentiated institutions matched and highly developed scientific technology by segmented individual roles, and a cosmopolitan outlook which highlights efficiency and progress." **(Cowgill, 1974)**

In the present scenario, as the community is influenced by modernization and westernization, the path from adolescence to adulthood is endowed with stress. This is true, especially in the case of adolescents as they have to face greater stress in the form of parental expectations and highly competitive academic and job environments. **(Watode *et al.* 2016)**

Modernization leads to dispute in peoples mind. Modernization has also caused many changes in the context of human nature, their work and their personality. Modern person lives in a complex society. There have been continuous struggles and disputes in their life. Students of today face a lot of challenge with the changes in automation, social structure, values and materialistic needs which create a situation of continuous stress and struggle among the students.

Feelings of stress are a part of life. Few levels of stress can actually be good for students, as the right kind of stress stimulates them toward growth and change. Stress is obligatory to challenge students to learn. Approaches are needed that decrease the negative aspects of stress which lessen students' learning and performance. The key to decreasing stress is providing students with a feeling of control over their information, education about what to expect, feedback regarding what can be done to refine their performance and acceptance of modernization. However, when stress exists for an extended period of time, they can become a burden or even a health risk.

A significant source of stress in students undergoing modernization is the increase in socioeconomic inequity that accompanies modernization. Commonly speaking, the distribution of wealth becomes more unequal, resulting in marked societal stratification where previously such stratification was, if not absent, at least muted. Current studies point to the effects of such stratification on cultural consonance as a potent source of stress.

Stress arises when the combination of internal and external pressures exceeds the individual's resources to cope with their situation **(Williams, 1999).** Students are very likely to experience some or many stressors which may test their ability to cope: becoming more independent, adapting to a new environment, making new friends, balancing a heavy work load, and dealing with a myriad of other issues.

Undergoing change at a rapid momentum during the college life often leave the students stressed. Our society is undergoing a transitional phase wherein the people are challenged with many needs, problems and responsibilities which lead to emotional instability and stress among them. There are major stressors are financial, family, social, educational, marriage, separation, bereavement, personal setback and stress regarding heath of others. Undergoing change at a rapid pace during the college life often leave the students stressed, they may be trapped by anxiety, depression, irritability or headache. Stress is a matter which is hard to avoid. The term stress has not only become a part of our conversation but has become a public issue to attract widespread media attention. Stress is described as anxieties, burdens, worries and pressures laid on a person which starts affecting his day to day functioning.

Some researchers differentiate two types of stress: acute and chronic. An acute stress occurs as single events like a life transition or an uncharacteristic event. Examples would be a sickness, first date or getting into trouble in college. Chronic stress is recurring demands such as academic concerns, financial difficulties, or disability. Acute stressors can convert into chronic stressors, if they prevail for a longer time. Primarily these stressors are produced as a result of modernization and ones inability to adjust to it.

Students react to college life in a variety of ways. For few students, college is stressful because it is an immediate change from high school, separation from home financial conditions, academic stress etc. For others, it might be a pleasurable time where one is exposed to new friends and new culture. Although some stress is mandatory for personal growth to occur, the amount of stress can overwhelm a student and affect his ability to manage.

College is a stressful period for many young adults as they go through the process of adapting to new social and educational environments. College may be even more stressful for students who have the added efforts of learning different educational knowledge in addition to academic preparation. Some students, the frustrations and challenges of campus life appear to lead to severe emotional problems.

For many college students, moving away from the comforts of home and into an on-campus dorm or apartment contribute to stress. Social challenges also contribute to college stress. Students are also mindful of disagreements with colleagues, and few students feel pressure to engage with peers who can get in the way of school in social outings.

Young adults in college have a distinctive array of negative interactions or stressors **(Garrett, 2001).** Every student has had it or has it in one point in their college life. According to **Ross *et al.* (1999)**, there are many clarifications for increased stress levels in college students. First, students have to make meaningful adjustments to college life. Second, due to the pressure of studies, there is strain placed on interpersonal relationships. Third, changes in lifestyle and housing arrangements give to stress experienced by college students. This is because of all the human factors in the educational network, the main role is performed by the students and it is only through them that the critical education process takes place. Today's students face new educational challenges, calling for greater student effort. In addition, the community has clear needs and expectations for students to play different tasks, many of which are contradictory, ambiguous and unachievable in our society's current bureaucratic, socio-cultural and economic environments, creating massive stress on students.

Stress affects the academic performance of students and people's jobs as well. Students in their teens are the ones who are going through the transitional stage, which is an intermediate of childhood and adulthood. Stress is believed to be caused by the several problems that exist such as problems at college, family problems, financial problems and problems in their surroundings, which obstructs their work and/or study. Stress can explode psychological disturbances among students when they are grown up. These disturbances will cause stress to the students in the future if they are not overcome.

Stress that can have a profound impact on college students' well-being. It is critical to be able to recognize the signs and symptoms of too much stress such as physical symptoms: Recurring colds and minor illness, Increased frequency of headaches, Frequent muscle aches and/or tightness, Fatigue and emotional symptoms: Anger, Being more irritable, Increased levels of frustration or disorganized than usual, Increased difficulty in getting things done, Feelings of hopelessness in coping with life, Greater sense of persistent time pressure **(The University of Illinois at Chicago, 2006).**

Such feelings can be extremely hazardous as students may turn to unhealthy choices to cope including alcohol or drug abuse, or worse. What's more, as a individual becomes stressed more and more frequently, it could cause long term health issues, including high blood pressure, heart problems, skin problems and chronic pain. There is even some evidence that chronic stress may lead to diabetes in some people **(Collingwood, 2007).**

There arises a need to timely intervene and equip the college students with the knowledge and strategies which might be adopted to handle stressful situation as stress is an inevitable part of growing up. A step taken in this direction within time will prove beneficial in not only lowering stress levels but also curtailing the incidence of stress leading to depression and anxiety.

There are hundreds of ways to deal with stress. One of the best ways is to simply walk away from the task for a few moments to calm down and collect your thoughts. Steps should be taken to introduce Stress Management Education in the curriculum. With the help of parents, family, friends, and perhaps campus stress-management resources, many students will be able to keep their stress levels relatively under control or even prosper in the college setting. Relaxation techniques prove to be an extremely valuable tool in stress management. Most of the techniques like self-hypnosis, counseling, yoga, meditation and deep muscle relaxation work in a similar fashion. The practice of one of these techniques on a regular basis will prove beneficial to provide a wonderfully calming and relaxing feeling which has a lasting effect an young minds. A best coping strategic plan is one which shows healthy ways to prevent stress from increasing or strategic plan for reducing tension when the stress level builds up beyond a moderate level. Learning of strategies for stress management thus became important during this period as it can save the students from the pressure and strain exerted by continuous stress in their life. There also arises a need to minimize the stressors so that the students can explore their full potential.

Justification-

India being a developing country is going through a period of rapid change in which the traditional ways of life are being rapidly replaced by the modern outlook. Modernization improves the lives of people in many tangible ways wherein higher standards of life, freedom, security and social justice are accepted goals of modernization. Modernization has its good and bad effects on people. It leads to greater benefits of science and technology but on the other hand, modernization breaks up the social ties that bind the society and our culture. It leads to many problems such as stress, anxiety, crime and break up of family groups. The onset of modernization has caused a significant amount of burgeoning rise in anxiety and stress among people. Stress is usually been researched focusing on major life events that produce change. Modernization and globalization have brought significant changes in the Indian society. One of such life events is adapting to change that the college life brings in. For many college students, new educational environment, social pressures and parental expectations/ aspirations can lead to stress. Stress caused during student life can lead to higher amount of risk taking behavior as well as depression. **Hughes (2005)** remarked that stress contributes to anxiety, which in turn interferes with students academic performance. Students, during their college life are generally stressed over grades, relationships, rising cost of studying, life on campus, uncertainty about job prospects and parental pressures, which they find difficult to cope with. We live in a culture that is obsessed with target grades where constant comparison has become a mode of life. Students by and large are suffering in silence as they are not only expected to perform socially but also academically. There is an alarming need to focus on students well-being and help them to develop their capabilities by equipping them with stress coping strategies so that the issue can be timely addressed and the incidence of psychological problems like depression, anxiety and suicidal ideation can be handled. Thus the present study aimed to assess the impact of attitude towards modernization on stress among students and to implement an intervention package to reduce stress among college students. The study was hence conducted with the following objectives-

OBJECTIVES-

1. To assess and find out the attitude of college students towards modernization across gender, socio economic groups and socio cultural settings.
2. To assess and find out the level and type of stress among college students across gender, socio economic groups and socio cultural settings.
3. To evaluate the impact of modernization on stress among the selected sample.
4. To implement the prepared intervention package to reduce stress among the selected sample.

5. To assess the efficacy of the intervention package in combating stress among the selected sample.

Chapter -II

REVIEW OF LITERATURE

Chahal *et al.* (2002) conducted a study on psychosocial effect on attitude towards modernization among college going boys and girls. Total survey of 80 respondents was selected through stratified random techniques. Results revealed that girl and boy did not differ significantly in their attitude towards modernization. There was statistically no significant effect of intelligence of college respondents. The achievement motivation of boy respondents had no significant effect on their attitude towards modernization. Attitude of boy respondents towards modernization differ with various levels of socio-economic groups and intelligence. Socio-economic groups and achievement motivation had no effect on attitude towards modernization.

Pierceall and Keim (2007) studied the stress and coping strategies among college going respondents. The aim of the current study was to determine the level of stress perceived by college students. Perceived Stress Scale was used to collect data from two hundred twelve respondents. Results highlighted that 75 percent respondents had moderate level stress, 12 percent high level stress, and 13 percent had low level of stress. Female respondents were more stressed as compared to male respondents, there were no significant differences between nontraditional and traditional college going students. The most often used strategies to cope with stress included talking to friends and family members, exercising and leisure activities. Less advisable coping strategies were smoking, taking illegal drugs and drinking alcohol.

Goyal and Gupta (2009) investigated the impact of modernization on aggression level of college students. Fifty male and fifty female respondents, in the age range of 18-21 years formed the sample of the current study. Low level of positive relationship was found between attitude towards aggression levels and modernization of college students. Boys and girls did not differ significantly in their attitude towards aggression level and modernization. Result revealed that there exists no statistically significant difference in the attitude of males and female respondents towards modernization. The girl respondents had positive and statistically significant attitude towards modernization in the area of religion, politics and parent child relationship as compared to male respondents who had more positive attitude in the dimension of marriage and status of women.

Kai-Wen (2009) conducted a study on sources of stress among college going respondents in Taiwan. A self prepared questionnaire was used to collect the data for the current study. A total sample of two hundred thirty questionnaires was distributed among respondents, and two hundred one responses were obtained. Research concluded that male respondents felt higher level of stress from family factor as compared to females. College students in higher levels felt higher level of more stress from mental, physical, college, and emotional factors and respondents who take a student loan also feel higher level of stress from mental, physical, college, and emotional factors as compared to those who do not.

Menon (2010) investigated the effect of modernization on values of college students. The data was collected from one thousand undergraduate college students within the age range of 17-22 years in which (500 girls and 500 boys) from government, private, urban and rural degree colleges participated. Proportionate Random sampling methods was used for the data collection. One way ANOVA was used for the study along with Pearson's product moment correlation matrix. The findings showed a statistically significant positive association between modernization and values, and among undergraduate students, a statistically significant impact of modernization on values was observed.

Marks (2010) studied a cross sectional study on finding modernization, meritocracy and students' occupational expectations among students. Research highlighted the socioeconomic background, effects of ability (measured by test scores) and gender on the level of socioeconomic group of students expected occupation at age thirty of approximately one lakh seventy thousand, 15-year respondents in thirty countries. The impact of ability relative to socioeconomic status was stronger in more economically developed communities. The impact of both socioeconomic background and ability were partially mediated by national academic systems. Ability also had a powerful influence on between-school differences in students' occupational expectations and negatively on 'not having an expected occupation'. A strong category of the meritocracy thesis was not justified by the albeit often small, effects of socioeconomic background and significant on students' occupational expectations seen in most of the countries in the world.

Abdulghani *et al.* (2011) conducted a study on stress and its effect on medical students: a Cross-sectional study at a medical college in Saudi Arabia. This cross-sectional study was conducted to find the extent of stress among medical students and to see the association between stress levels and their academic achievement as well as their stress. All the students from 1-5 year from University were taken for the study. K10 i.e. Kessler10 psychological distress inventory, was to measure the stress level among the respondents. The extent of stress was measured and compared with variables, such as gender, academic year, academic grades, regularity to course attendance, and perceived physical problems. Eighty seven percent sample respondents to the study (n=892). The total extent of stress was 63 percent, and the prevalence of severe stress was 25 percent. The extent of stress levels was higher among females (75.7 percent) than male their counterparts (57 percent). The stress level significantly reduced as the year of study rise, except for the final year student. The extent of stress level was higher during the preparatory 3 years of study and among the female respondents. Physical problems were related with high level of stresses. It was concluded that preventive mental health services, could be made an important part of routine clinical services for medical students, particularly in the initial educational years, to prevent stress.

Malini (2011) reviewed Modernization of English Language Teaching. The dimensions like free practice, modernized approaches, restricted practice, and conventional teaching. These perspectives of communicative teaching had their relevance to English Language in today's time. Teaching practices which paves a new way to solve the drawbacks of conventional and restricted teaching methods. Besides, the introduction of more student focused teaching method with few modernized beliefs such as free practice of class room conversation, student friendly approach and regulator like work of the teacher were all the necessary advancement in the field. Result showed that the stress should be laid on the modernization of communicative teaching method.

Ji and Zhang (2011) carried out a study on stress and coping strategies and investigated the mental stresses of students and discussed 04 sources of stresses. The questionnaire contained 20 questions in four areas: employment situations, study conditions, personal factors and economic conditions. The samples sizes were eight hundred students. Results found a remarkable positive correlation between mental stresses of students, employment situations and a positive correlation between mental stresses and study conditions. Though, there was a positive correlation between mental stresses, personal factors and economic conditions respectively, the differences were eminent for students.

Chawla and Kang (2012) studied the attitude towards modernization among males and females. The sample comprised of sixty adults (thirty females and thirty males) within the age of 35-45 years belonging to middle socio economic group from Ludhiana city in Punjab. The data from the sample was collected using the socio-economic status scale developed by **Bhardwaj (2001)** and the Comprehensive Modernization Inventory (CMI) developed by **Ahluwalia and Kalia (1981).** t-test was used to examine the attitude of females and males towards modernization in their city. Results revealed a significant difference in males and females with regard to their attitude towards modernization. Male respondents were more predisposed towards status of women, marriage and politics while female respondents possessed a more modern perspective towards education. Females and males respondents did not differ significantly in their attitude towards religion, socio-culture factor and parent-child relationship.

Bhat and Naseem (2012) conducted a study on modernization among higher secondary students in relation to subject choice and sex. In this research study, the sample was collected through stratified random sampling technique. A total of eighty students from various schools were selected. Data was collected through Modernization Scale developed by **Singh *et al.* (1979).** Results found that the boy students differ significantly from girl students on the total modernization. The girls from Science and Arts stream did not differ significantly on the total modernization. Similarly, the boys from Science and Arts stream did not differ significantly on the scores of total scores of modernization. The Science and Arts stream students did not differ significantly on the total scores of modernization. The female and male higher secondary students of Arts differ significantly on the total scores of modernization. The female and male higher secondary students from Science stream differ significantly on the total scores of modernization.

Mazumdar *et al.* (2012) carried a comparative study on stress and its factors among the under-graduate and post-graduate college going students. Total 250 students were selected for this research survey. From the total sample, 100 students were male and 150 students were female.

For the survey, questionnaire set were used with two parts. Part one was related to various symptoms and Part two measured level of stress in student's life in colleges. Out of two hundred fifty respondents, 60 percent female respondents were prone to the given symptoms whereas 40 percent male respondents were prone to these stress related symptoms. In government colleges, under-graduate and post-graduate included 20 percent and 8 percent male respondents respectively whereas graduate and post-graduate comprised of 8 percent and 15 percent of female respondents respectively. Out of two hundred fifty respondents private college graduate comprised 15 percent and 12 percent of male respondents and female respondents respectively.

Singh (2012) studied the impact of parental education on Ranchi students' modernity. The aim of the study was to determine the influence of parental education on the modernity of the college respondents selected. Total 120 students were included in the research study samples. There were 2 groups of college students, the first group of sixty college students was the son of highly educated parents, and the second group of sixty students was the son of illiterate parents. The age of the students was 19 to 25 years. Attitudinal Modernity Scale and Information Questionnaire were used. The result revealed that 1st group were more modern because their parents and as they both were highly educated.

Mahmoudi (2012) conducted a study on modernization and environmental awareness among adolescent students. This study was aimed to find out the effect of modernization and the environmental awareness among students. A total sample of two hundred adolescent students of high school from 3 private school and 3 governments and were selected. t-test was used for analysis of data. The result showed that the sensitivity of both private and government school students was almost the same for the climate, but the average score of adolescents in private school was more than the adolescents in government school for modernization, symbolising that private school students were more modern in their approach than their counterparts.

Waghachavare ***et al.*** **(2013)** examined stress among professional college students from an Indian urban area. The objective of the current present was to find out the stress among students of different professional colleges and its consistency with various social, health-related factors and academic. Cross-sectional study was conducted among students of engineering, dental and medical colleges from the urban area. The total sample size was twelve hundred. A self-prepared questionnaire was used for the data collection. Out of the 1,224 samples, two hundred ninty-nine (24.4 percent) experienced stress. Among them eighty two (27.4 percent), one hundred two (34.1 percent) and one hundred fifteen (38.5 percent) were engineering, medical and dental students, respectively. There was significant association between education and stress. Stress was assessed in one hundred twelve (20.4 percent) males and one eighty seven (27.7 percent) females. By applying binary logistic regression, academic factors, health medical studies, and lifestyle factors were the statistically significant medium for stress.

Kumar and Bhukar (2013) investigated the level of stress and coping strategies of students belonging to Engineering professions and Physical Education. Total sample of sixty respondents was randomly selected from the Engineering Institute and Physical Education. Each profession group had thirty respondents (fifteen females and fifteen males) in age group of 21 to 23 years. Stress scores due to: 1) compulsive, 2) overload and 3) frustration and inhibition, aggressive behavior and time-urgent were measured for the selected respondents using the questionnaire. Two way ANOVA showed that stress was statistically significantly higher among females in comparison to males. Coping strategy was higher in males as compared to females of their respective profession, but Physical Education females had higher coping strategy than males and females of Engineering. Thus, it was concluded that Physical Education college students had better coping strategy in comparison to the Engineering college going girls and boys.

Malik *et al.* (2013) researched in order to find out the attitude of graduate students towards modernization. Total populations of two hundred graduate college respondents (hundred girls and hundred boys) were selected by using simple random sampling from different colleges. The Modernization Scale by **Singh *et al.* (1979)** was used to find out modernization among respondents. Results revealed that selection of stream had no impact whereas gender affected the attitude of graduate college students towards modernization.

Patel (2013) conducted a study on attitude of adolescent students towards modernization in relation to certain variables. Descriptive-survey Method was used for the study. The total research sample was 3357 students. Socio economic status scale by Dr. Pallavi Ben and Self prepared modernization attitude scale and Patel was used. The result indicated that the urban respondents have high modernization attitude as compared to rural respondents. The male respondents of urban area have high level of modernization attitude than rural area. Female respondents of urban have high level of modernization attitude than rural area. The female adolescent respondents of urban area have high level of modernization attitude than male adolescent respondents. Upper socio economic status respondents have high level of modernization attitude than respondents of middle socio economic status and low socio economic status.

Peerzada (2013) examined the modernization of female and male school going students. Total sample consisted sixty higher secondary school going students i.e. thirty girls and thirty boys students. Modernization Scale developed by **Singh *et al.* (1979)** was used for study. Results revealed that boy respondents have significantly higher mean scores as compared to female students in terms of modernization. Males have more freedom in employment, politics and marriage than females.

Yazawa ***et al.* (2013)** investigated the impact of lifestyle changes on stress in a modernizing rural population of China. EBV antibody titer was measured in dried blood spot samples collected from two hundred forty adults living in rural society of Hainan Island. Measures of two major lifestyle changes in rural communities i.e., commercial goods possession and diet, were scrutinized by using information on the weekly frequency of pork consumption and monthly mobile phone fees. Both parameters were standardized to create 2 composite scores: an investment tendency index and a total affluence index. Least-squares regression analysis was used to find out the association between EBV antibody titer and its lifestyle parameters. A positive association was found between EBV antibody titer and frequency of pork consumption while a negative association was found between EBV antibody titer and mobile phone fees. A negative association was also seen between EBV antibody titer and ITI. Psychological stress among local resident respondents was linked to the manner of lifestyle changes they had experienced, where acquiring a more irrespective of current affluence, market-oriented lifestyle, was correlated with less psychological stress.

Kumar and Mittal (2014) studied the modernization, aggression and religious attitude, modernization of college students and its effect on their academic performance. Normative survey method was used for the current study. Aggression Scale by **Ojha (1990)** and

Comprehensive Modernization Inventory, Attitude Scale towards Religion by **Ahluwalia & Kalia (1985)** were used. Total sample of two hundred respondents (hundred muslin and hundred hindu) were selected. Random sampling technique was used for collecting data. The Modernisation, violence and religious attitude of Muslim and Hindu respondents were found to differ significantly. Muslim boys and girls do not vary in their academic achievement, whereas Hindu women and men have been found to differ substantially in their academic achievement. It was seen that significant positive correlation existed between academic performance and modernization of respondents. Academic achievement of Hindu college going students was found to be correlated with modernization and religious attitude.

Patnam and Bangale (2014) investigated the academic stress among graduate students and its influencing factors. Total sample of two hundred graduate college going students in the age group of 18 to 23 years of 5 colleges of Maharashtra State comprised the sample. The data was collected by personally interviewing the sample respondents based on open ended interview schedule and by the Socio-Economic Status Scale and Battery of Academic Stress Scale (BASS). Ninety percent of the respondents rated to have high level of academic stress followed by average level of academic stress. Socio economic group of both boys and girls respondents and inter personal relations maintained by girl respondents with neighbors, teachers and peers seemed to have significant negative correlation with their academic stress. Academic frustration was significantly higher in male respondents as compared to female respondents. The parenting practices and types of family adopted for the college going male students also had significant negative correlation with their academic stress.

Kaur (2014) conducted a study on impact of modernization on level of aggression among college students. In the current study random sampling technique was used, a total sample of two hundred students (hundred females and hundred males) belonging to high school were selected. The Aggression scale developed by **Pal and Tasneem (1971)** and Modernization Scale developed by **Singh *et al.* (1979)** were used. The result revealed that modernization does not differ among male and female respondents. In females, modernization is high but not much as compared to males. This may be due to some reason; first, today technology is very vast and rapidly changing. Second, their life style and way of thinking is same about to modernization. Both boys and girls adopt modern living styles. Third, in modern days facilities regarding daily living and education are adequately same as compared to traditional times. There exists negative impact of modernization on level of aggression among samples. The result revealed that modernization creates aggression among college going males and females.

Menhas (2014) studied the impact of modernization on Pakistani women and examined the impact of modernization regarding their lifestyle. The total sample of 100 females was selected through convenience sampling method. Self prepared questionnaire was used for the data collection. Results revealed that maximum of the respondents i.e. 42 percent prefer arrange marriage; maximum of the respondents i.e. 42 percent wear jeans and 50 percent respondents stated that vulgarity is prevailing among females in the society.

Akande *et al.* (2014) investigated the sources and level of stress among school going students. Descriptive survey was used. Samples of eighteen secondary schools out of the fifty nine public senior secondary schools were selected for the survey with a total of five hundred forty male and female respondents. Self-prepared questionnaire was designed for data collect. The results showed that secondary school respondents had a average level of stress and significant sources of stress included environmental, academic and intra-personal. A significant gender difference in the stress level and also some sources of stress among selected respondents was observed.

Kaur (2015) conducted a study on the modernisation of gender among young boys and girls. The purpose of the study was the comparison among respondents of the magnitude of modernisation. Total sample of 200 boys and girls of intermediate class compressed the sample for the study. It was seen that the girls had high level of modernization as compared to male students. Out of seven dimensions of modernization, mean score difference was seen to be significant in four dimensions i.e., politics, parent child relation, religion and marriage. Females mean scores were higher than males which indicated that females were more modern than their male counterparts.

Singal (2015) investigated the effect of modernization on value pattern of college going boys and girls. The current study aimed to assess and compare the modernization with value pattern of college going students. Total hundred respondents were selected from different schools of Bathinda district. The data was divided into female/male and urban/rural. The Value-Pattern Scale developed by **Ojha (1977)** and modernization scale developed by **Singh *et al.* (1979)** were used. The statistical analysis was meanly based on average, standard deviation and t-test. There was no noticeable difference between adolescent college going girls and boys on the variable of values and modernization.

Dhillon and Moga (2015) conducted a modernization research on youth issues. The research aimed at exploring young people's issues with respect to modernisation. There were selected a total of two hundred Punjab high school students. Comprehensive Modernization Inventory developed by **Ahluwalia & Kalia (1985)** and Youth Problem Inventory developed by **Sharma (1986)** was used. Results revealed no significant difference in the mean scores of youth problems of selected respondents. The girls and boys respondents had the similar means on their personal problems. The mean scores of girl respondents in case of socio emotional, educational problems and family were more than boys which was found to be statistically non significant. Results also showed that there was no major difference between the average scores of rural and urban respondents. There was also no substantial difference in family and personal issues among interviewees belonging to modern and low modernised categories. Significant difference was seen between the two groups with reference to educational and socio-emotional problems. High modernized category had high educational and socio-emotional problems as compared to the low modernized category respondents.

Singh and Singh (2015) conducted a study of modernity behaviour of university going students in relation to activism and altruism. Total sample of one hundred eighty university going students was selected through stratified random sampling methods. The Self-Report Altruism Scale developed by **Rushton *et al.* (1981)**, Sharma Student Activism Scale developed by **Sharma (1988)** and Attitudinal Modernity Scale by **Sharma (1979)** were used for the study. Descriptive research method was used. The results revealed non-significant gender differences were seen as well as the modernity behavior among university going students did not seem to relate to altruism.

Dhull and Kumari (2015) examined the academic stress among adolescent boys and girls. The sample of the current study consisted of high school students. Four public schools were taken randomly and from each public school about fifty three samples were also selected. Stress inventory for school students developed by **Rani and Singh (2012)** was used. Results of the current study showed that, there was significant difference between academic stress of boys and girls respondents. Female respondents were found to have more academic stress as compared to the male respondents.

Kaur (2015) investigated the relationship between attitude of boys and girls towards modernization in relation to emotional maturity and intelligence. The total population comprised of two hundred respondents from Hoshiarpur district which were selected randomly. The sample consists of both boys and girls respondents studying in private and government schools. Comprehensive modernization inventory developed by **Ahulwalia & Kalia (1971),** Group test of intelligence test developed by **Jalota (2010)** and Emotional maturity scale developed by **Singh & Bhargava (2010)** were used for current study. The outcome revealed a substantial correlation between respondents' attitude to intellect and modernization, and no significant correlation was found between respondents' attitude to emotional maturity and modernization. There was no substantial difference in the attitude of respondents towards gender-based modernization. Significant difference existed in the attitude of respondents towards modernization among those studying in private and government schools.

Gupta *et al.* (2015) investigated the factors causing stress among medical college students and also find out the reliability of MSSQ-40 (Medical Students' Stressor Questionnaire). The overall stress was ninety one percent and majority of respondents were stressed because of academic performance. High level of academic stress level was found among respondents who were not conversant with resided in a hostels, experienced a change in medium of teaching from elementary school to medical school and the local area language. Early screening and remedying stressors was found to assist in mental health and building physical in students.

Kumar and Rout (2015) carried out a study on the attitude of Muslim society towards modernization of madarasa education and to compare the attitude of various groups such as parents, maulavis, students of the Muslim community and teachers towards Modernization of Madarasa Education. Total two hundred fifty populations from the Muslim community were selected. Equal numbers of students, teachers, maulavis and parents, teachers were selected. Self prepared 5-point attitude scale was used. Results indicated that various groups of the Muslim society vary in their attitude and Muslim society has high positive attitude towards modernization of Madarasa education yet the difference was not significant.

Jain and Garg (2015) conducted a study on attitude of post-graduate students towards modernization. Total sample of hundred respondents including fifty females and fifty males were selected for the study by using simple random sampling technique. Respondents from urban socio cultural settings were significantly higher in attitude towards modernization as compared to respondents from rural socio cultural settings. Modernization scale developed by **Singh *et al.* (1979)** was used. Statistical tools such as Mean, Standard Deviation and t-test were used for data analysis. Research revealed that no significant difference between post graduate girls and boys in relation to modernization.

Devi and Mohan (2015) conducted a study on stress and its effects on college going students in between the age category of 18 to 21 years. Sample comprised of 200 students. Convenience sampling techniques was used for collection of data. Result showed that the major reasons of stress were family factors, academic factors, emotional factors, social factors, financial factors and emotional factors.

Ahmad and Jan (2016) studied on the level of modernization and social awareness college going boys and girls. The total sample compromised of hundred college going boys and girls. Modernization scale prepared by **Singh *et al.* (1979)** and social awareness scale prepared by Nadeem Ijalal were used for data collection and for statistical analysis 't' test was used. The results indicated that boy and girl respondents did not differ significantly on the levels of modernization as well as social awareness.

Sharma (2016) investigated the stress level of among the college going boys and girls. The goal of the current study was to determine the level of stress among respondents and to evaluate the level of physical stress, pressure, anger and anxiety among the samples selected. Descriptive research method was used. The total sample size of two hundred fourteen respondents in the age range of 19 to 22 years was selected. Stress Scale prepared by Lakshmi and Narain was used. Result highlighted that maximum respondents had average level of stress.

Rathour and Kang (2016*)* *investigated the profile and attitude of male and female students towards various dimensions of modernization and also compared the modernization of students in aspect of locale and gender. Total sample of four hundred students was selected from government colleges in rural and urban cultural settings were selected for the study. Comprehensive Modernization Inventory prepared by* ***Ahluwalia and Kalia (1985)* *was used for measuring the attitude towards modernization. Result highlighted a significant difference college boys and girls which showed that college respondents vary in their level of modernization. Boys had high level of modernization than the girl. The results also indicated significant difference of modernization among urban and rural respondents which highlighted that urban and rural respondents vary in their level of modernization.*

Watode *et al.* (2016) examined the prevalence of stress among school students. Cross-sectional survey method was used for the study. Simple random sampling technique was used. A self-prepared questionnaire was used. Percentage and chi-square test was used to analyse the data. Among the out of total sample of three hundred ninety seven respondents of the study, three hundred forty eighty respondents were high level of stress. Stress was seen in one hundred thirty nine girl and two hundred nine male respondents thus, the association with gender was not significant. Association between stress and education of parents was not seen. Academics, Parents, academics, friends and teachers were facing high level of stress. School going boys and girls were exposed to stress. Girls were at higher risk as compared to boys. Introduction of stress management techniques in academic curriculum could be helpful in lowering stress of among students.

Shameem (2017) studied the attitude towards modernization of college girls belonging to urban and rural cultural settings. The sample comprised of fifty college females (twenty five urban and twenty five rural) randomly selected from towns and villages. Result highlighted that the mean scores of rural girl respondents on attitude towards modernization was one hundred fourteen which was comparatively a low number on the scale. Result also explained that urban and rural cultural setting had a significant impact on the attitude of college going females towards modernization.

Sagar and Singh (2017) concluded a research on academic stress level among higher secondary school students. Descriptive research technique and stratified random sampling methods was used. Total sample size of one hundred eighty respondents was selected from ten higher secondary schools. The sample was collected though self prepared Academic Stress Scale. t-test and analysis of variance were used as statistically tools. Result showed a high significant difference between the academic stress level of girl and boy respondents of higher secondary school students as well as no significant difference existed among academic stress of commerce, science and arts stream respondents. Result found that there was no significant difference between urban and rural socio cultural setting students, self finance school going respondents and academic stress of government aided.

Gupta (2017) *analyzed the* attitude of under-graduate students of towards modernization in which a total sample of four hundred students from different eight colleges, were selected randomly. The purpose of research was to study gender difference in the attitude towards modernization and also to compare of attitude of family type wise, student's stream wise (arts and science) and region wise. Statistical tools such as mean, standard deviation (SD) and t test were used for the study. Results revealed that there was difference in attitude of college going boys and girl respondents, urban and rural socio cultural setting respondents, arts and science under-graduates and graduates of nuclear and joint family. It was also found that no significant difference in the attitude of college going boys and girls of nuclear family as well as joint family.

Ninaniya *et al.* (2017) conducted a study on attitude of college going adolescent boys and girls towards modernization. A total number of two hundred respondents between the age ranges of 16 to17 years were selected for the study. Comprehensive Modernization Inventory designed by **Ahluwalia and Kalia (1998)** was used to find out the attitude of respondents towards modernization. The results highlighted that urban adolescents had favourable attitudes on parent child relationship, education, the status of women and politics dimensions of modernization towards compared to their rural counterparts. It was also seen that urban adolescents were more positive towards parent child relationship, education and status of women as compared to rural adolescents.

Shaikh ***et al.*** **(2018)** conducted a study on stress, stressors, anxiety and depression among rural students. Total four hundred sixty one respondents were selected from the rural cultural setting of Nanded district, Maharashtra. A self constructed stress scale-21 and Marathi depression anxiety questionnaire including correlated factors to find out the magnitude of stress, anxiety and depression and its stressors was administered to the sample. The prevalence of stress, anxiety and depression among the selected respondents was 54 percent, 60 percent, and 44 percent, respectively. Rural respondents reported the significantly higher levels of stress than the respondents studying in the rural setting. Tobacco use, harsh parenting, disturbed family, negative feeling about academic performance and past adverse event experiences were found to be significantly associated with higher level of stress. Results highlighted that the mental health status of the respondents was alarming which requested prompt measures.

Camille ***et al.*****, (2019)** studied the level of stress among school going adolescents. Class 12th students were selected to respond to questionnaires in rating scale survey form. Results highlighted that there was no significant difference in stress between gender, attitude and the skills of school going students. As well as, there was no significant difference in stress level when 12th class was classified according to strand by performance or skill, attitude and content. With regards to content, attitude and financial status was seen to be significant among respondents and skills or performance had no significant relation with the financial status of the respondents.

Mehmet ***et al.*****, (2019)** examined the predictors of academic level of stress among college going adolescents. The aim of the current study was to assess the factors predictive of college respondents' academic stress level. Total sample of 307 graduate college adolescents comprising of 128 girls were actively innovated in this research. Results revealed that girl respondents had higher level of academic stress as compare to boys. For statistical analysis, correlations and multiple regression analyses were used which revealed that, locus of control, gender and life satisfaction were positively significant predictors of academic stress among the respondents.

Chapter-III

MATERIALS AND METHODS

Research involves formulating the problem to be investigated, selecting a suitable research design, applying appropriate procedures for data collection, finding the results and presenting them through a written report. The purpose of this chapter is to

- Describe the research methodology used for the present study,
- Explain the sample selection,
- Describe the procedure used in collecting the data, and
- Provide an explanation of the statistical procedure used to analyze the data.

The methodology followed during the course of the present study is discussed under the following sections

3.1 Research design

3.2 Sampling procedure

  3.2.1 Locale of the study

  3.2.2 Selection of sample

  3.2.3 Sample distribution

3.3 Variables

3.4 Tools and Tests

3.5 Data collection

3.6 Statistical procedures

3.1 Research Design

An action research design was followed to conduct the present study. Action research design involves a research initiated to solve an immediate problem by collecting information and outcomes, analyzing the information, developing a plan to improve it, collecting changes after a new plan is implemented and developing conclusions regarding the improvements.

Survey method was used for the present study and Questionnaires were used to gather information from the respondents. Surveys are a method of gathering information from individuals which are conducted to gather information through a printed questionnaire or interviews in some structured format. Standardized procedures were used wherein every participant was asked the same questions in the same way.

3.2 Sampling procedure

3.2.1 Locale of the study-

The state of Uttar Pradesh was purposively selected for the study owing to its large population. The Prayagraj (Allahabad) district of Uttar Pradesh was systematically randomly selected for the study. Systematic random sampling method was also followed for the selection of Blocks, Villages, Wards, and Primary Sampling Units (PSUs) from Prayagraj (Allahabad) district.

Systematic random sampling is the sampling method that required selecting samples based on a system of intervals in a numbered population. This type of sampling ensures that all outcomes are given equal chance of getting selected in the sample. One tehsil was covered from the selected district and two blocks were selected from the identified tehsil.

Prayagraj (Allahabad) has been divided into several blocks within Tehsils. There are 20 blocks under eight Tehsils namely- Bara, Handia, Karchana, Koraon, Meja, Phulpur, Sadar and Soraon. Allahabad has three major suburbs namely Jhusi, Naini and Phaphamau. Karchana Tehsil was purposively selected for the present study to comprise the rural cultural setting. Karchana is in the central part of Allahabad district and is situated 21 km south of Allahabad, the district headquarters.

Table 3.1 Sampling procedure for the selection of District, Blocks, Villages, Wards, PSUs

Level		Name	No	Sampling Methods
State		Uttar Pradesh	01	Purposive Sampling
District		Prayagraj	01	Systematic Random Sampling
Rural	**Blocks**	Karchana	01	Systematic Random Sampling
	Villages	1. Bendo 2. Lohari 3. Sonai	03	Systematic Random Sampling
Urban	**Wards**	18, 37, 40, 55, & 63, 71	06	Systematic Random Sampling
	PSUs	Baghambari (ward 18) Katra (ward 37) Mutthiganj part-1(ward 40) Medical College Area(ward55) Karela Bagh (ward 63) Beniganj (ward 71)		Systematic Random Sampling

Selection of District

The demographics of Uttar Pradesh are a complex topic, which is undergoing dynamic change. Uttar Pradesh is India's most populous state. Uttar Pradesh is divided into 75 districts in which purposively one district was selected. Prayagraj (Allahabad) district was purposively selected to carry out the present research on the basis of population, sex-ration and literacy rate because as of the 2011 census, Prayagraj (Allahabad) is the most populous district of Uttar

Pradesh and also Prayagraj's (Allahabad) educational system is distinct from Uttar Pradesh's other cities, with an emphasis on broad education.

Table 3.2 District-wise distribution of population, sex-ration and literacy rate

District	Population	Sex Ratio	Literacy Rate	District	Population	Sex Ratio	Literacy Rate
Agra	4,418,797	868	71.58%	Kannauj	1,656,616	879	72.70%
Aligarh	3,673,889	882	67.51%	Kanpur Dehat	1,796,184	865	75.78%
Allahabad	**5,954,391**	**901**	**72.32%**	Kanpur Nagar	4,581,268	862	79.65%
Ambedkar Nagar	2,397,888	978	72.23%	Kanshiram Nagar	1,436,719	880	61.02%
Auraiya	1,379,545	864	78.95%	Kaushambi	1,599,596	908	61.28%
Azamgarh	4,613,913	1,019	70.93%	Kheri	4,021,243	894	60.56%
Baghpat	1,303,048	861	72.01%	Kushinagar	3,564,544	961	65.25%
Bahraich	3,487,731	892	49.36%	Lalitpur	1,221,592	906	63.52%
Ballia	3,239,774	937	70.94%	Lucknow	4,589,838	917	77.29%
Balrampur	2,148,665	928	49.51%	Mahamaya Nagar	1,564,708	871	71.59%
Banda	1,799,410	863	66.67%	Mahoba	875,958	878	65.27%
Bara Banki	3,260,699	910	61.75%	Mahrajganj	2,684,703	943	62.76%
Bareilly	4,448,359	887	58.49%	Mainpuri	1,868,529	881	75.99%
Basti	2,464,464	963	67.22%	Mathura	2,547,184	863	70.36%
Bijnor	3,682,713	917	68.48%	Mau	2,205,968	979	73.09%
Budaun	3,681,896	871	51.29%	Meerut	3,443,689	886	72.84%
Bulandshahr	3,499,171	896	68.88%	Mirzapur	2,496,970	903	68.48%
Chandauli	1,952,756	918	71.48%	Moradabad	4,772,006	906	56.77%
Chitrakoot	991,730	879	65.05%	Muzaffarnagar	4,143,512	889	69.12%
Deoria	3,100,946	1,017	71.13%	Pilibhit	2,031,007	895	61.47%
Etah	1,774,480	873	70.81%	Pratapgarh	3,209,141	998	70.09%
Etawah	1,581,810	870	78.41%	Rae Bareli	3,405,559	943	67.25%
Faizabad	2,470,996	962	68.73%	Rampur	2,335,819	909	53.34%
Farrukhabad	1,885,204	874	69.04%	Saharanpur	3,466,382	890	70.49%
Fatehpur	2,632,733	901	67.43%	Sant Kabir Nagar	1,715,183	972	66.72%
Firozabad	2,498,156	875	71.92%	Sant Ravidas Nagar	1,578,213	955	68.97%
Gautam B. Nagar	1,648,115	851	80.12%	Shahjahanpur	3,006,538	872	59.54%
Ghaziabad	4,681,645	881	78.07%	Shrawasti	1,117,361	881	46.74%
Ghazipur	3,620,268	952	71.78%	Siddharthnagar	2,559,297	976	59.25%
Gonda	3,433,919	921	58.71%	Sitapur	4,483,992	888	61.12%
Gorakhpur	4,440,895	950	70.83%	Sonbhadra	1,862,559	918	64.03%
Hamirpur	1,104,285	861	68.77%	Sultanpur	3,797,117	983	69.27%
Hardoi	4,092,845	868	64.57%	Unnao	3,108,367	907	66.37%
Jalaun	1,689,974	865	73.75%	Varanasi	3,676,841	913	75.60%
Jaunpur	4,494,204	1,024	74%				
Jhansi	1,998,603	890	75.05%				
Jyotiba Phule Nagar	1,840,221	910	63.84%				
Gorakhpur	4,440,895	950	70.83%				
Hamirpur	1,104,285	861	68.77%				

*As of the 2011 census

Selection of Blocks

Prayagraj (Allahabad) district was divided broadly into two clusters- the Trans Ganga region and the Trans Yamuna region. Trans Ganga comprises of 11 blocks and Trans Yamuna comprise of nine blocks. The researcher selected one block from Trans Yamuna region through systematic random sampling method. The Trans Yamuna region comprised of Karchana, Chaka, Meja, Jasra, Uruwan, Kaudhiyara, Manda, Koraon and Shankargarh blocks. Karchana block was selected from the Trans Yamuna region through systematic random sampling method.

Selection of Villages

Three villages each were selected from the identified block through systematic random sampling. The villages Bendo, Lohari and Sonai were selected from Karchana block.

Selection of Wards and Primary Sampling Units (PSUs)

For the selection of wards, Prayagraj (Allahabad) district was divided into two zones- The Northern Prayagraj Junction and the Southern Prayagraj Junction. A total of six wards were selected from both the zones through systematic random sampling to identify the urban college going students for the study. The six wards selected were ward no. 18, 37, 40, 55, 63 and 71. From each of these wards one PSU was selected through systematic random sampling. A total six PSUs were selected for the study. The PSUs selected were Baghambari, Katra, Mutthiganj, Medical College Area, Karela Bagh and Beniganj.

Table 3.3 Selected Blocks, Villages, Wards and PSUs of Prayagraj (Allahabad) district

State Uttar Pradesh		
District Prayagraj (Allahabad)		
Rural	**Urban**	
Trans Yamuna Region	Northern Prayagraj Junction	Southern Prayagraj Junction
Block Karchana	Wards 18, 37, 40	Wards 55, 63, 71
Villages Bendo Lohari Sonai	**PSUs** Baghambari Katra Mutthiganj	**PSUs** Medical College Area Karela Bagh Beniganj

3.2.2 Selection of sample- A total of 300 respondents from three socio-economic classes (lower, middle and upper socio-economic groups) in the age group of 17-21 years belonging to rural and urban cultural backgrounds were selected from different colleges in the selected areas of Allahabad District through stratified random sampling techniques. Stratified random sampling is a method when there are different subgroups in the population. Stratified random sampling divides a population into subgroups, and random samples are taken, in proportion to the population, from each of the strata created.

3.2.3 Sample distribution- For the current analysis, a total of 300 samples were chosen, consisting of 150 students from rural cultural backgrounds and 150 students from urban cultural backgrounds. The 150 college students from rural as well as urban cultural background were further divided into 75 boys and 75 girls from each group, (25 each from the lower, middle and upper socio-economic categories) were selected from different colleges in the Prayagraj District using stratified random sampling methods namely-

- University of Allahabad (Science Faculty), Katra, Prayagraj city
- Arya Kanya Degree College, Mutthiganj, Prayagraj city
- Divyabha Girls Degree College, Baghambari, Prayagraj city
- Thakur Har Narayan Singh Degree College, Karela Bagh, Prayagraj city
- Kulbhashkar Ashram Degree College, Medical College area, Prayagraj city
- Allahabad Degree College (Law Faculty), Beniganj, Prayagraj city
- Sardar Patel Degree College, Sonai, Karchana
- Kalawati Shikshan Sansthan (BTC College), Sonai, Karchhana
- Srimati Jayapatti Smarak Mahavir Degree College, Lohari, Karchhana
- Prayag Institute of Technology & Management, Bendo, Karchhana
- Shivaji Polytechnic, Bendo, Karchhana

Table 3.4 Sample collections from Urban Cultural Setting

Sr No.	Name of Colleges	Socio Economic Status					
		Boys			Girls		
		LSES	MSES	USES	LSES	MSES	USES
1.	Arya Kanya Degree College	-	-	-	4	4	5
2.	Thakur Har Narayan Singh Degree College	7	6	7	4	5	4
3.	Divyabha Girls Degree College	-	-	-	6	4	5
4.	Kulbhashkar Ashram Degree College	6	7	6	4	4	3
5.	Allahabad University (Science Faculty)	6	7	6	5	3	3
6.	Allahabad Degree College (Law Faculty)	6	5	6	2	5	5
Total		25	25	25	25	25	25

Table 3.5 Sample collections from Rural Cultural Setting

Sr No.	Name of Colleges	Socio Economic Status					
		Boys			Girls		
		LSES	MSES	USES	LSES	MSES	USES
1.	Sardar Patel Degree College, Sonai	4	5	6	5	5	6
2.	Kalawati Shikshan Sansthan (BTC College), Sonai	6	3	5	4	4	5
3.	Srimati Jayapatti Smarak Mahavir Degree College, Lohari	5	7	5	6	6	4
4.	Prayag Institute of	4	2	4	5	5	8

	Technology& Management, Bendo						
5.	Shivaji Polytechnic, Bendo	7	8	5	5	5	2
Total		**25**	**25**	**25**	**25**	**25**	**25**

3.3 Variables

For the analysis, a set of independent and dependent variables were chosen. The dependent variables represent the output or effect or are tested to see if it is the effect. The independent variables represent the input and causes, or are tested to see if they are the cause.

Independent variables

- Socio Cultural Setting
  - Urban
  - Rural
- Gender
  - Boys
  - Girls
- Socio Economic Status
  - Upper Socio Economic Status
  - Middle Socio Economic Status
  - Lower Socio Economic Status
- Modernization

Dependent variables

- Stress

3.4 Tools and Tests

3.4.1 Socio Economic Status Scale

The socioeconomic status of the sample was defined by means of **Gururaj and Maheshwaran (2014) (Annex I)** revised socioeconomic condition of **Kuppuswami (1962).** The updated socioeconomic scale reflects a three-index evaluation inventory – occupation, schooling and family income. The socio-economic status of the family is determined by each of the three variables. The scale limit is 29 with minimum 3. The ratio is 29. The subjects were classified into three sub categories based on the results obtained, i.e. Lower Socio Economic Status, Middle Socio Economic Status, Upper Socio Economic Status.

- **Reliability**

It was found that when all four dimensions (education, income and occupation) were being used multiple, bi-serial R is 0.885 while it is 0.733 when occupation is measured. The inference (r1.23=0.534, r2.13=4.78 and r3.63=4.88) was substantiated by the partial correlation.

- **Validity**

Various methods were used to test the validity of this scale-

a. Matching against outside criterion

The validity of the socio economic scale was tested by requesting several number of teachers and college going students in the university campus area to give the class/status estimate of the persons they know well and then the actual occupation, income and education were ascertained and the class estimate given on the socio economic status scale.

b. Distribution patterns

The scales have been given to the children's families. It was found to have usual probability distributions as regards socio-economic status among the parents of children studying in school and high schools. In addition, in the two distributions the proportions are more or less the same.

3.4.2 Comprehensive Modernization Inventory

Ahluwalia and Kalia (1985) used a comprehensive inventory of modernization to determine students' attitude to modernization as set out in (**Appendix II**). For building up the Modernization Collection, the books, tests and other literature compiled 112 statements on the seven fields of modernization (politics, education, parent-child relations, women's status, marriage, faith in God, socio-cultural factors). On the seven sub-scales of modernization, 112 items were written.

- **Reliability**

Based on the accurate measurement of its capacity (Garrett, 1973) the reliability of the test or any measuring instrument depends upon it. In 100 cases the overall value of the test was 0.82, and this was calculated using a standardized test method with an interval of 15 days. This is very high and important at a confidence level of .01. Coefficients were seen for the interaction of various sub-scales.

- **Validity**

Three types of modernization inventory validities were developed namely face validity, content validity and construct validity.

Face Validity- Twenty educational, psychological and sociological experts were initially given the list of 112 statements to determine the importance of subject-matter of a small sub-scale. This experts' unanimity on the items was regarded as a symbol of the inventory's validity.

Content Validity- The inventory's content areas have been evaluated systematically. The opinion of 20 experts in the psychological, educational and sociological fields supported the empirical validity and substance of the Modernization Inventory.

Face validity- Material validity- Validity building-The building

Construct Validity- By measuring the correlation between various parts of the modernization inventory and overall size, the validity of the modernization inventory was calculated.

Table 3.6 Area-wise and Type-wise Distributions of Items

Sr. No.	Area	Type of Items	Item wise Serial No.		
I.	**Education**	Positive	1, 13, 18, 32	4	7
		Negative	3, 12, 19	3	
II.	**Parent-Child relationship**	Positive	2, 16, 30, 31, 44	5	7
		Negative	17, 43	2	
III.	**Politics**	Positive	4, 21, 33, 45	4	7
		Negative	5, 20, 46	3	
IV.	**Status of Women**	Positive	6, 7, 22	3	7
		Negative	9, 23, 34, 35	4	
V.	**Marriage**	Positive	8, 25, 37, 47	4	7
		Negative	24, 36, 38	3	

VI.	Religion	Positive	10, 27, 39, 49	4	7
		Negative	11, 26, 40	3	
VII.	Socio-cultural factors	Positive	15, 29, 41, 42, 48	5	7
		Negative	14, 28	2	
			Total	**49**	**49**

- **Scoring Procedure**

The method of score is very simple. Both positive and negative items are included in the modernization inventory. For a positive item, the maximum scoring is 5 and the minimum is 1. The scoring method should be reversed in the case of negative things as seen in the table. The number of the total score for 7 dimensions gives the overall score for modernization.

3.4.3 Student's Stress scale

Agrawal (2012) has developed the student stress scale to measure the level of distress among college students as in **Appendix III.** The scale consists of 64 life events (including 9 major categories) which must be scored on a 7-point scale. Scale points description was 1, stress was not enough at all; 2, stress was very low; 3, stress was a little; 4, stress was average; 5, stress was too high, 6, and stress was too low, while 7, stress was too great. All questions are mandatory.

- **Reliability-**

Reliability can be measured in many ways: Internal consistency reliability using Cronbach Alpha is the most widely accepted measure.

Internal coherence- The uniformity of the internal coherence- The homogeneousness of the items in question is concerned. An internally consistent scale is insofar as its papers are highly interrelated. Internal consistency is usually equated to the alpha coefficient of Cronbach; it is the most commonly used reliability metric. The estimated Cronbach alpha coefficient was 0.964.

Test-Retest Reliability- It is an indicator of the consistency of a metric over time that corresponds to the outcomes of two measurement occasions. A random study of 250 students was used to assess the reliability of the SSS for tests at a 6-week interval. The obtained reliability factor was 0.88. Both scores show that SSS is highly accurate.

- **Validity-**

The calculated value of a tool is said to be accurate. The authenticity of the face shall be used to verify SSS authenticity. It has been developed based on the stress. This method, it was believed, made its target population "cultural appropriateness" scale. Therefore, the scale can be assumed to be face validity. In addition, stress dimensions have been empirically evaluated for their predictive stress value, and only those dimensions have been selected that predict strains best.

Table 3.7 Descriptions of Sub-scales

Sr. No.	Sub-scale	Item numbers
1.	Financial	1,2,3,4,60
2.	Family	5,6,7,8,12,20,59,63
3.	Social	9,11,41,43
4.	Education	
a).	Education: Not attaining educational objectives	23,24,44,45,46,48,56
b).	Education: Irregular university functioning	47,49,58
c).	Education: Lack of study facilities	51,52,53,54,55,57
d).	Education: Teacher student relationship	10,21,50
5.	Ego Threat	13,14,15,16,18,19,22,26,61
6.	Bereavement	28,29,30,31
7.	Separation	32,33,42
8.	Personal Setback	17,25,27,34,35,62,64
9.	Health of others	36,37,38,39,40

4 Scoring Procedure

The results for each respondent are determined by adding the cumulative rating of all conditions or incidents encountered by the respondent. Later, total scores were percentile scores. In this regard, the percentile value is determined for every respondent and is then compared to the percentile stage. The total score ranges from 0 (when the respondent is unable to have an event) to 448 (when all events have an intolerable stress).

3.5 Procedure of Data Collection

The entire study was conducted in five phases.

Phase 1

After seeking permission from the principals of the respective colleges, the boy and girl students of under graduation were contacted and briefed about the study. The 150 college students from rural as well as urban cultural background were further divided into 75 boys and 75 girls from each group, (25 each from upper , middle and lower socio-economic categories) were selected from different colleges in the Prayagraj District using stratified random sampling techniques which was done with the help of implementing the revised version of Socio Economic Status Scale devises by **Kuppuswami (1962)** and revised by **Gururaj and Maheshwaram (2014)**. The first and foremost step after the selection of respondents was to build rapport with all students and seek their trust before talking to them about their stress. Each participant was contacted separately in the college and the desired information was sought, beginning from the general/ background information to specific information through questionnaire. The researcher assured to keep the responses confidential as well as to be used only for research purposes. Wherever necessary, the questions were explained in their own local language i.e. hindi. The doubts of the participants regarding any question were made clear during the interview session.

Phase 2

Comprehensive Modernization Inventory by **Ahluwalia and Kalia (1985)** was implemented to assess the attitude of students regarding modernization in seven areas- i.e. education, parents- child relations, politics, status of women, marriage, religion and socio cultural. Student Stress Scale devised by **Agrawal (2012)** was also implemented during this phase to assess the level of distress among the college students. The sub scale of the test includes the following dimensions-Financial, Family, Social, Education, Ego threat, Bereavement, Separation, Personal Setback and Health of others.

Phase 3

During the third phase an intervention package to reduce stress among the respondents **(Appendix IV)** was planned and implemented for a period of three months to all the selected respondents.

5 Individual and group counseling session were held for the college students in regarding what concerns them the most.

6 Yoga and meditation session was conducted on a regular basis for three months for reducing stress among students as it could help to quiet busy minds, balance the nervous system, and promotes feelings of calm and peace which reduces the stress level.

7 A video was designed and developed in a simple yet interesting manner for reducing stress level. Video contained easily comprehensible language. Picture, data, motivational thoughts and suggestions for a stress free life. Video was added for efficient explanation to the students.

Intervention Package

1). Counseling session were designed in such a way that they provided a safe and confidential environment to the respondents to express their ideas and thoughts so that counseling might help the students for reducing their stress level and also provide right and positive way for their life. Counseling was aimed to explore the feeling and behaviour of the students, identify aspects of their lives that they would to change, set personal goals and work towards desired change.

Group counseling sessions were led by the researcher which were planned to provide opportunities to the students to come in contact with others who were also facing similar stress and share their thoughts and problems without any hesitation because many times students think that their problem is unique and no one is suffering this situation.

The most important thing that was kept in mind while counseling the students individually or in group was that stress can be reduced by implementing proper strategies to improve the existing situation. During the counseling session the students were helped to resolve issues related to academic, social, family and relationship problems.

As s part of group counseling session students were encouraged to create a social circle of good friend so as to share their whereabouts worries and anxieties. The students were explained the importance of good friends which can be a key to reduce stress in any situation.

2). Students were also asked to develop hobbies which gives them relaxation and enjoyment. Activities like painting, singing, dancing, photography, gardening, writing, cooking and playing games were also encouraged.

3). Yoga and meditation sessions were held for reducing stress level among students. Yoga requires concentrating and focusing the mind to a single point, which is excellent for stress reduction level. Yoga and meditation helps quiet busy minds, balances the nervous system, and promote feelings of calm and peace which reduces the stress level. During intervention, researcher did child's pose (Balasana), Eagle pose (Garudasana), Standing forward fold (Uttanasana), Kapalbharti Pranayam and Anulom Vilom Pranayam and meditation and also motivated for any physical activities like exercise, aerobics, zumba and dance.

4). The developed video film was shown to the respondents which talked about stress management and way a person should function in times of stress and face every challenge in life as a learning lesson.

Table 3.8 Timeline of the intervention activities conducted on the urban and rural college students

S. No	Activities	Urban	Rural
1.	Counseling sessions (Individual and Group)	24 days (3 days in each PSU) (3*8)	20 days (5 days in each village) (5*4)
2.	Relaxation activities session	16 days (2 days in each PSU) (2*8)	16 days (4 days in each village) (4*4)
3.	Yoga and meditation	24 days (3 days in each PSU) (3*8)	20 days (5 days in each village) (5*4)
4.	Information imparted through a short film	16 days (2 days in each PSU) (2*8)	16 days (4 days in each village) (4*4)
5.	Awareness campaign	16 days (2 days in each	16 days (4 days in each

		PSU) (2*8)	village) (4*4)

Intervention was given to the students by seeking their permission, making adjustment according to their class (period) schedule and using their free class so as to get the maximum output of the intervention package.

Phase 4

During this phase, the efficacy of intervention package was assessed after providing intervention for reducing stress level among the college students. It was conducted after a gap of one month from the last day of the intervention programme.

Phase 5

Data analysis and report writing was done during the fifth phase of the study.

3.6 Statistical procedures used for data analysis

Data collection was coded, tabulated and analyzed using appropriate statistical techniques like mean, standard deviation (SD), t-test, p-value, ANOVA and correlation.

Mean:

Arithmetic mean is the quotient that results when a sum of all the items in the series is divided by the number of items (N). The formula for finding out arithmetic mean is

$$\bar{x} = \frac{\sum x}{n}$$

Where,

$\bar{X}$= X= score in distribution

Standard deviation (SD):

It is the square-root of the arithmetic mean squares of deviation from arithmetic mean. In short, SD may be defined as "Root Mean Square Deviation from Mean".

$$SD = \sqrt{\frac{\sum(x-\bar{x})^2}{n}}$$

Where,

SD	=	Standard deviation
X	=	Value of variable
$\bar{X}$	=	Arithmetic Mean
n	=	Total number of observations

t-Test:

The t-test as used with small sample (n<30) and was worked out by W. S. Gossett whose pen name was 'student'. Hence, this test is also called "Student's t-test".

$$t = \frac{x_1 - x_2}{\sqrt{\frac{S_1^{\,2}}{N_1} + \frac{S_2^{\,2}}{N_2}}}$$

Where,

$\bar{X}$	=	mean of sample 1
$\bar{X}$	=	mean of sample 2
N1	=	number of subjects in sample 1
N2	=	number of subjects in sample 2
$S1^2$	=	variance of sample 1

$S2^2$ = variance of sample 2

P value:

The p-value is the level of marginal significance within a statistical hypothesis test representing the probability of the occurrence of a given event. It is used as an alternative to rejection points to provide the smallest level of significance at which the null hypothesis would be rejected.

Some groups find it helpful to use the asterisk rating system as well as quoting the P value-

$P < 0.05$ *

$P < 0.01$ **

$P < 0.001$

Most authors refer to statistically significant as $P < 0.05$ and statistically highly significant as $P < 0.001$ (less than one in a thousand chance of being wrong).

Analysis of Variance (ANOVA) test:

An analysis of variance table called as ANOVA table was prepared for performing the test of significance to draw the conclusions about the various factors.

Source of variance	Degree of freedom	Sum of square	Mean sum of square	F(cal.) = M.S.S./E.S.S.	F(tab.) 1%

Correlation:

`Correlation is a statistical technique that is used to measure and describe the strength and direction of the relationship between two variables. Correlation requires two scores from the same individuals.

$$r = \frac{n(\Sigma xy) - (\Sigma x)(\Sigma y)}{\sqrt{[n\Sigma x^2 - (\Sigma x)^2]\,[n\Sigma y^2 - (\Sigma y)^2]}}$$

Where,

n	=	number of pairs of scores
Σxy	=	sum of the products of paired scores
Σx	=	sum of x scores
Σy	=	sum of y scores
Σx2	=	sum of squared x scores
Σy2	=	sum of squared y scores

Paired t-Test:

The paired t-test also called the dependent sample t-test, is a statistical procedure used to determine whether the mean difference between two sets of observations is zero. In a paired sample t-test, each subject or entity is measured twice, resulting in pairs of observations.

$$t = \frac{\Sigma d}{\sqrt{\frac{n\left(\Sigma d^2\right)-\left(\Sigma d\right)^2}{n-1}}}$$

Where,

d	=	difference per paired value
n	=	number of samples

Critical Difference:

The critical difference (CD), the smallest difference between sequential laboratory results which is associated with a true change in the patient, is commonly calculated by assuming the same standard deviation (SD) for the initial and subsequent measurements. The calculation of the CD is re-examined without making this assumption.

$$\mathbf{CD_{95}{}^{\%} = 2.77 \times \sqrt{(CV_a^2 + CV_i^2)}}$$

Where,

CV_a = analytical coefficient of variation

CV_i = CV of within-subject biological variation

Chapter-IV

RESULTS AND DISCUSSION

This chapter deals with the detailed description of the present investigation. The data collected was coded, tabulated and analyzed by using appropriate statistical techniques.

Table 4.1 and **figures 4.1** to **4.4** highlights the frequency and percentage distribution of respondents belonging to different socio economic groups from urban and rural background on the basis of modernization in education. It is clear from the table that in case of urban boys, maximum percent i.e. 56 percent of those belonging to upper socio economic group possessed high level of modernization followed by 48 percent of boys belonging to middle socio economic group and 40 from lower socio economic group. In among the rural boys it was witnessed that in the educational aspect, 52 percent of the upper socioeconomic strata, 52 percent of the middle socioeconomic group and 40 percent of respondents from the lower socioeconomic group had a high degree of modernisation. In case of girls belonging to urban background, it was witnessed that 76% of the upper socio-economic group and 64% of the middle socio-economic group of girls and 60% of the lower socio-economic group possessed high level of modernization attitude towards education wherein maximum modernization was found respondents belonging to upper socio economic group from both from urban and rural cultural settings. Girls were found to have better attitude towards modernization towards education as compared to their male counterparts. It was noted that 72% of the upper socio-economic community, 64% of the middle socio-economic group and 52% of the lower socio-economic strata had a better attitude towards education in the case of girls from rural settings. Different research has correlated with the study that boys have been found to be less driven than girls and less optimistic about school **(Davies, 1984; Darom & Rich, 1988; Cox, 2000; Francis, 2000; Warrington *et al.*, 2000).**

The table further highlighted that average level of modern attitude towards education was possessed by 44 percent urban boys belonging to upper socio economic group, followed by 44% of urban boys belonging to the upper socio-economic category, followed by 52% from the middle socio-economic category and 60 urban boys from the lower socio-economic category represented an average level of modernization, while 48% from the upper and middle socio-economic categories and 60% from the lower socio-economic category displayed an average level of modernization in the case of boys from rural backgrounds. In the case of urban girls, 24 per cent of the upper socio-economic group, 36 per cent of the middle socio-economic group and 40 per cent of the lower socio-economic group represented an average level of modernization in education, while in the case of rural girls, 28 per cent of the upper socio-economic class, 36 per cent of the middle socio-economic class and 48 per cent of the middle socio-economic class were identified. Girls were found to have more positive attitude towards education. None of the respondents from urban as well as rural cultural setting were found to be possessing low level of attitude towards educational modernization. Girls showed more modern attitude towards educational aspects. The better educational performance of women represents an inherent women's academic dominance, which has emerged through current gender equality education policies. **Fergusson and Horwood (1997).**

Table 4.1 Frequency and percentage distribution of urban and rural respondents belonging to various socio-economic classes on the basis of their attitude towards modernization in education

Level of Modernization	Urban Respondents (n=150)												Rural Respondents (n=150)											
	Upper socio economic group				Middle socio economic group				Lower socio economic group				Upper socio economic group				Middle socio economic group				Lower socio economic group			
	Boys (n=25)		Girls (n=25)		Boys (n=25)		Girls (n=25)		Boys (n=25)		Girls (n=25)		Boys (n=25)		Girls (n=25)		Boys (n=25)		Girls (n=25)		Boys (n=25)		Girls (n=25)	
	F	%	F	%	F	%	F	%	F	%	F	%	F	%	F	%	F	%	F	%	F	%	F	%
High (35-26)	14	56	19	76	12	48	16	64	10	40	15	60	13	52	18	72	13	52	16	64	10	40	13	52
Average (25-16)	11	44	06	24	13	52	09	36	15	60	10	40	12	48	07	28	12	48	09	36	15	60	12	48
Low (15-07)	00	00	00	00	00	00	00	00	00	00	00	00	00	00	00	00	00	00	00	00	00	00	00	00

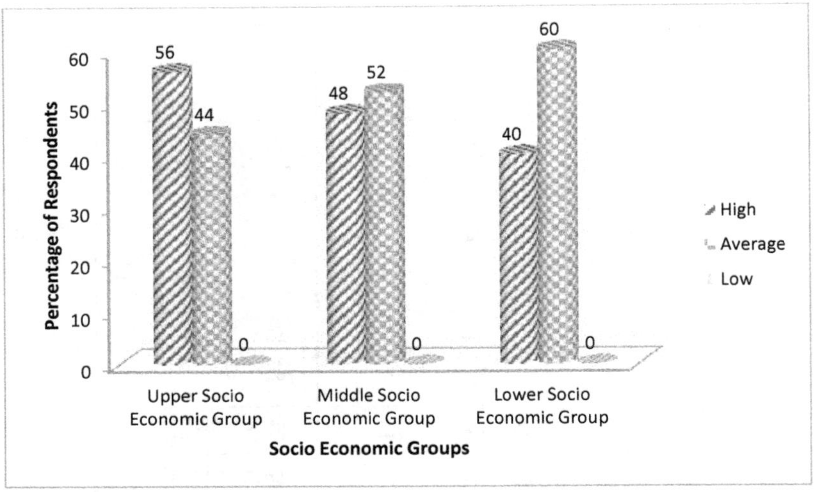

Fig 4.1 Distribution of urban boys on the basis of their attitude towards modernization regarding education

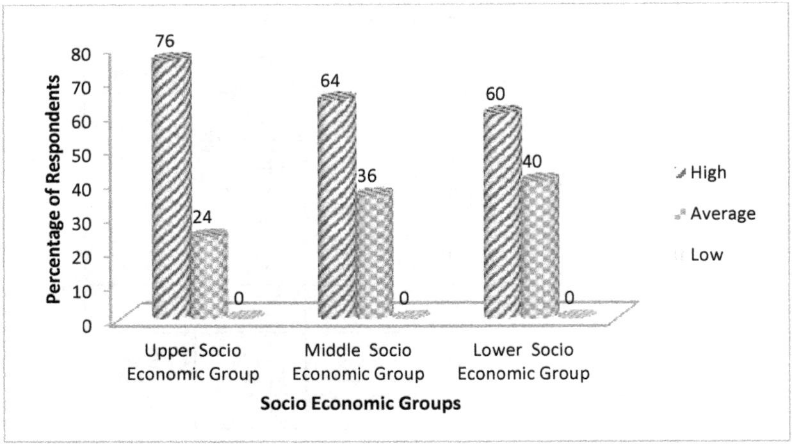

Fig 4.2 Distribution of urban girls on the basis of their attitude towards modernization regarding education

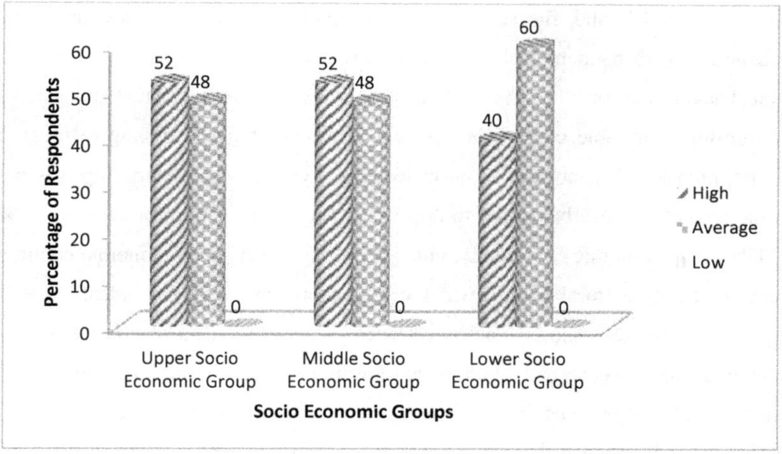

Fig 4.3 Distribution of rural boys on the basis of their attitude towards modernization regarding education

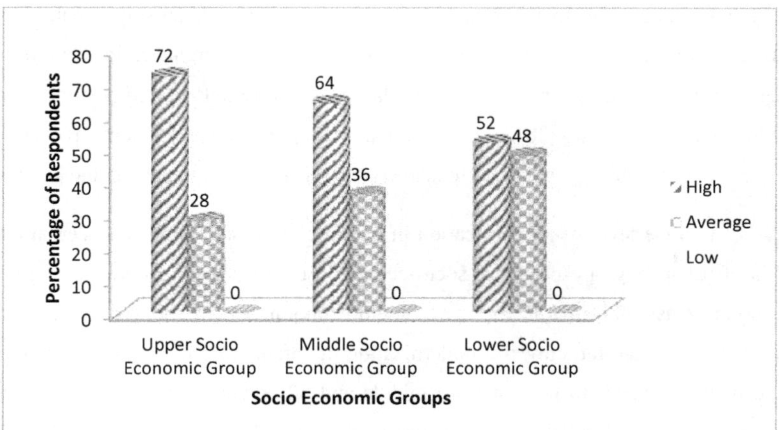

Fig 4.4 Distribution of rural girls on the basis of their attitude towards modernization regarding education

Table 4.2 and **figures 4.5** to **4.8** highlights the frequency and percentage distribution of respondents belonging to different socio economic groups from urban and rural background on the basis of attitude towards modernization in parents child relationship. The table clearly showed that in case of boys belonging to urban cultural setting, high level of modernization concerning parents child relationship was possessed by 68 percent of those belonging to upper socio economic group followed by 60% of the middle socio-economic community, and 40% of the lower socio-economic community. In the case of rural cultural boys, it was shown that 60 percent of respondents from both the upper and middle socio-economic categories and 40 percent from the lower socio-economic category each had a high level of attitude towards modernization with regard to parents child relationships. As far as girls were concerned, it was reflected from the table that 84 percent urban girls from upper socio economic group followed by 80% of the middle socio-economic class and 56% of the lowest socio-economic class had higher level of attitude towards modernization in the aspect of parents child relationship whereas in case of rural girls it was seen that 80 percent from upper, 76 percent from middle and 52 percent from lower socio economic group had high level of modernization wherein girls were more modern in their attitude toward parents child relationship because generally girls are submissive and obedient to their parents and learn parents child relationship from their family very earlier in their age. Similar results were obtained by a study carried out by **Shaban and Mattoo (2017)** which revealed the parent child relationship varies greatly in the use of the child's symbolic punishment, rejection, love component and gender.

Average level of modernization in parent child relationship was seen among only 25% of urban boys in the upper socio-economic community, 32% in the middle socio-economic class and 56% in the lower socio-economic class whereas among rural boys average level of attitude toward modernization in parent child relationship was seen in 36 percent from upper, 40 percent from middle and 52 percent from lower socio economic group. In case of girls belonging to urban background, It was observed that 16 percent of the upper and middle socio-economic class and 36 percent of the lower socio-economic class each had an average degree of modernization of parent-child relationships, while 20 percent of the upper socio-economic category, 24 percent of the middle socio-economic category and 48 percent of the lower socio-economic category had an average level of modern attitude towards parents child relationship.

Low level of modernization in aspects of parent child relationship was witnessed in 8 percent urban boys each from upper and middle socio economic group and only 4 percent from lower socio economic group were identified with low level of modern attitude regarding parents child relationship. In case of boys from rural cultural setting, it was seen that 04 percent from upper, none of respondents in the middle socio-economic class and 08% in the lower socio-economic class had low level of modern attitude toward parents child relationship. As far as girls were concerned, none of the girls in the upper socio-economic strata, 04 percent of the middle socio-economic strata and 08 percent of urban girls in the lower socio-economic strata were possessed low level of attitude towards parents child relationship whereas in case of rural girls, it was seen that none of respondents from all three socio economic group possessed low level of attitude towards modernization parents child relationship.

Families have significantly changed after the traditional stay at home and at home with the worker. **Gerson (2012)** found that both men and women often shared fairly well balanced parenting behaviours. Mothers spend much more time on average than parents looking after children. **(Craig, 2006)**. It may fellows, since children spent more time with their mothers, their mothers would feel more emotionally closer than their father. According to **Dalton *et al.*, (2006)** reports of In relation to the nature of the current relationships with the romantic partners, parental fathers, but not mothers, and father's parentage often related to self-image as closely and firmly linked. The study proves that adolescents are developing a modern attitude towards parent child relationship as well.

Table 4.2 Frequency and percentage distribution of urban and rural respondents belonging to various socio-economic classes on the basis of their attitude towards modernization in parents child relationship

Level of Modernization	Urban Respondents (n=150)												Rural Respondents (n=150)											
	Upper socio economic group				Middle socio economic group				Lower socio economic group				Upper socio economic group				Middle socio economic group				Lower socio economic group			
	Boys (n=25)		Girls (n=25)		Boys (n=25)		Girls (n=25)		Boys (n=25)		Girls (n=25)		Boys (n=25)		Girls (n=25)		Boys (n=25)		Girls (n=25)		Boys (n=25)		Girls (n=25)	
	F	%	F	%	F	%	F	%	F	%	F	%	F	%	F	%	F	%	F	%	F	%	F	%
High (35-26)	17	68	21	84	15	60	20	80	10	40	14	56	15	60	20	80	15	60	19	76	10	40	13	52
Average (25-16)	06	25	04	16	08	32	04	16	14	56	09	36	09	36	05	20	10	40	06	24	13	52	12	48
Low (15-07)	02	08	00	00	02	08	01	04	01	04	02	08	01	04	00	00	00	00	00	00	02	08	00	00

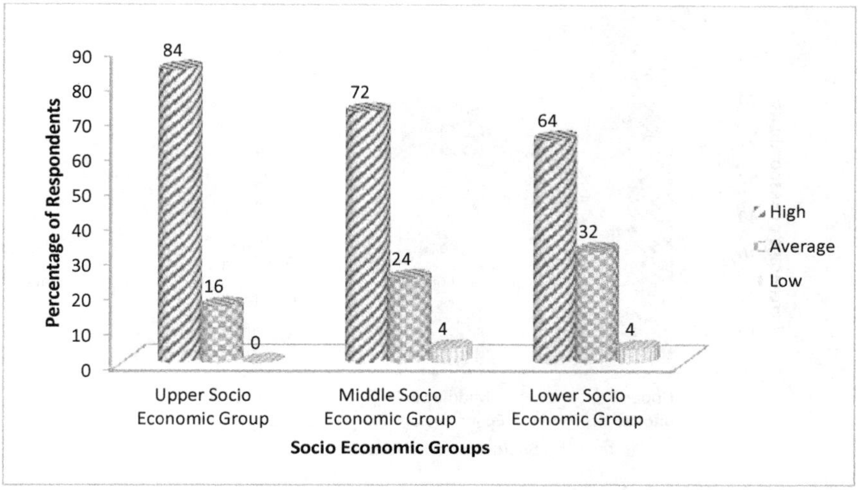

Fig 4.5 Distribution of urban boys regarding their attitude towards parents child relationship across three socio-economic groups

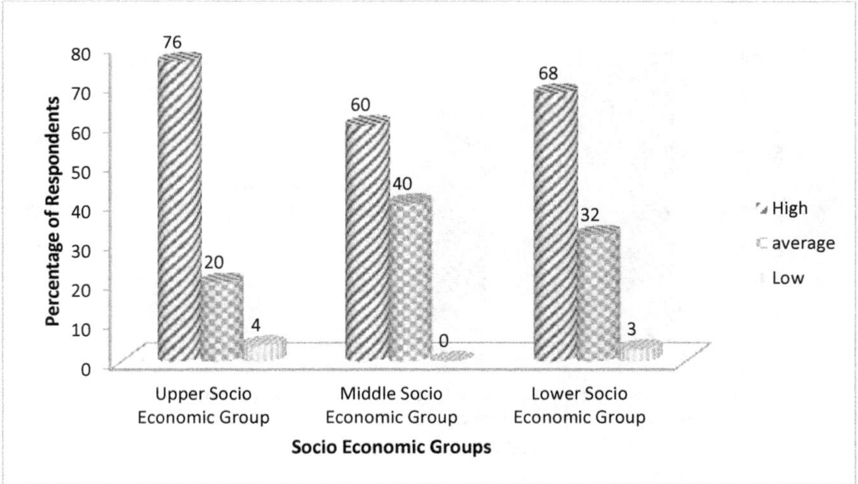

Fig 4.6 Distribution of urban girls regarding their attitude towards parents child relationship across three socio-economic groups

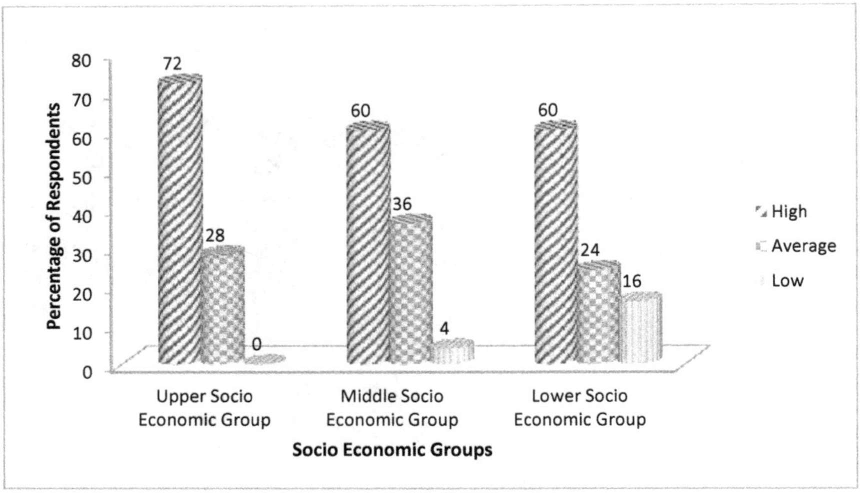

Fig 4.7 Distribution of rural boys regarding their attitude towards parents child relationship across three socio-economic groups

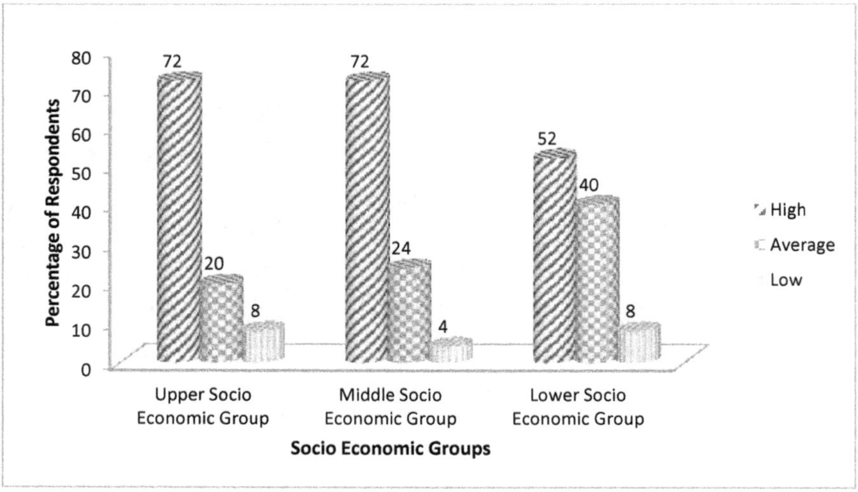

Fig 4.8 Distribution of rural girls regarding their attitude towards parents child relationship across three socio-economic groups

Table 4.3 and illustrations in **figures 4.9 to 4.12** highlights the frequency and percentage distribution of urban and rural adolescents belonging to different socio economic groups (the lower socio-economic class, the middle socio-economic class and the upper socio-economic class respectively) focused on the their attitude towards modernization in politics. The data represented in the table indicated that in case of boys belonging to urban background, it was noticed that 84 percent belonging to upper socio economic group, 72 percent from middle and 64 percent from lower socio economic strata possessed high level of modern attitude towards politics, whereas, among the rural boys, it was seen that 72 percent from upper socio economic group, 60 percent each from middle as well as lower socio economic group had high modern attitude towards politics. In case of girls belonging to urban cultural setting, it was found that 76 percent from upper, 60 percent from middle and 68 percent from lower socio economic strata had highly modern attitude towards politics whereas among girls from rural background, it was found that 72 percent each from upper as well as middle socio economic group and 52 percent respondents from lower socio economic group had high level of modernization as far as politics was concerned. This might be due to the fact that upper socio economic groups are highly educated which aids them in their decision to exercise their voting rights and not be confused and convinced by misleading advertisements in print and electronic media. Similar results found by **Chadha (2014)** in her study that the number of women as voters has risen dramatically. Women are nearly equal to men in their engagement as voters.

Average category of modernization towards politics was seen among 16 percent urban boys from upper socio economic group followed by 24 percent from middle and 32 percent from lower socio economic strata whereas in case of rural boys, it was seen that average level of modern attitude towards politics was possessed by 28% of the upper socio-economic class, 36% of the middle socio-economic class and 24% of the lower socio-economic class were boys. As far as girls were concerned, it was noticed that in case of urban girls, 20% of the upper socio-economic community, 40% of the middle socio-economic community, and 32% of the lower socio-economic community possessed average level of modernization towards politics. In case of rural girls, the table highlighted that 20% of the upper socio-economic community, 24% of the middle socio-economic community and 40% of the lower socio-economic community had an average level of modern attitude towards politics. Politics was historically an occupation by gender. Men and women are traditionally conditioned to believe that men are qualified to vote politically. The problem is that unhealthy differentiation has been formed from a young age in an institutional context. A new approach to politics assumes that women who have been integral to the development of contemporary political parties are present and accept their contribution.

Very few respondents from both rural and urban cultural setting were found to have low level of modern attitude towards politics. In case of urban boys, none of respondents found from upper socio economic group, 04 percent each from middle and lower socio economic strata possessed low level of modern attitude towards politics. Among the rural boys, it was seen that none from the upper socio-economic class, 4% from the middle socio-economic class and 16% from the lower socio-economic class were seen to have a low attitude towards political modernization. As far as urban girls were concerned, it was noticed that only 04 percent from upper socio economic strata and none of respondents from middle as well as lower socio economic group had low level of attitude towards political modernization. Only 08 percent rural girls belonging to upper socio economic group, 04 percent belonging to middle socio economic group and 08 percent belonging to lower socio economic group had low level of attitude towards political modernization. Modernization is a concept of a gradual transformation from a "premodern" or "traditional" society into a "modern" society.

The women's booking bill was a political bill that facilitated the inclusion of women in different areas. The participation of women in politics is essential for their overall growth and empowerment in the present scenario. Finding of the study coincides with the study conducted by **Tootell (2015)** who reported that Women have no negative government consequences. As a category, of course, women are not less eligible as members of the public service than men. That is why women participate not only at lower but also higher levels in the political sector of the country.

Table 4.3 Frequency and percentage distribution of urban and rural respondents belonging to various socio-economic classes on the basis of their attitude towards modernization in politics

Level of Modernization	Urban Respondents (n=150)												Rural Respondents (n=150)											
	Upper socio economic group				Middle socio economic group				Lower socio economic group				Upper socio economic group				Middle socio economic group				Lower socio economic group			
	Boys (n=25)		Girls (n=25)		Boys (n=25)		Girls (n=25)		Boys (n=25)		Girls (n=25)		Boys (n=25)		Girls (n=25)		Boys (n=25)		Girls (n=25)		Boys (n=25)		Girls (n=25)	
	F	%	F	%	F	%	F	%	F	%	F	%	F	%	F	%	F	%	F	%	F	%	F	%
High (35-26)	21	84	19	76	18	72	15	60	16	64	17	68	18	72	18	72	15	60	18	72	15	60	13	52
Average (25-16)	04	16	05	20	06	24	10	40	08	32	08	32	07	28	05	20	09	36	06	24	06	24	10	40
Low (15-07)	00	00	01	04	01	04	00	00	01	04	00	00	00	00	02	08	01	04	01	04	04	16	02	08

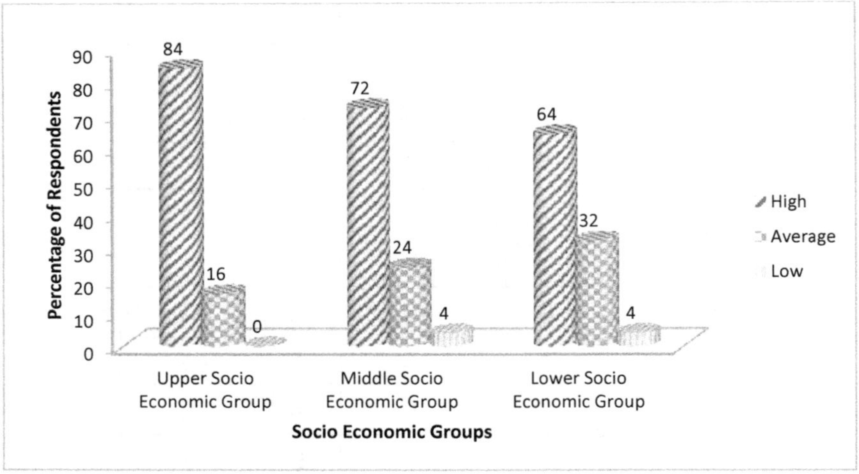

Fig 4.9 Distribution of urban boys regarding their attitude towards politics across three socio-economic groups

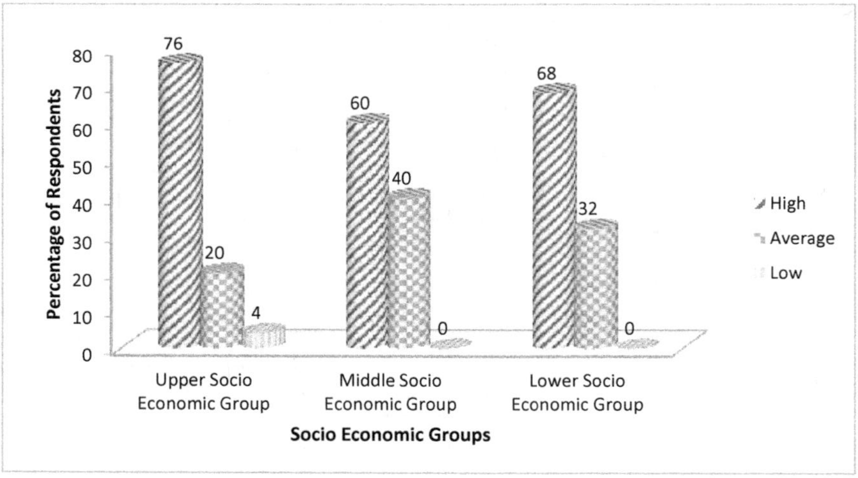

Fig 4.10 Distribution of urban girls regarding their attitude towards politics across three socio-economic groups

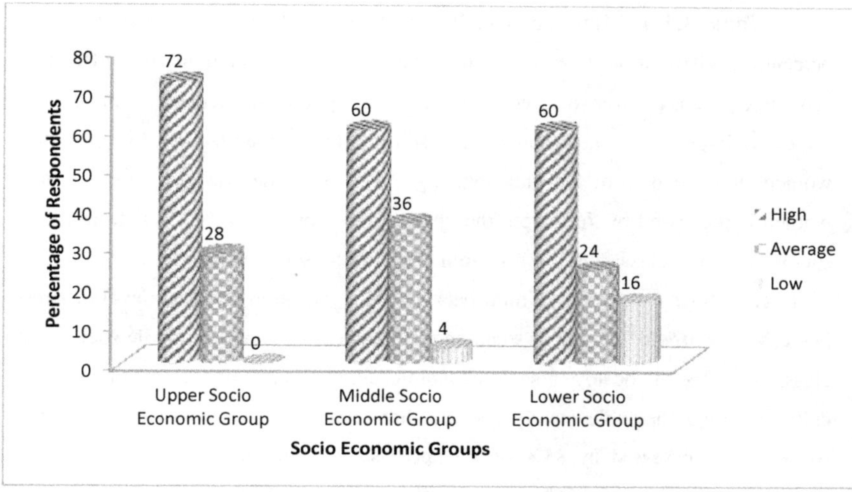

Fig 4.11 Distribution of rural boys regarding their attitude towards parents politics across three socio-economic groups

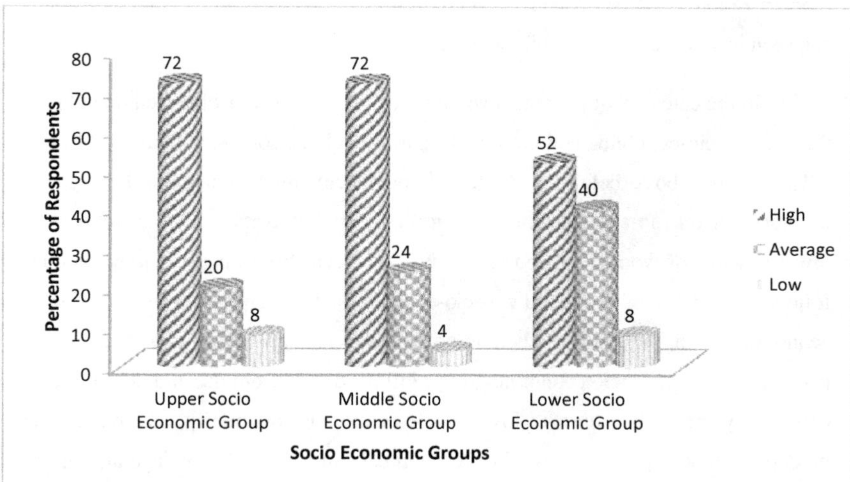

Fig 4.12 Distribution of rural girls regarding their attitude towards politics across three socio-economic groups

Table 4.4 and illustration in figures **4.13** to **4.16** highlights the frequency and percentage distribution of urban and rural adolescents belonging to different socio economic groups (Lower socio-economic community, middle socio-economic community, upper socio-economic community) focused on the modernization towards status of women. It is seen from the data that high level of modernization regarding status of women is possessed by 76% from the upper socio-economic class, 52% from the middle socio-economic class, and 40% from the lower socio-economic class. In case of adolescents boys from rural cultural background it was seen that high level of stress was possessed by 56% of the upper socio-economic class, 44% of the middle socio-economic class, and 32% of the lower socio-economic class. In case of girls belonging to urban cultural setting the table clearly showed that high level of modernization in status of women was possessed by 84% of the upper socio-economic class, 68% of the middle socio-economic class, and 56% of the lower socio-economic class. In the case of girls with a rural cultural history, 60% from the upper socio-economic class, 56% from the middle socio-economic class and 48% from the lower socio-economic class had high level of modernization in status of women where in maximum modernization in status of women can seen in girls belonging to all the three socio economic strata.

In the category of average level of modernization, it was observed that only 24% of the upper socio-economic community, 44% of the middle socio-economic community, and 52% of urban boys belonging to lower socio economic community belonged to this category whereas in case of rural boys, it was seen that average level of modern attitude towards status of women was possessed by 44 percent from upper socio economic group followed by 56% of the middle socio-economic group and 68% of the lower socio-economic group. Among girls belonging to urban background, it was witnessed that 12 percent from upper socio economic group, followed 24% from the middle socio-economic community and 36% from the lower socio-economic community had average level of modern attitude towards status of women. In case of rural girls, average attitude towards status of women was seen among 36 percent from upper socio economic group followed by 44 percent each from lower and middle socio economic group.

In the modern era, the condition of women is changed by the constitutional rules, the advancement of innovations, globalization and commercialism. The concerted intervention of feminist critics, women's freedoms, the security of rights, constitutional guarantees and genuine efforts, through various schemes and programmes, between central and state governments, has contributed to giving women in our country modern status. Similar results were obtained by a study carried out by **Ghosh and Roy (1997)** which revealed that the as a consequence of urbanization and growth, educated middle and upper class women have increased their economic and social status.

The table also indicates that low level of modernization in status of women was present in none of the urban boys from upper socio economic class, 04% in the middle socio-economic class and 08% in the lower socio-economic class. Low level of modern attitude towards status of women was witnessed among none of rural boys belonging to upper, middle and lower socio economic group. In case of girls from urban cultural setting, it was noticed that 04 percent from upper socio economic group and 08 percent each from middle and lower socio economic group possessed low level of modernization attitude towards status of women whereas in case of rural girls low modernization was seen among 04 percent in upper socio economic group whereas none of respondents were found in this category among the middle socio economic group and only 08 percent from lower socio economic group possessed low level of modern attitude towards stats of women. In dynamic society such as India, women's status is not standardized. Since then women's patriarchal roles have changed a few times as a result of financial needs and little effort to improve society in general. The respondents were optimistic about a new, well-equipped and equitable status for women that provide a ray of hope for change in the near future.

Women's status is one of the key criteria for assessing a specific country's level of women's growth. The government has enacted numerous legislative initiatives aimed at providing support services, particularly to women in households, to provide equal protection, counter social inequality and numerous types of crime, abuse and to enhance women's status. Finding of the study coincides with the study conducted by **Liu (1994)** discovered that, There was a wider difference between men and women in family income and reproduction management and a wider parental income regulation, but economically developed rural areas were similar to urban areas and clarified the rural families' status related to women's income and children and education beyond high school. The differences between men and women were more important than urban areas.

Table 4.4 Frequency and percentage distribution of urban and rural respondents belonging to various socio economic classes on the basis of their attitude towards modernization in status of women

Level of Modernization	Urban Respondents (n=150)												Rural Respondents (n=150)											
	Upper socio economic group				Middle socio economic group				Lower socio economic group				Upper socio economic group				Middle socio economic group				Lower socio economic group			
	Boys (n=25)		Girls (n=25)		Boys (n=25)		Girls (n=25)		Boys (n=25)		Girls (n=25)		Boys (n=25)		Girls (n=25)		Boys (n=25)		Girls (n=25)		Boys (n=25)		Girls (n=25)	
	F	%	F	%	F	%	F	%	F	%	F	%	F	%	F	%	F	%	F	%	F	%	F	%
High (35-26)	19	76	21	84	13	52	17	68	10	40	14	56	14	56	15	60	11	44	14	56	08	32	12	48
Average (25-16)	06	24	03	12	11	44	06	24	13	52	09	36	11	44	9	36	14	56	11	44	17	68	11	44
Low (15-07)	00	00	01	04	01	04	02	08	02	08	02	08	00	00	01	04	00	00	00	00	00	00	02	08

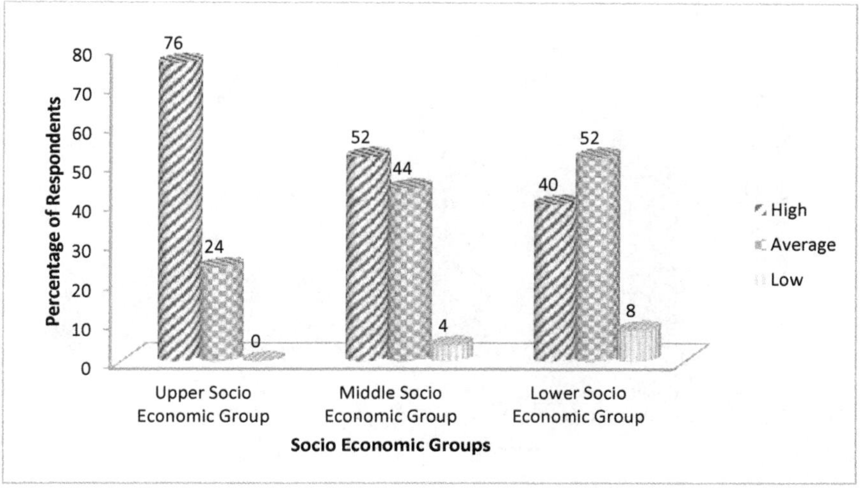

Fig 4.13 Distribution of urban boys regarding modernization in status of women across three socio-economic groups

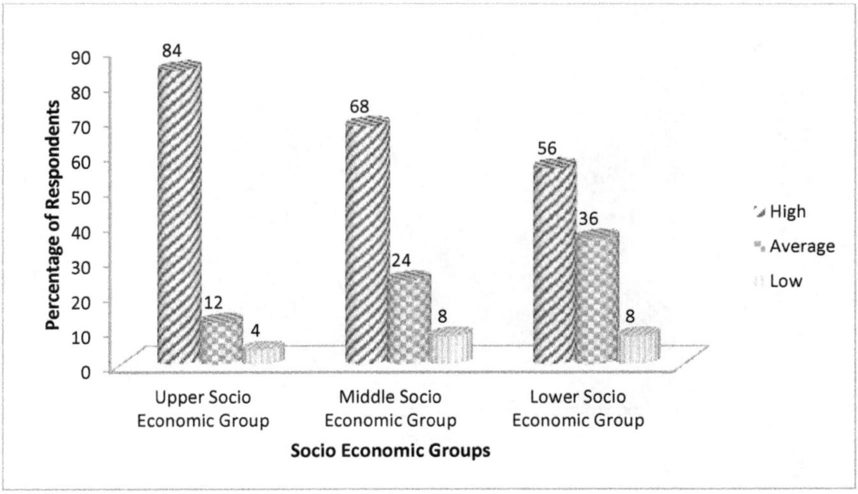

Fig 4.14 Distribution of urban girls regarding modernization in status of women across three socio-economic groups

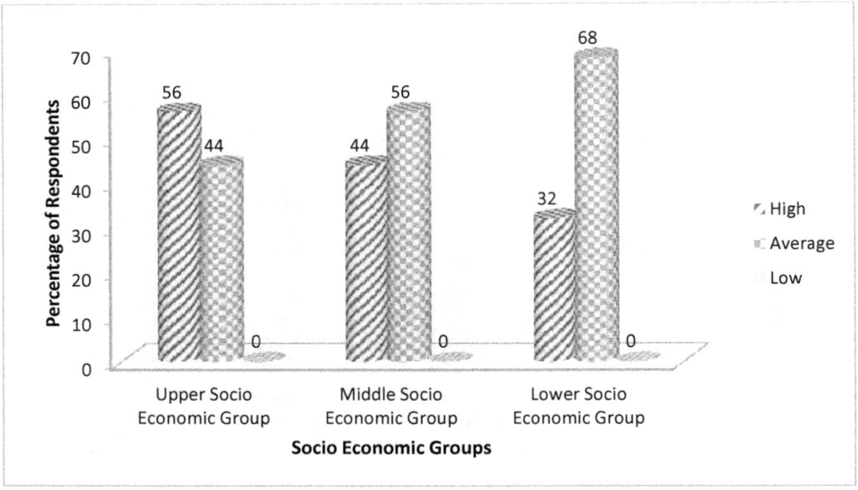

Fig 4.15 Distribution of rural boys regarding modernization in status of women across three socio-economic groups

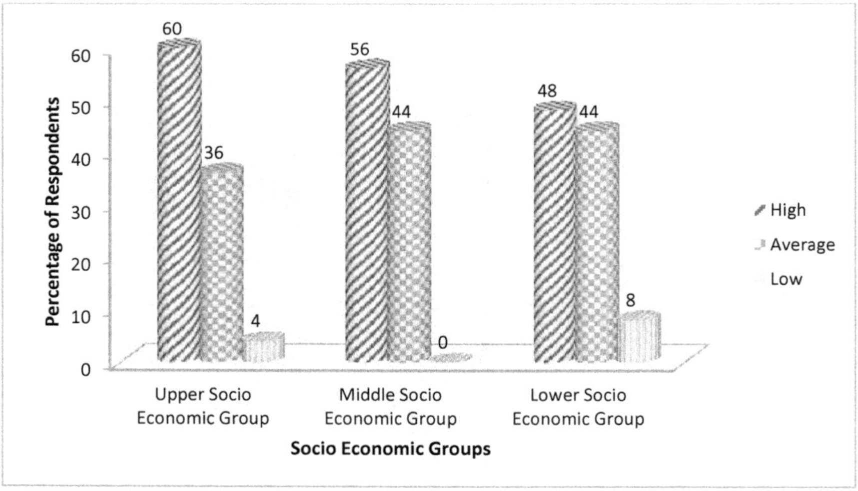

Fig 4.16 Distribution of rural girls regarding modernization in status of women across three socio-economic groups

Table 4.5 and illustration depicted in figures **4.17** to **4.20** highlights the frequency and percentage distribution of respondents belonging to different socio economic groups from urban and rural background on the basis of attitude towards modernization in marriage. The table clearly showed that in case of urban boys high level of modernization towards marriage is possessed by 40 percent each from upper and middle socio economic group, 32 percent from lower socio economic group. In case of boys from rural cultural setting, it was clear from the data depicted in the table that high level of modernization towards marriage was possessed by 40 percent respondents from upper socio economic group, 36 percent each from middle and lower socio economic group. In case of girls belonging to urban cultural background, maximum number of respondents in all socio-economic classes were found to possess high level of modern attitude towards marriage i.e. 64 percent, 64 percent and 32 percent respectively in upper, middle and lower socio economic group wherein most positive attitude could be seen among respondents belonging to upper and middle socio economic group. In case of girls belonging to rural cultural setting, high level of modernization towards marriage levels was noted among 44 percent, 40 percent and 36 percent respondents respectively from upper, middle and lower socio economic group wherein most positive attitude towards could be seen among respondents belonging to upper socio economic group. Girls learn earlier to take care of their family, household work, responsibilities of their parents hence they had a more positive and modern attitude towards marriage as compared to boys. Similar results were obtained by a study carried out by **Klein (2006)** which revealed that women undergraduate students had more optimistic attitudes towards marriage than men. Finding of the coincides with the study conducted by **Smock and Manning (1997)** who found that women from low economic backgrounds would choose to marry with the notion that marriage is a traditional breadwinner, for example the male.

In case of urban boys, average level of modernization in marriage was possessed by 60 percent boys belonging to upper socio economic community, 44% of the Middle Socio-Economic Community and 52% of the Lower Socio-Economic Community whereas in case of boys belonging to rural background, it was witnessed that 40 percent, 56 percent and 52 percent respectively from upper, middle and lower socio economic groups possessed average level of modern attitude towards marriage. In the category of average level of modernization it was noticed that in case of the girls respondent from urban background 32 percent respondents from upper socio economic community, 28% of the

Middle Socio-Economic Community and 60% of the Lower Socio-Economic Community possessed average level of modernization on marriage. Average modernization on marriage was also seen that 52 percent each respondents from upper and middle socio economic group and 60 percent of rural girls belonging to lower socio economic group.

Low level of modernization on marriage was found that none of the respondents were found in upper socio economic group and 16 percent urban boys each from middle and lower socio economic group. In case of rural boys, it was noticed that low modernization on marriage was possessed by 20 percent boys in the upper socio economic community, 08% of the Middle Socio-Economic Community and 12% of the Lower Socio-Economic Community Table also highlighted that in case of urban girls, only 04 percent respondents from upper socio economic group and 08 percent each from middle and lower socio economic group possessed low modernization on marriage whereas in case of their rural counterparts it was seen that 04 percent, 08 percent and 04 percent respectively upper, middle and lower socio economic group possessed low modernization on marriage.

Result showed that girls have had stronger intentions to marry than boys, as marriage is a significant part of Indian society, so girls are feeling the pressure of their family and social classes to marry, not only in their lower but also medium and higher socioeconomic groups. Finding of coincides with the study conducted by **Dennison and Koerner (2008)** many studies in the field of marital attitudes have identified significant differences between young males and females' attitudes towards marriage.

Table 4.5 Frequency and percentage distribution of urban and rural respondents belonging to various socio-economic classes on the basis of their attitude towards modernization in marriage

Level of Modernization	Urban Respondents (n=150)												Rural Respondents (n=150)											
	Upper socio economic group				Middle socio economic group				Lower socio economic group				Upper socio economic group				Middle socio economic group				Lower socio economic group			
	Boys (n=25)		Girls (n=25)		Boys (n=25)		Girls (n=25)		Boys (n=25)		Girls (n=25)		Boys (n=25)		Girls (n=25)		Boys (n=25)		Girls (n=25)		Boys (n=25)		Girls (n=25)	
	F	%	F	%	F	%	F	%	F	%	F	%	F	%	F	%	F	%	F	%	F	%	F	%
High (35-26)	10	40	16	64	10	40	16	64	08	32	08	32	10	40	11	44	09	36	10	40	09	36	09	36
Average (25-16)	15	60	08	32	11	44	07	28	13	52	15	60	10	40	13	52	14	56	13	52	13	52	15	60
Low (15-07)	00	00	01	04	04	16	02	08	04	16	02	08	05	20	01	04	02	08	02	08	3	12	01	04

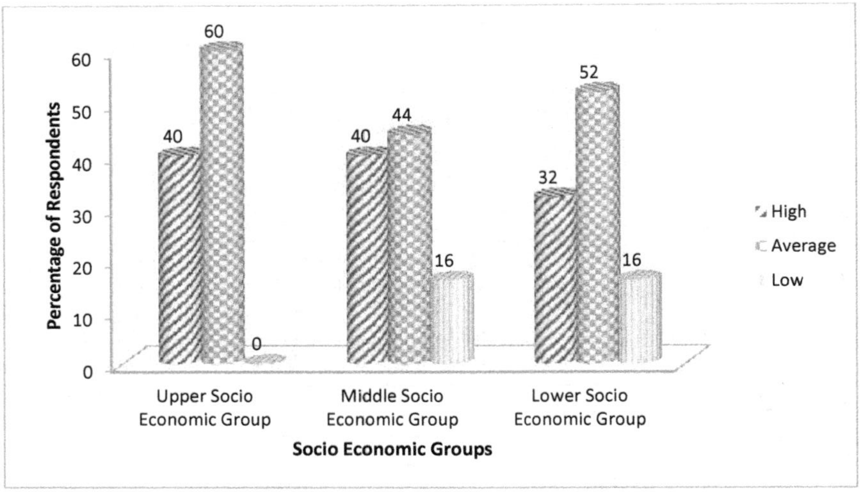

Fig 4.17 Distribution of urban boys regarding modernization in marriage across three socio-economic groups

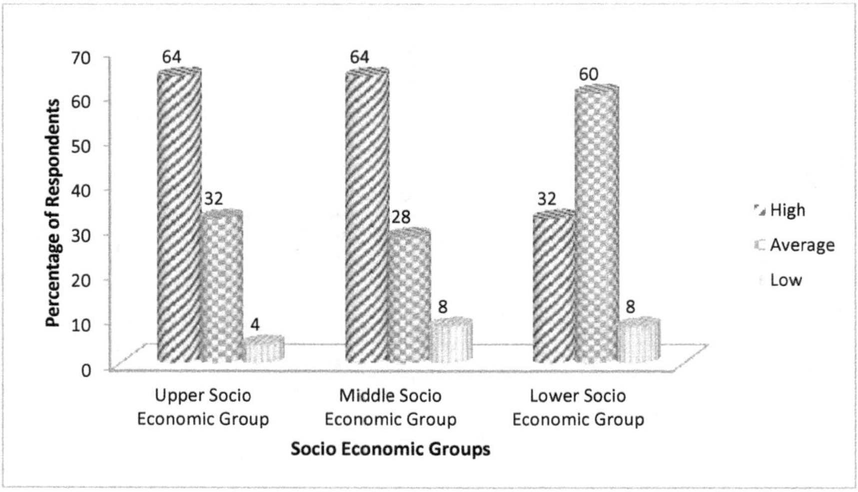

Fig 4.18 Distribution of urban girls regarding modernization in marriage across three socio-economic groups

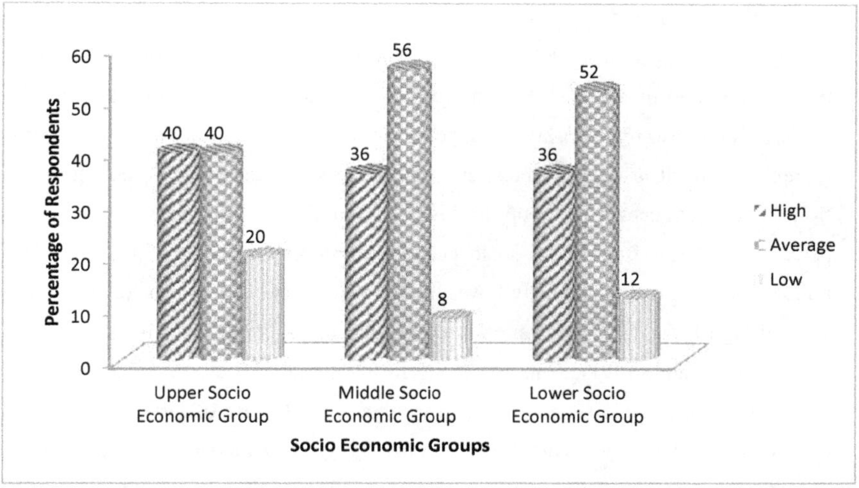

Fig 4.19 Distribution of rural boys regarding modernization in marriage across three socio-economic groups

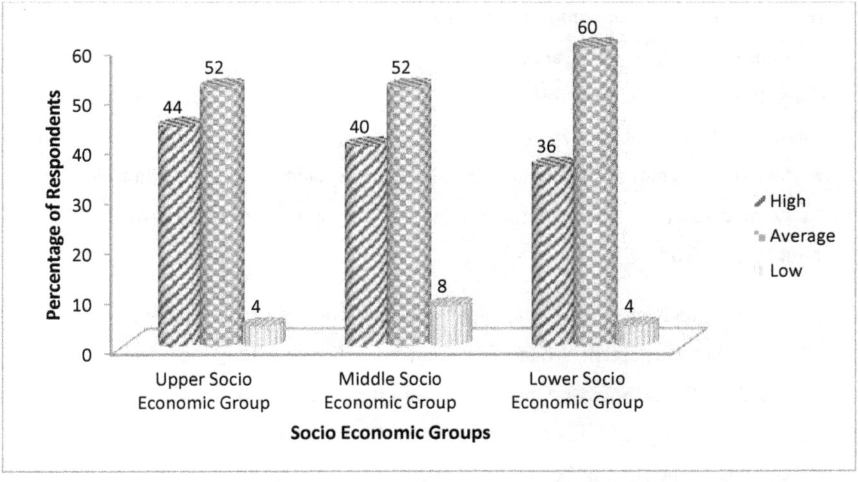

Fig 4.20 Distribution of rural girls regarding modernization in marriage across three socio-economic groups

Table 4.6 and figures **4.21** to **4.24** highlights the frequency and percentage distribution of respondents belonging to different socio economic groups from urban and rural background on the basis of faith in God. The table clearly shows that high level of modernization towards faith in God is possessed by 24 percent from upper socio economic group, 52 percent urban boys belonging to middle socio economic group and 40 percent from lower socio economic group. In the case of rural adolescent boys, it was seen that 20 percent rural boys from upper socio economic group, 60 percent of those belonging to middle socio economic group followed by 48 percent from lower socio economic group showed high level of modernization towards faith in God wherein maximum faith in God can be seen among respondents belonging to middle and lower socio economic group as compare to upper socio economic group in high level. In case of girls belonging to urban cultural setting the table clearly showed that high level of modernization towards faith in God is possessed by 60 percent from upper socio economic group, 68 percent girls from middle socio economic group followed by and 56 percent from lower socio economic group wherein maximum faith in God can seen in girls belonging to middle socio economic strata. Among the rural adolescent girls, it was seen that 64 percent of those belonging to upper socio economic group had high modernization towards faith in God followed by 52 percent from the middle socio economic group and 44 percent from lower socio economic group had high modernization towards faith in God. In higher society also females are emotional. Many times they are not able to explain their problems or situations to others so they worship and feel psychologically stronger. Finding of the study coincides with the study conducted by **Damor (2013)** which revealed a significant difference in faith in God between the average scores of girl respondents and boys. Respondents of girls were highly positive about faith in God.

As far as average level of modernization towards faith in God was concerned, it was witnessed that 68 percent urban adolescent boys from upper socio economic community, 36% of the Middle Socio-Economic Community and 56% of the Lower Socio-Economic Community belonged to this category wherein highest level of modernization towards faith in God was found among boys from upper socio economic group. Among the rural boys, average level of modernization towards faith in God i.e. 72 percent was elicited among upper socio economic group followed by 36 percent from middle and 40 percent from lower socio economic strata. Among the female respondents from urban background, it was witnessed that 24 percent each from upper and middle socio economic and 44 percent girls from lower socio economic group had average level of modernization towards faith in God whereas, among the rural girls average level of modernization towards faith in God was seen among 32 percent each from middle and upper socio economic strata and 52 percent girls belonging to lower socio economic group.

As far as low modernization towards faith in God was concerned 08% of the upper socio-economic class, 12% of the middle socio-economic class and 04% of urban boys in the lower socio-economic class belonged to this category. Among the rural boys were concerned 08 percent from upper socio economic strata, only 4 percent from middle socio economic group and 12 percent respondents from lower socio economic group showed positive attitude towards low level of modernization whereas among the urban girls showed positive attitude towards low level of modernization was seen among 16 percent girls belonging to upper socio economic group followed by 8 percent from middle socio economic group and none respondents from lower socio economic strata. Table also showed that 04 percent respondents from upper socio economic group, 16 percent of rural girls belonging to middle socio economic group and 4 percent respondents from lower socio economic group had low level of modernization towards faith in God.

Girls and boys have been socialized differently in the family and have always had a different function and in this group women are submissive and passive as compared to boys. Similar results were obtained by a study carried out by **Carapina (2015)** which explained in his study that women living in small sites gained higher ritual scores than people living in big sites that suggested that church influence was stronger in smaller squares. Social dynamics were intensive in the smaller communities so that the group's pressure to accept or to reject certain comportments could prove that members were sensitive to the rules.

Current IOE 2015 survey estimates that 60% of females and 35% of males believe life after death has come. 54% of men and 34% of women registered agnostic or atheist treatment. It is complicated to have a connation between religion and modernization and social change. The trust in God and religious beliefs may be a catalyst for change. People with a modern viewpoint and the intellectuals of have a deep faith in the teachings of all religions, who stress universal brotherhood and a compassionate viewpoint, and not very hard on their religion's practices. Trust in God, religious teachings are the ultimate force of daily life. The Modern vision indicates that the divine is found everywhere in religious institutes, temples, churches, and mosques **(Novak, 2012)**.

Table 4.6 Frequency and percentage distribution of urban and rural respondents belonging to various socio-economic classes on the basis of their attitude towards modernization in faith in God

Level of Modernization	Urban Respondents (n=150)												Rural Respondents (n=150)											
	Upper socio economic group				Middle socio economic group				Lower socio economic group				Upper socio economic group				Middle socio economic group				Lower socio economic group			
	Boys (n=25)		Girls (n=25)		Boys (n=25)		Girls (n=25)		Boys (n=25)		Girls (n=25)		Boys (n=25)		Girls (n=25)		Boys (n=25)		Girls (n=25)		Boys (n=25)		Girls (n=25)	
	F	%	F	%	F	%	F	%	F	%	F	%	F	%	F	%	F	%	F	%	F	%	F	%
High (35-26)	06	24	15	60	13	52	17	68	10	40	14	56	05	20	16	64	15	60	13	52	12	48	11	44
Average (25-16)	17	68	06	24	09	36	6	24	14	56	11	44	18	72	08	32	09	36	08	32	10	40	13	52
Low (15-07)	02	08	04	16	03	12	02	08	01	04	00	00	02	08	01	04	01	04	04	16	03	12	01	04

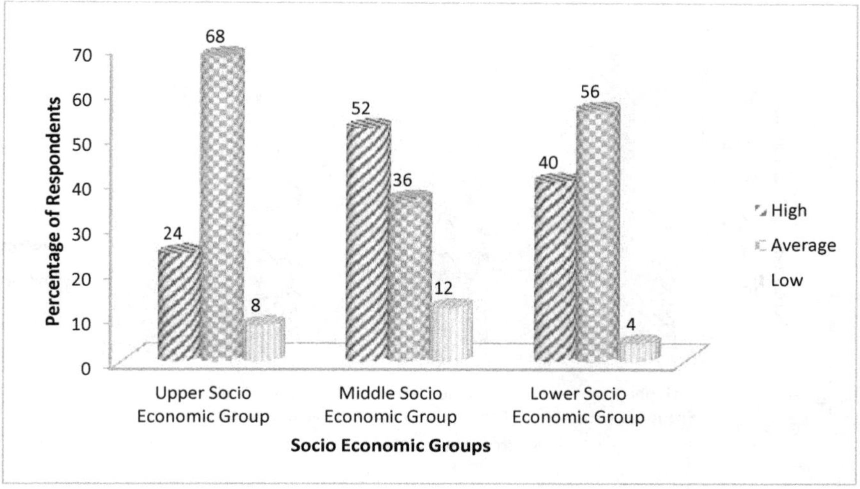

Fig 4.21 Distribution of urban boys regarding modernization in faith in God across three socio-economic groups

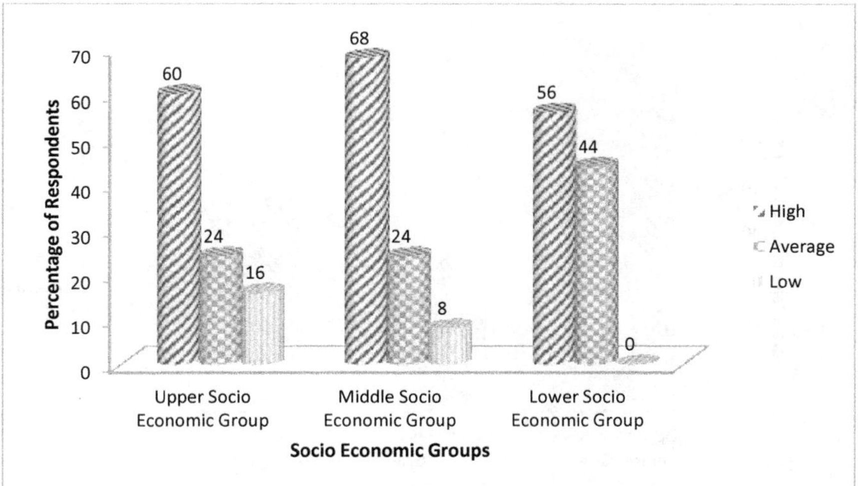

Fig 4.22 Distribution of urban girls regarding modernization in faith in God across three socio-economic groups

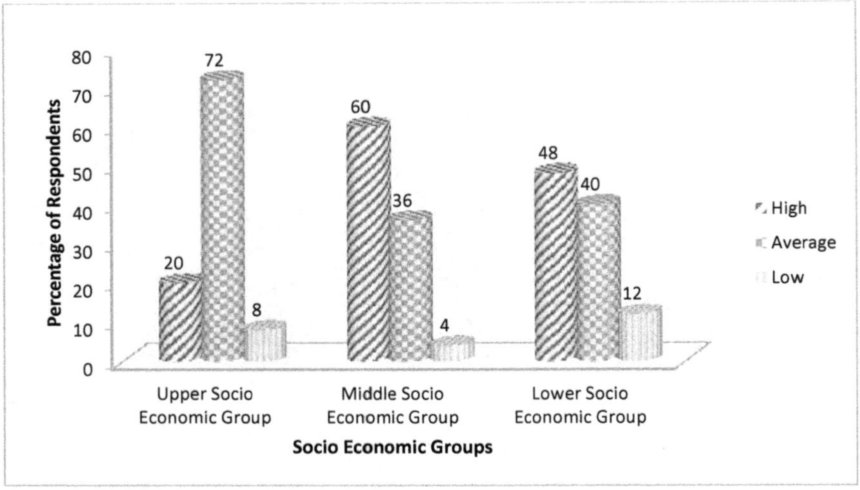

Fig 4.23 Distribution of rural boys regarding modernization in faith in God across three socio-economic groups

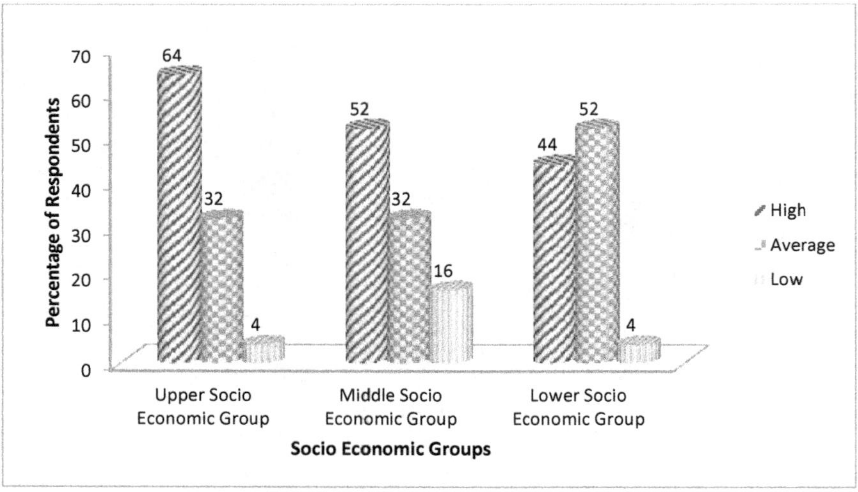

Fig 4.24 Distribution of rural girls regarding modernization in faith in God across three socio-economic groups

Table 4.7 and figures **4.25** to **4.28** highlights the frequency and percentage distribution of respondents belonging to different socio economic groups from urban and rural background on the basis of modernization pertaining to socio cultural factor. The table clearly showed that among the boys belonging to urban cultural setting, 40% of the upper socio-economic community, 32% of the middle socio-economic community, and 12% of the lower socio-economic community possessed high level of modernization regarding socio cultural factor wherein maximum modernization could be seen among boys belonging to the upper socio economic groups. In the case of rural adolescent boys 36 percent, 24 percent and 28 percent respectively from upper, middle and lower socio economic group displayed high level of modernization pertaining to socio cultural factors. Among the urban adolescent girls 56 percent, 44 percent and 36 percent respectively from upper, middle and lower socio economic group showcased high level of modernization in socio cultural factors whereas in the case of rural girls, data depicted that 44 percent, 40 percent and 08 percent respectively from upper, middle and lower socio economic group had high level of modernization towards socio cultural factor wherein girls were better than boys regarding modernization pertaining to socio cultural factors.

With regard to the average level of modernization regarding socio cultural factor it was witnessed that 52 percent, 65 percent and 68 percent urban boys respectively from upper, middle and lower socio economic group belonged to this category, whereas, 48 percent, 60 percent and 68 percent rural boys respectively from upper, middle and lower socio economic group possessed average level of modern attitude towards socio cultural factors. Average level of modernization regarding socio cultural factor was found to be possessed by 40 percent, 48 percent and 52 percent urban girls belonging to upper, middle and lower socio economic group respectively wherein girls belonging to lower socio economic group were found to be more modern in their outlook. Forty eight percent rural girls belonging to upper socio-economic community, 44% of the upper socio-economic community, 84% of the lower socio-economic community also showed average level of modernization regarding socio cultural factors, wherein, rural girls from lower socio economic group were more modern in their perspective.

Low modernization levels were depicted by 08 percent from upper socio economic group, 04 percent from middle socio economic strata and 20 percent urban boys from lower socio economic group. In view of rural boys, it was seen that low modernization levels regarding socio cultural factor was seen among 16 percent respondents each from upper and middle socio economic group followed by only 4 percent respondents from lower socio economic group. Low level of modernization regarding socio cultural factor was found in 04 percent urban girls from upper socio economic group, 08 percent urban girls from middle socio economic group followed by only 04 percent respondents from lower socio economic group. As far as rural girls were concerned, it was seen that in the category of low modernization level 08 percent from upper socio economic group, 16 percent respondents In the middle socio-economic class and 08% in the lower socio-economic class belonged to this category.

Man is genetically engaged in the development, reproduction and transmission of culture. The complex principles, patterns of behaviour, and norms that govern people's relationships and attitudes to nature and society are defined by culture. Culture We may also conclude that culture is a dynamic social heritage that provides social experience as a succession.

Customs, behaviours and beliefs characterizing a culture are socio-cultural influences. Culture includes more importantly aesthetics, education, language, law and politics, religion, technology and material culture, values and behaviour. Social influences include families, responsibilities and social standing. Most people from the urban and rural fields have a high-to-average modern attitude towards socio-cultural influences, reflecting the fact that society is in a state of transition, where people follow a lifestyle that is most feasible to them and that is in keeping with the environment.

The drops in birth rates have decreased families **(Martin *et al.*, 2003).** The standard and amount of training (i.e. years spent in education) have also increased. According to **Juhn and Potter (2006)** participation in women's labour force increased. Relationship dynamics were also modified and divorce became more common. **(Amato, 2010)** and marriage and birth was delayed in later ages **(Martin *et al.*, 2003)**.

Table 4.7 Frequency and percentage distribution of urban and rural respondents belonging to various socio-economic classes on the basis of attitude towards modernization pertaining to socio cultural factors

Level of Modernization	Urban Respondents (n=150)												Rural Respondents (n=150)											
	Upper socio economic group				Middle socio economic group				Lower socio economic group				Upper socio economic group				Middle socio economic group				Lower socio economic group			
	Boys (n=25)		Girls (n=25)		Boys (n=25)		Girls (n=25)		Boys (n=25)		Girls (n=25)		Boys (n=25)		Girls (n=25)		Boys (n=25)		Girls (n=25)		Boys (n=25)		Girls (n=25)	
	F	%	F	%	F	%	F	%	F	%	F	%	F	%	F	%	F	%	F	%	F	%	F	%
High (35-26)	10	40	14	56	08	32	11	44	03	12	11	36	9	36	11	44	6	24	10	40	07	28	02	08
Average (25-16)	13	52	10	40	16	65	12	48	17	68	13	52	12	48	12	48	15	60	11	44	17	68	21	84
Low (15-07)	02	08	01	04	01	04	02	08	05	20	01	04	04	16	02	08	04	16	04	16	01	04	02	08

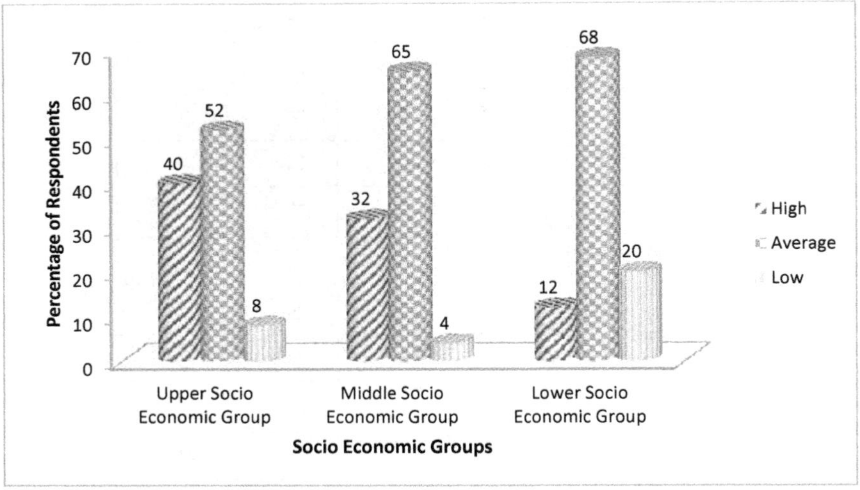

Fig 4.25 Distribution of urban boys regarding modernization in socio cultural factor across three socio-economic groups

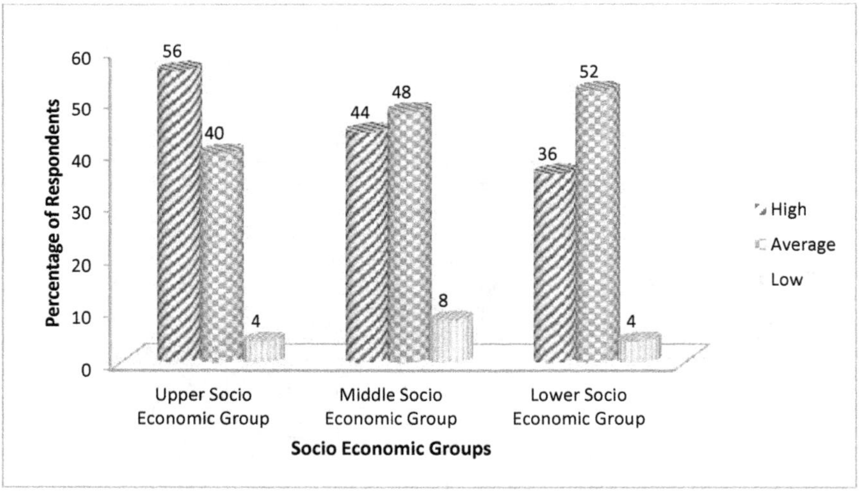

Fig 4.26 Distribution of urban girls regarding modernization in socio cultural factor across three socio-economic groups

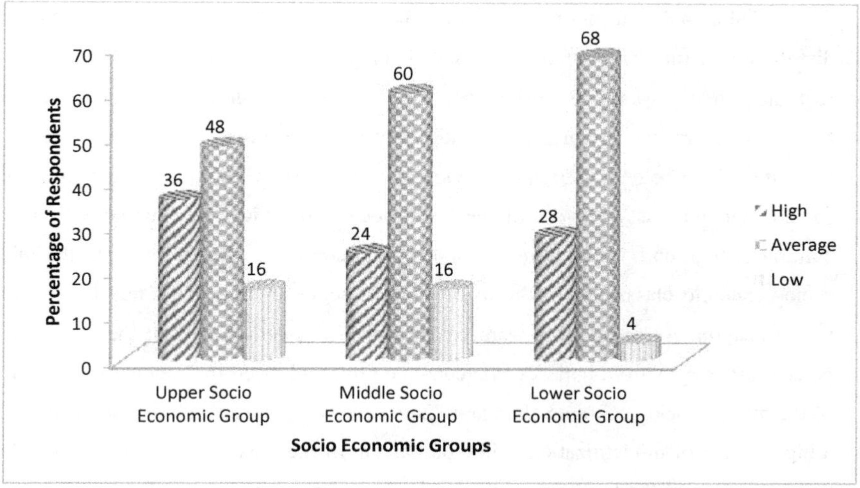

Fig 4.27 Distribution of rural boys regarding modernization in socio cultural factor across three socio-economic groups

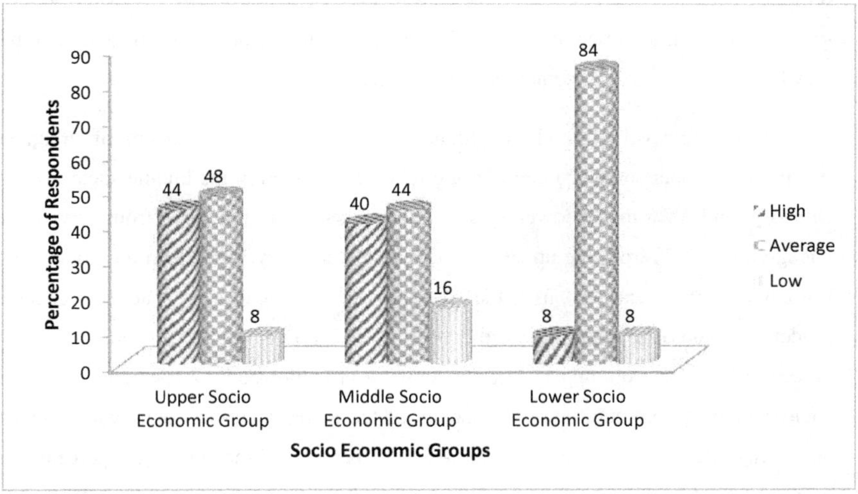

Fig 4.28 Distribution of rural girls regarding modernization in socio cultural factor across three socio-economic groups

Table 4.8 and **figures 4.29 to 4.32** highlights the frequency and percentage distribution of rural and urban respondents belonging to different socio economic groups regarding their towards modernization. The table clearly shows that in case of boys belonging to urban cultural setting a high level of modernization was depicted by 72 percent of those belonging to upper socio economic class followed by 64% of the middle socio-economic class and 48% of the lower socio-economic class. For boys from rural cultural backgrounds, 64% from the upper socio-economic class, 52% from the middle socio-economic class and 48% from the lower socio-economic class had high level of modernization. As far as girls were concerned, it was reflected from the table that 80 percent urban girls from upper socio economic group followed by an equal i.e. 80 percent of the middle socio-economic class and 72 percent of the lower socio-economic class had a high degree of modernization, while 68 percent of the upper, 40 percent of the middle and 52 percent of the lower socio-economic class were seen to be modernised in the case of rural girls, had high level of modernization. On the whole it was witnessed that girls were more modern in their attitude as compared to boys. This may be because the orthodox pattern they are held in since ages is nourished by women. They want society to grant them equal, dignified and respectful status. In comparison to their male counterparts, they have a high degree of contemporary attitude.

Average level of modern attitude was seen among 24 percent of urban boys belonging to upper socio economic group followed by 28% in the middle socio-economic category, and 48% in the lower socio-economic category. For boys from rural cultural backgrounds, 36% from the upper socio-economic category, 40% from the middle socio-economic category and 48% from the lower socio-economic category had average level of modern attitude. As far as girls were concerned, it is reflected from the table that only 16 percent urban girls from upper socio economic group followed by 20 percent of the middle socio-economic community and 28 percent of the lower socio-economic community had an average degree of modernization, while 32 percent of the upper, 60 percent of the middle and 40 percent of the lower socio-economic community were seen to be modernized in the case of rural girls, had average level of modernization.

Low level of modern attitude was seen among 04 percent urban boys from upper, 08 percent middle socio economic group and 12 percent from lower socio economic group. In case of boys from rural cultural setting, it was seen that none of respondents from upper socio economic class, 08% of the middle socio-economic class and 04% of the lowest socio-economic class had low level of attitude towards modernization. As far as girls were concerned, it was noticed that only 04 percent from upper socio economic group and none of the urban girls belonging to lower and middle socio economic group possessed low level of modernization whereas, in case of rural girls, it was seen that none of respondents from upper as well as middle socio economic group and only 08 percent from lower socio economic group possessed low level of modernization. Modernization is a phase of transformation from conventional to some form of technology and growth as well as the consequent changes in social structure, beliefs, intentions, achievement and expectations. Now parents are conscious of their children and provide education equally, not only for boys, but for girls. Similarly **Chandalia (2015)** revealed that major modernization disparities with regard to both rural and urban young people as well as **Ninaniya *et al.,* (2017)** also indicated that in contrast to rural youth, urban youth had a greater approach to modernization based on socio-cultural circumstances. **Jogsan (2015)** revealed in his study that there was a substantial gap in modernization between boys and girls.

Table 4.8 Frequency and percentage distribution of urban and rural respondents belonging to various socio-economic classes on the basis of their attitude towards modernization

Level of Modernization	Urban Respondents (n=150)												Rural Respondents (n=150)											
	Upper socio economic group				Middle socio economic group				Lower socio economic group				Upper socio economic group				Middle socio economic group				Lower socio economic group			
	Boys (n=25)		Girls (n=25)		Boys (n=25)		Girls (n=25)		Boys (n=25)		Girls (n=25)		Boys (n=25)		Girls (n=25)		Boys (n=25)		Girls (n=25)		Boys (n=25)		Girls (n=25)	
	F	%	F	%	F	%	F	%	F	%	F	%	F	%	F	%	F	%	F	%	F	%	F	%
High (245-180)	08	72	20	80	16	64	20	80	12	48	18	72	16	64	17	68	13	52	10	40	12	48	13	52
Average (179-114)	06	24	04	16	07	28	05	20	10	40	70	28	09	36	08	32	10	40	15	60	12	48	10	40
Low (113-49)	01	04	01	04	02	08	00	00	03	12	00	00	00	00	00	00	02	08	00	00	01	04	02	08

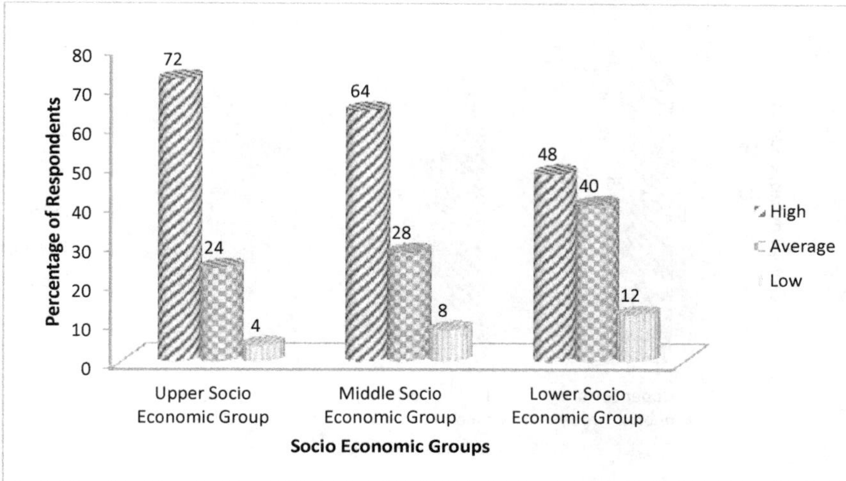

Fig 4.29 Distribution of urban boys regarding modernization across three socio-economic groups

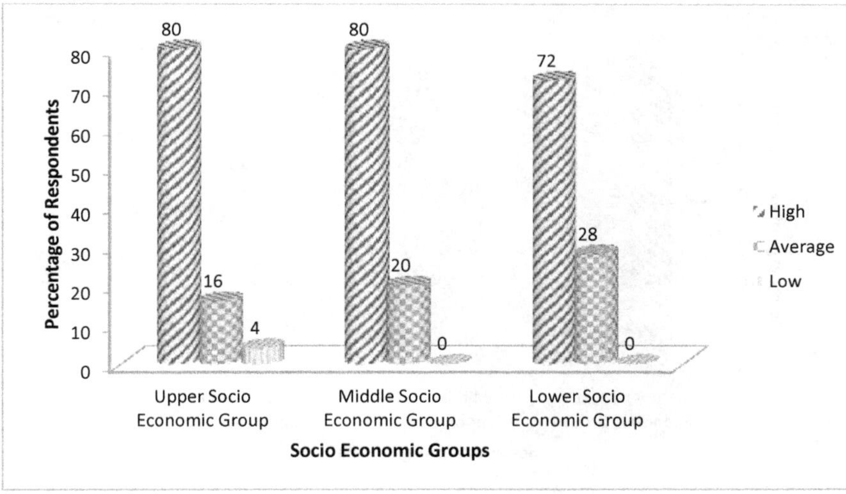

Fig 4.30 Distribution of urban girls regarding modernization across three socio-economic groups

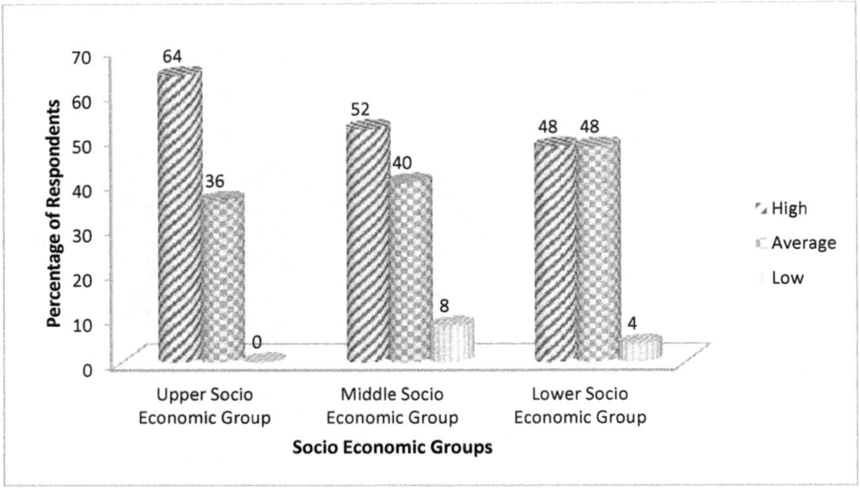

Fig 4.31 Distribution of rural boys regarding modernization across three socio-economic groups

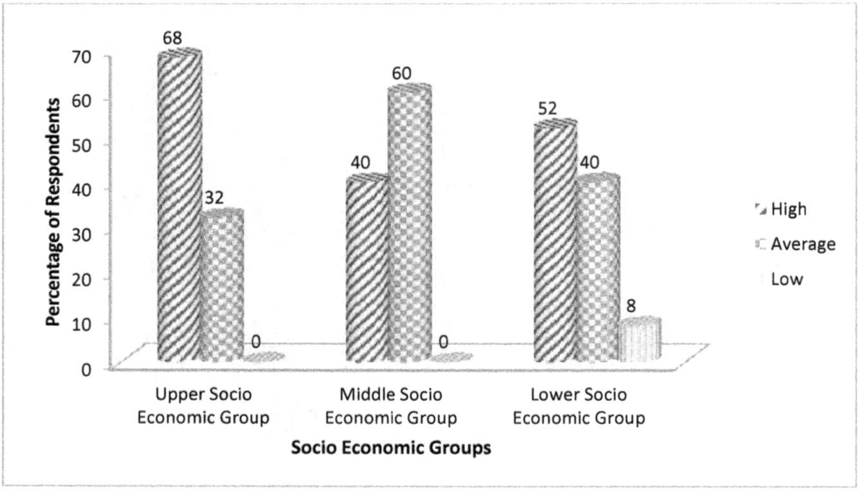

Fig 4.32 Distribution of rural girls regarding modernization across three socio-economic groups

Table 4.9 Comparison of urban and rural boys and girls belonging to different socio economic groups based on their attitude towards education

Socio economic Status	Socio cultural setting	Boys n=150		Girls n= 150		t-cal	p-value
		Mean	Standard Deviation	Mean	Standard Deviation		
Upper socio economic status (n=100)	Urban (n=50)	23.40	3.40	26.80	4.21	3.13**	0.002
	Rural (n=50)	22.36	2.84	25.16	2.82	3.49**	0.000
Middle socio economic status (n=100)	Urban (n=50)	22.40	2.27	25.04	4.37	2.67*	0.009
	Rural (n=50)	19.92	2.85	21.36	4.47	1.35NS	0.181
Lower socio economic status (n=100)	Urban (n=50)	20.00	1.50	24.08	4.11	4.66**	0.000
	Rural (n=50)	17.04	2.74	20.12	4.38	2.97*	0.004

** Highly Significant

*Significant

NS Non Significant

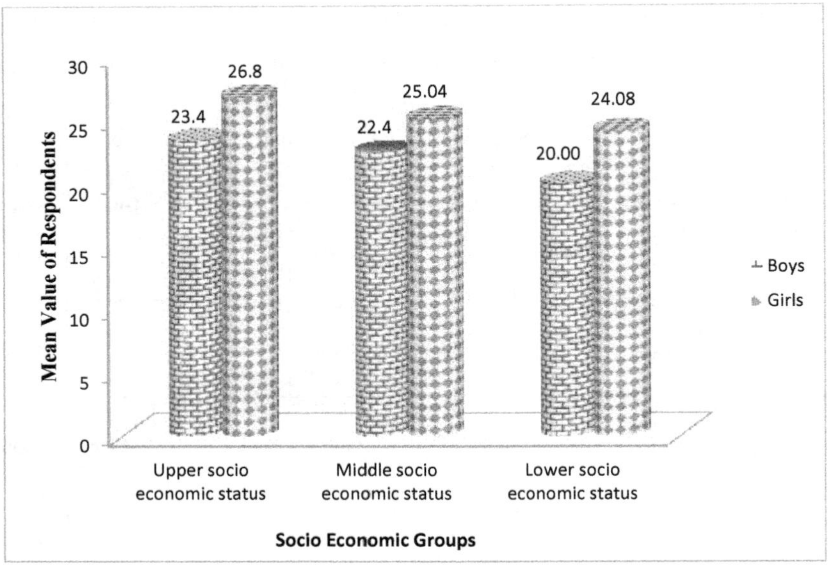

Fig 4.33 Attitude towards education of urban adolescents across three socio economic groups

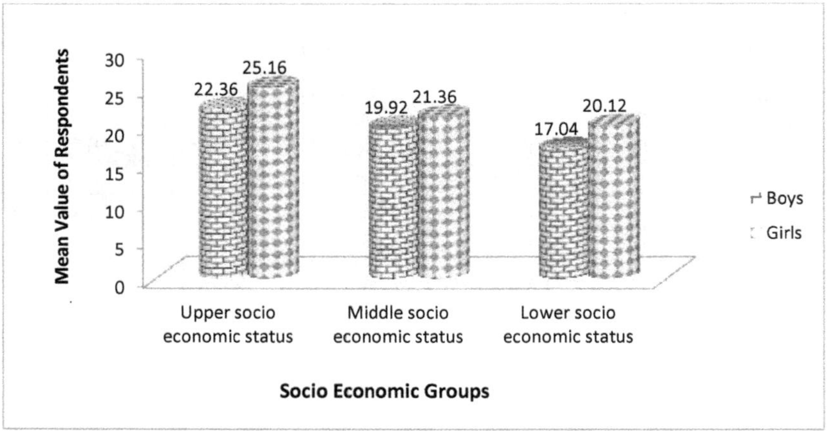

Fig 4.34 Attitude towards education of rural adolescents across three socio economic groups

The above **table 4.9** and **figure 4.33** and **4.34** indicates the comparison of urban and rural boys and girls belonging to different socio economic group based on their attitude towards education. In case of respondents belonging to upper socio economic group, there lies a significant gender difference both among the urban and rural masses (t= 3.13, p=0.002 and t= 3.49, p= 0.000 respectively) regarding their attitude towards education. The mean value depicted in the table further clarifies that girls in all the socio economic strata have better attitude towards education as compared to their male counterparts.

Among the respondents of middle socio economic strata a non significant gender variance is noted in the urban boys and girls as the t value is 2.67 and p value is 0.009 signifying a significant gender variance. The mean value further indicated that girls have better attitude towards education as compared to their male counterparts. Among the rural respondents belonging to middle socio economic class, it is considered that a non significant gender variance existed as for as attitude towards education was concerned as the t value was found to be 1.35 and p value was 0.181. The mean value further depicted that girls had a slightly better attitude towards education in the rural masses also as compared to their male counterparts.

The table also reflects that there is a significant difference among boys and girls belonging to both urban and rural background among the respondents from lower socio economic group as the t-value for urban group was found to be 4.66 and p value was 0.000 and so was the case with rural respondents wherein the t-value was 2.97 and p value was 0.004 signifying a significant gender difference among both the groups with regard to their attitude towards education. Among the urban masses it was seen that girls possessed a better attitude towards education as compared to their male counterparts whereas in case of rural respondents from lower socio economic group it was also noticed that female possessed better attitude towards education when compared to their male counterparts. Finding of the study coincides with the study conducted by **Cresswell *et al.* (2002)** suggests that In particular in the reading field where girls are above boys at all levels, there are major gender gaps. This table also indicates that the attitude of respondents towards education increases as the socioeconomic level rises. A constructive educational approach increases young people's academic achievement. Parents have recognized the need to educate the girl and hence the view of girls has dramatically shifted to their education. Study conducted by **Das *et al.* (2014)** highlights that the factors that build obstacles for academic achievements include anxiety, socioeconomic strata, familial environment, form of school etc. Statistics indicate that the attitudes of boys and girls to schooling and academic performance vary greatly.

Table 4.10 Comparison of urban and rural boys and girls belonging to different socio economic groups based on their attitude towards parents child relationship

Socio economic Status	Socio cultural setting	Boys n= 150		Girls n= 150		t-cal	p-value
		Mean	Standard Deviation	Mean	Standard Deviation		
Upper socio economic status (n=100)	Urban (n=50)	23.96	3.29	25.48	4.06	1.78*	0.002
	Rural (n=50)	23.36	2.09	25.44	3.93	2.33*	0.022
Middle socio economic status (n=100)	Urban (n=50)	22.48	2.27	24.48	4.21	2.08*	0.009
	Rural (n=50)	19.88	2.86	21.68	3.38	2.02	0.047
Lower socio economic status (n=100)	Urban (n=50)	20.60	1.75	23.12	3.85	2.97*	0.000
	Rural (n=50)	16.56	2.97	22.20	3.85	5.79	0.000

*Significant

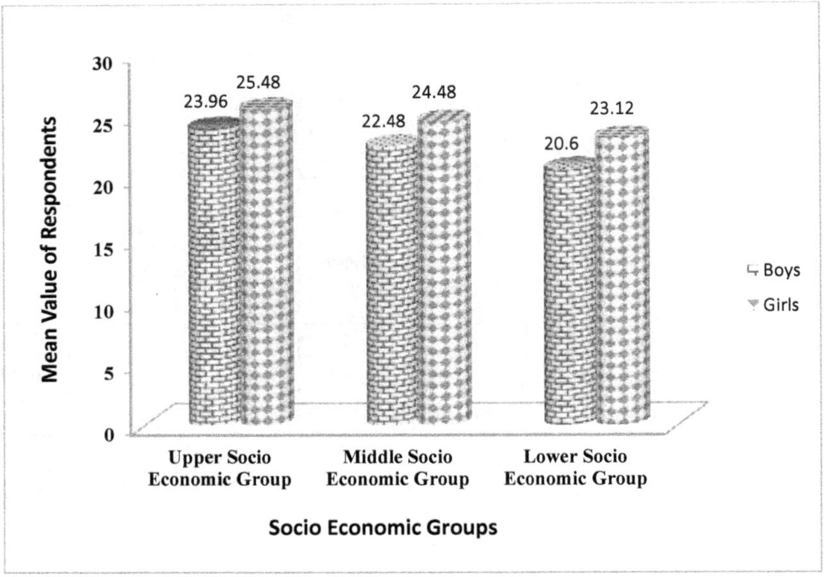

Fig 4.35 Attitude towards parents child relationship of urban adolescents across three socio economic groups

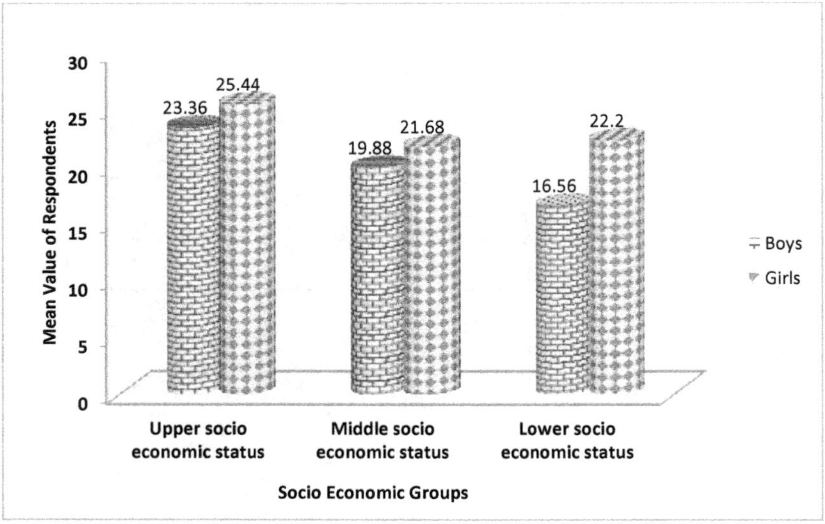

Fig 4.36 Attitude towards parents child relationship of rural adolescents across three socio economic groups

Table 4.10 and **figure 4.35** and **4.36** shows the comparative analysis of urban and rural boys and girls belonging to various socio-economic classes on the basis of their respective characteristics towards parents child relationship. In case of respondents from the upper socio economic group it was evident from the table that there lies a significant gender variance in parents child relationship among the urban masses (t=1.78, p= 0.002) as well as rural masses (t= 2.33, p= 0.22) showing a significant difference among boys and girls with regard to parent child relationship. The mean values indicated that girls in this group possessed a slightly better attitude regarding parents child relationship as compared to their male counterparts. The explanation is maybe that girls are closer to their families and support mothers work in the home and can therefore spend more time with their families and share more closeness to their parents in the bargain. The healthy relationship between parents has a positive influence on children's self-esteem, school success, cognitive growth, and child behaviour. **Kerr *et al.* (2012)** reported that, while parent attitudes influence child behaviour, the relationship changes as a child develops with adolescent behaviour influencing the parenting style and attitudes. Children's behaviour influences that of their parent.

A significant gender variance regarding parents child relationship was also evident among both the urban and rural masses belonging to the middle socio economic group t=2.08, p= 0.009 and t= 2.02, p= 0.047 for urban and rural category respectively signifying a significant gender variance in both the groups. Girls in these groups were also found to have better attitude towards parents child relationship as compared to the boys.

From the table it is evident that there lies a significant difference among boys and girls both from urban and rural background belonging to lower socio economic group with regard to their attitude towards parent child relationship as the t-value was found to be 2.97 and p-value 0.000 for the urban respondents and t-value 5.79 and p-value 0.000 for the rural masses indicating a highly significant gender variance. The mean values further indicated that girls in both the rural and urban group have better attitude towards parents child relationship as compared to their male counterparts.

The findings of the current research are consistent with the study conducted by **Suri *et al.* (2016)** which revealed a disparity in parent child relationship between male and female adolescents.

Table 4.11 Comparison of urban and rural boys and girls belonging to different socio economic groups based on their attitude towards politics

Socio economic Status	Socio cultural setting	Boys n= 150		Girls n= 150		t-cal	p-value
		Mean	Standard Deviation	Mean	Standard Deviation		
Upper socio economic status (n=100)	Urban (n=50)	24.80	4.12	25.28	3.33	0.45NS	0.654
	Rural (n=50)	23.28	2.93	23.76	3.70	0.50NS	0.618
Middle socio economic status (n=100)	Urban (n=50)	22.72	2.47	23.64	4.26	0.93*	0.355
	Rural (n=50)	20.60	3.75	21.36	2.13	0.88*	0.038
Lower socio economic status (n=100)	Urban (n=50)	20.60	1.78	23.60	3.32	3.97**	0.000
	Rural (n=50)	17.36	2.36	21.88	4.32	4.58**	0.000

** Highly Significant

*Significant

NS Non Significant

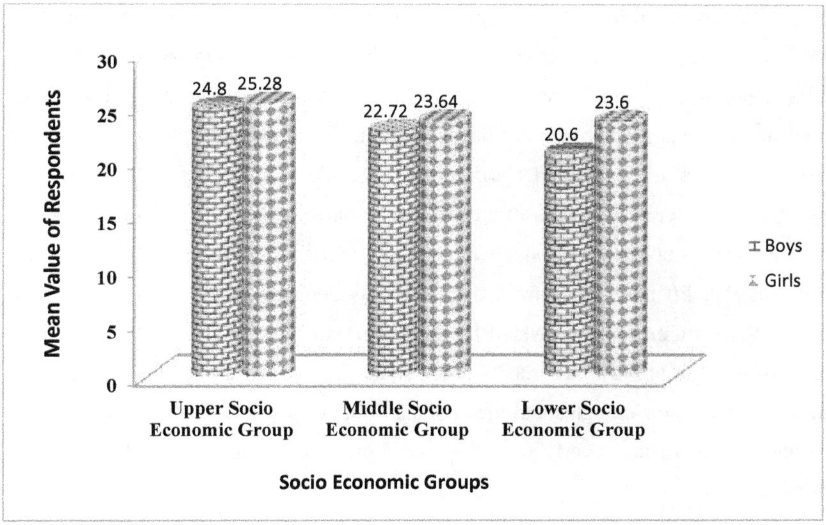

Fig 4.37 Attitude towards politics of urban adolescents across three socio economic groups

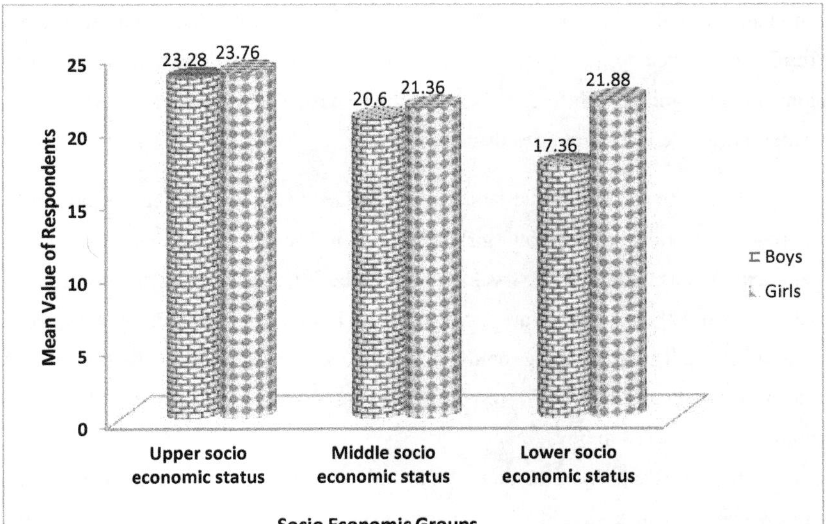

Fig 4.38 Attitude towards politics of rural adolescents across three socio economic groups

The above **table 4.11** and **figure 4.37** and **4.38** reveals the comparison of urban and rural boys and girls belonging to different socio economic group based on their attitude towards politics. Among the respondents from upper socio economic sector it was seen that there lies a non significant gender difference among the urban group (t= 0.45, p= 0.654) and also a non significant gender difference was evident among the rural masses (t= 0.50, p= 0.618) with regards to their attitude towards politics wherein girls had a slightly better attitude towards politics than boys which is an important determinant of modernization as feminists still lift their voice from the grassroots demanding gender equality in modern times. Women are now empowered by education and socially driven by working people. The Constitution has also accorded women equal rights. Political attitudes are changing as girls can voice their thoughts and viewpoints. Politics modernization is seen in fields such as health, extremism, poverty reduction and family and community welfare that discuss global agenda.

Data depicted in the table showed a non significant gender variance among urban boys and girls from middle socio economic group as t-value was 0.93 and p value was 0.355. Mean values indicated that girls had slightly better approach towards politics as compared to their male counterparts. A significant gender variance was seen among the rural masses belonging to middle socio economic as t-value was 0.88 and p= 0.038 indicating a significant difference between the groups. Mean value indicated that girls have better attitude regarding politics than boys.

It is witnessed from the table that there lies a highly significant gender difference among urban and rural boys and girls belonging to lower socio economic strata regarding concern towards politics as the t-value for urban boys and girls was found to be 3.97 and p-value was 0.000 and among rural boys and girls t-value was found to be 4.58 and p value was 0.000 indicating a strong significant gender difference among the respondents. The mean value revealed that girl respondents were found to have better attitude towards politics as compared to boys.

Similar results were obtained by a study carried out by **Zeng (2014)** who reported that women's participation in politics has been increased to a certain degree, in particular at the level of municipalities and districts, mostly due to women 's electoral quota. However, at the base level there has been no significant change (in some cases even negative movement). Views can change drastically based on how people feel about politics and the immediate climate.

Table 4.12 Comparison of urban and rural boys and girls belonging to different socio economic groups based on their attitude towards status of women

Socio economic Status	Socio cultural setting	Boys n=150		Girls n=150		t-cal	p-value
		Mean	Standard Deviation	Mean	Standard Deviation		
Upper socio economic status (n=100)	Urban (n=50)	25.00	2.94	24.56	3.29	0.49NS	0.625
	Rural (n=50)	23.12	1.96	24.16	3.84	1.20NS	0.233
Middle socio economic status (n=100)	Urban (n=50)	22.28	2.39	25.60	3.65	3.80**	0.000
	Rural (n=50)	20.36	2.98	22.60	2.97	2.65*	0.009
Lower socio economic status (n=100)	Urban (n=50)	20.36	1.70	23.44	3.34	4.10**	0.000
	Rural (n=50)	17.28	2.31	21.96	3.31	5.79**	0.000

** Highly Significant

*Significant

NS Non Significant

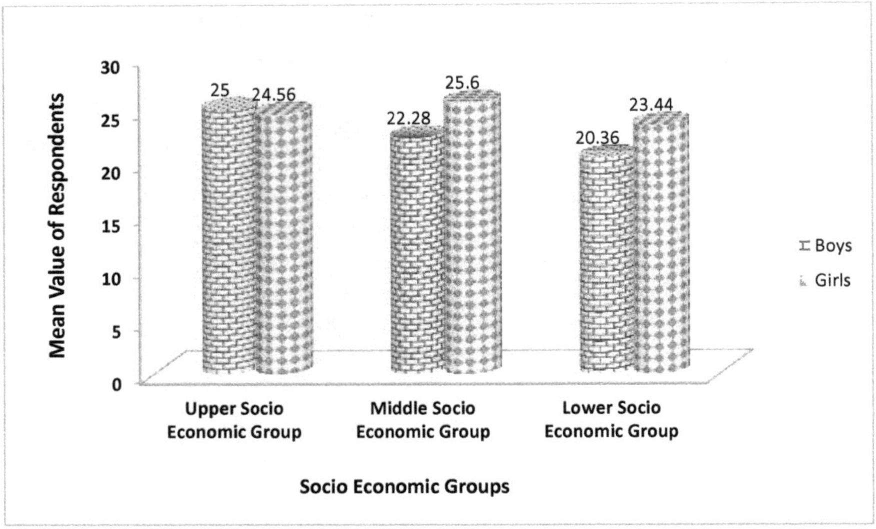

Fig 4.39 Attitude towards status of women of urban adolescents across three socio economic groups

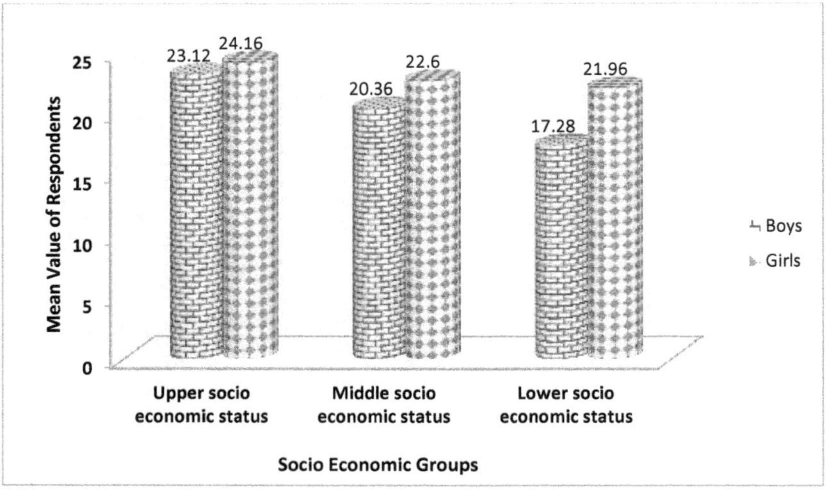

Fig 4.40 Attitude towards status of women among rural adolescents across three socio economic groups

The above **table 4.12** and **figure 4.39** and **4.40** shows the comparative analysis of urban and rural boys and girls belonging to various socio-economic classes on the basis of their respective characteristics attitude towards status of women. In case of respondents from the upper socio economic group, it was evident from the table that there lies a non significant gender variance in status of women among the urban masses (t=0.49, p= 0.625) as well as rural masses (t= 1.20, p= 0.233) although the mean values indicated that boys in this group possessed a slightly better positive attitude towards status of women as compared to their female counterparts.

A significant gender variance regarding status of women was also evident among the urban and rural masses belonging to the middle socio economic group where t value was 3.80, p value was 0.000 and t value was 2.65, p value was 0.009 respectively. Girls in these groups were also found to have better positive attitude towards status of women as compared to the boy respondents.

From the table it was evident that there lies a significant differences among boys and girls both from urban and rural background belonging to lower socio economic group with regard to their attitude towards status of women as the t-value was found to be 4.10 and p-value 0.000 for the urban respondents and t-value 5.79 and p-value 0.000 for the rural masses indicating a highly significant gender variance. The mean values further indicated that girls in both the rural and urban groups have better attitude towards status of women as compared to their male counterparts.

Since independence the condition of Indian women has changed drastically. Women in the fields of education, jobs and political engagement in the constitution are now granted equal opportunities. Internal reforms must also be ignored to boost women's status and reduce the rate of violence by women. A study conducted by **Shettar (2015)** revealed that with a single dimension, women's status cannot be seen but as multi-dynamic, and their status will bring about a better understanding in relation to different components of women's lives. **Loo and Thorpe (1998)** also revealed that the attitudes towards the role of women in society have been liberalized since the mid 1990's in terms of perceptions towards both genders and that gender differences have been decreased in the 1990's.

Table 4.13 Comparison of urban and rural boys and girls belonging to different socio economic groups based on their attitude towards marriage

Socio economic Status	Socio cultural setting	Boys n= 150		Girls n= 150		t-cal	p-value
		Mean	Standard Deviation	Mean	Standard Deviation		
Upper socio economic status (n=100)	Urban (n=50)	24.60	3.31	24.76	3.01	0.55NS	0.583
	Rural (n=50)	22.64	2.70	24.52	4.28	1.85NS	0.068
Middle socio economic status (n=100)	Urban (n=50)	22.16	2.23	25.32	4.56	3.11**	0.002
	Rural (n=50)	20.52	2.75	23.44	3.35	3.36**	0.001
Lower socio economic status (n=100)	Urban (n=50)	27.60	1.96	23.68	3.55	3.59**	0.000
	Rural (n=50)	17.48	2.77	20.64	3.59	3.48**	0.000

** Highly Significant

NS Non Significant

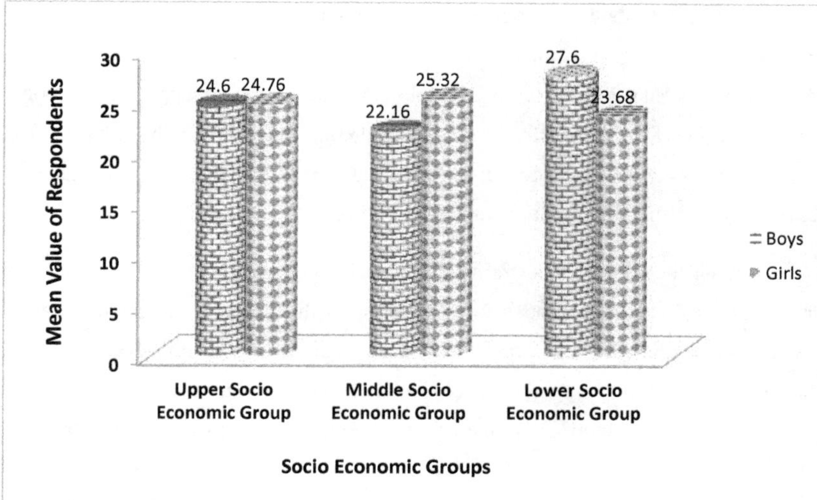

Fig 4.41 Attitude towards marriage of urban adolescents across three socio economic groups

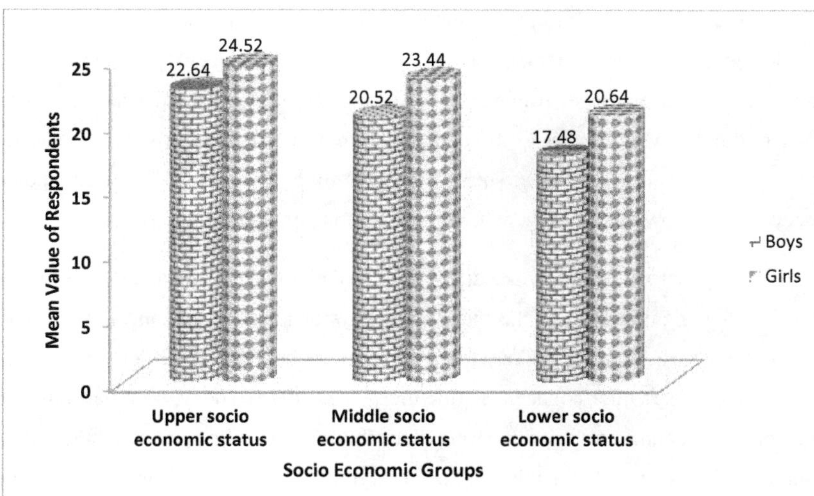

Fig 4.42 Attitude towards marriage among rural adolescents across three socio economic groups

The above **table 4.13** and **figure 4.41** and **4.42** indicates the comparison of urban and rural boys and girls belonging to different socio economic group based on their attitude towards marriage. In case of adolescents belonging to upper socio economic group, there lies a non significant gender difference both among the urban and rural masses where t value was 5.55, p value was 0.583 and t value 1.85, p value 0.068 respectively regarding their attitude towards marriage.

Among the respondents, from middle socio economic strata a significant gender variance is noted in the urban boys and girls as the t value was 3.11 and p value was 0.002 whereas among the rural boys and girls the t value was 3.36 and p value was 0.001 indicating a significant gender difference. The mean value further depicted that girls had a better attitude towards marriage in the urban as well as rural masses as compared to their male counterparts.

The table reflected that there was a significant difference among boys and girls belonging to urban and rural background among the respondents from lower socio economic group as the t-value for urban group was found to be 3.59 and p value was 0.000 and so was the case with rural respondents where the t value was 3.48 and p value was 0.000 signifying a significant gender difference among both the groups with regard to their attitude towards marriage. Among the urban masses, it was seen that boys possessed a better attitude towards marriage as compared to their female counterparts whereas, in case of rural respondents from lower socio economic group, it was noticed that girls possessed better attitude towards marriage when compared to their male counterparts.

In recent years the gender differences in the attitude of adolescents to matrimony have shifted significantly. In the mid 1970s, boys and girls were equivalent to marriage support, but girls were more likely to postpone marriage or to pursue jobs relative to girls until several years after college. **(Schulenberg *et al.* 1995)** Today, however, boys tend to be optimistic about marriage more often than children. **(Flanigom *et al.* 2005)** and a large number of girls are of the opinion of boys in wanting to delay marriage. According to **Bae *et al.* (2000)** the recent rise in the percentage of girls who are likely to choose to postpone marriage reflects new opportunities for education and jobs available to women, as well as wider social values that emphasize gender equality and empowerment.

Table 4.14 Comparison of urban and rural boys and girls belonging to different socio economic groups based on their attitude towards faith in God

Socio economic Status	Socio cultural setting	Boys n= 150		Girls n= 150		t-cal	p-value
		Mean	Standard Deviation	Mean	Standard Deviation		
Upper socio economic status (n=100)	Urban (n=50)	25.04	3.28	25.84	3.18	0.87NS	0.387
	Rural (n=50)	23.44	2.32	25.48	4.70	1.94NS	0.056
Middle socio economic status (n=100)	Urban (n=50)	21.88	1.92	28.72	3.83	7.97**	0.000
	Rural (n=50)	21.28	2.54	23.48	3.46	2.22*	0.029
Lower socio economic status (n=100)	Urban (n=50)	20.08	2.06	24.52	4.31	4.64**	0.000
	Rural (n=50)	16.68	2.11	23.44	4.36	6.97**	0.000

** Highly Significant

*Significant

NS Non Significant

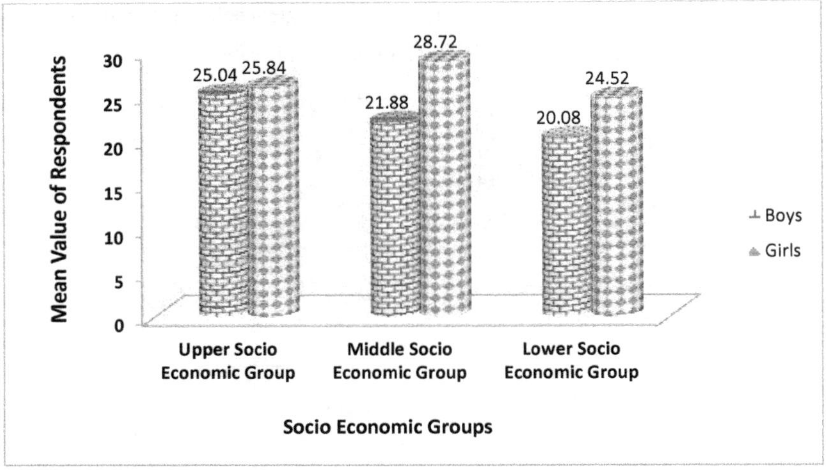

Fig 4.43 Attitude towards faith in God of urban adolescents across three socio economic groups

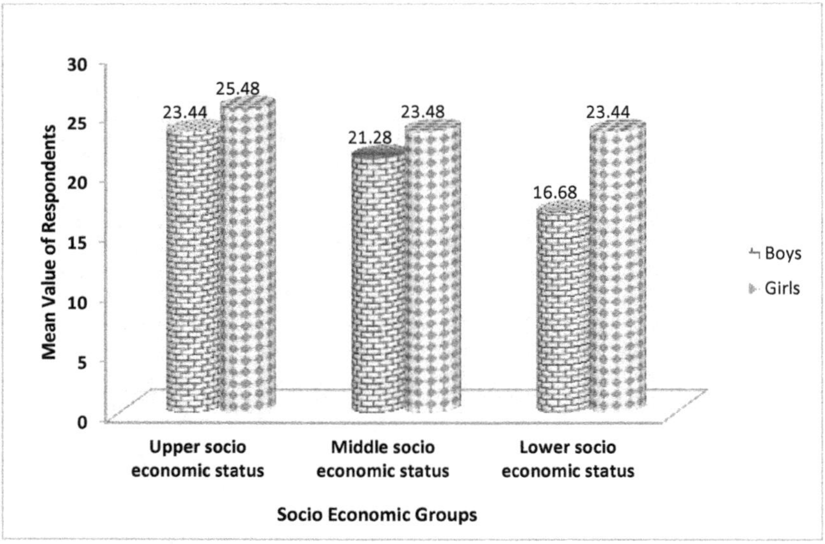

Fig 4.44 Attitude towards faith in god among rural adolescents across three socio economic groups

Table 4.14 and **figure 4.43** and **4.44** shows the comparative analysis of urban and rural boys and girls Belonging to various socio-economic classes on the basis of their respective characteristics attitude towards faith in God. In case of respondents from the upper socio economic group it was evident from the table that there lies a non significant gender variance in faith in God among the urban masses ($t=0.87$, $p= 0.387$) as well as rural masses ($t=1.94$, $p=0.056$) although the mean values indicated that girls in this group also possessed a slightly more faith in God as compared to their male counterparts.

A significant gender variance regarding faith in God was also evident among both the urban and rural masses belonging to the middle socio economic group ($t=7.97$, $p= 0.000$ and $t= 2.22$, $p= 0.029$) for urban and rural category. Girls in this group were also found to have more faith in God as compared to the boys.

From the table it is evident that there lies a significant difference among boys and girls both from urban and rural background belonging to lower socio economic group with regard to their attitude towards faith in God as the t-value was found to be 4.64 and p value 0.000 for the urban respondents and t-value 6.97 and p value 0.000 for the rural masses indicating a highly significant gender variance. The mean value further indicates that girls in both the rural and urban group have more faith in God as compared to their male counterparts.

Girls are influenced more religiously than boys as they believe and respect religious education and preaching and therefore grow faith in God. Women in all communities, cultures and religions are more religious than men. The study by **Schnabel, (2015)** , found that women tended to record daily prayers more often than men, obtained similar results. These results problematize the notion that the religiosity of biology is inherent and provide a theoretical framework for potential attempts to understand.

Table 4.15 Comparison of urban and rural boys and girls belonging to different socio economic groups based on their attitude towards socio cultural factors

Socio economic Status	Socio cultural setting	Boys n=150		Girls n=150		t-cal	p-value
		Mean	Standard Deviation	Mean	Standard Deviation		
Upper socio economic status (n=100)	Urban (n=50)	25.52	3.13	25.36	2.97	0.18NS	0.857
	Rural (n=50)	23.20	1.89	25.84	4.49	2.70**	0.008
Middle socio economic status (n=100)	Urban (n=50)	22.52	1.58	25.16	3.53	3.41**	0.001
	Rural (n=50)	21.68	3.14	21.76	2.74	0.09NS	0.0928
Lower socio economic status (n=100)	Urban (n=50)	19.36	1.89	22.76	4.21	3.67**	0.000
	Rural (n=50)	17.60	2.48	21.32	3.60	4.25**	0.000

** Highly Significant

NS Non Significant

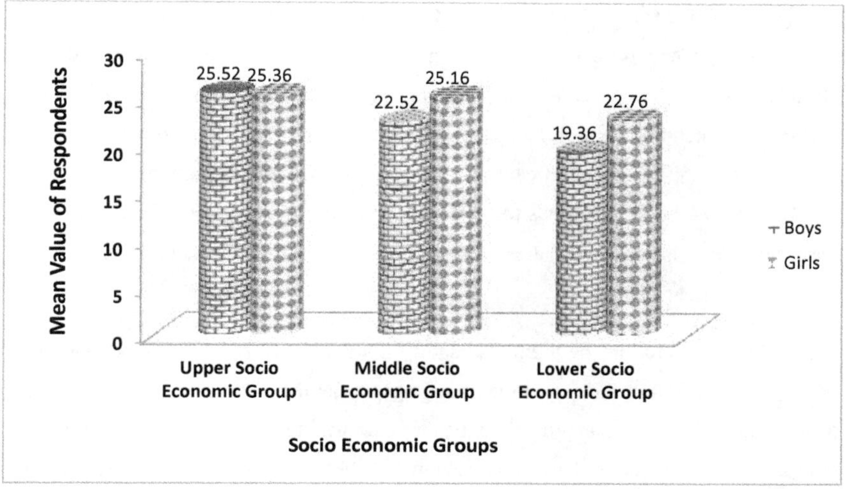

Fig 4.45 Attitude towards socio cultural factor of urban adolescents across three socio economic groups

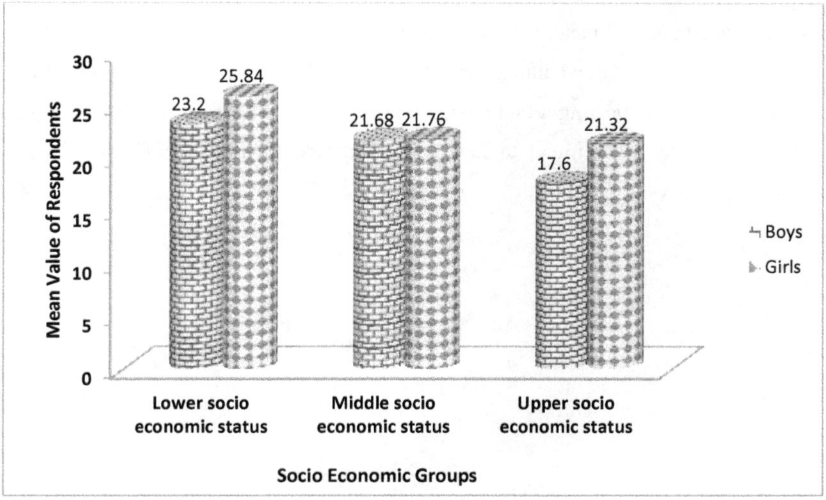

Fig 4.46 Attitude towards socio cultural factor among rural adolescents across three socio economic groups

The above **table 4.15** and **figure 4.45** and **4.46** indicates the comparison of urban and rural boys and girls belonging to different socio economic group based on their attitude towards socio cultural factor. Among the respondents from upper socio economic sector it was seen that there lies a non significant gender difference among the urban group ($t= 0.18$, $p= 0.857$) and a significant gender difference was evident among the rural masses ($t= 2.70$, $p= 0.008$) with regards to their attitude towards socio cultural factors wherein it was seen that girls were of a better frame of mind than boys as far as socio cultural factors were concerned.

Data depicted in the table also shows a significant gender variance among urban boys and girls from middle socio economic group as the t-value was 3.41 and $p=0.001$. Mean values indicate that girls had better approach towards socio cultural factors as compared to their male counterparts. A non significant gender variance was seen among the rural masses belonging to middle socio economic status.

It is witnessed from the table that their lies a significant gender difference among urban and rural boys and girls belonging to lower socio economic strata with concern towards socio cultural factors as the t-value for urban boys and girls was found to be 3.67 and p value was 0.000 and among rural boys and girls t-value was found to be 4.25 and p value was 0.000 indicating a highly significant gender difference among the respondents. Girl respondents were found to have better attitude towards socio cultural factors as compared to boys.

Table 4.16 Comparison of boys and girls belonging to different socio economic groups based on their attitude towards total modernization

Socio economic Status	Boys n=150		Girls n=150		t-tab	p-value
	Mean	SD	Mean	SD		
Upper socio economic status (n=100)	167.40	8.07	176.22	18.23	3.12**	0.002
Middle socio economic status (n=100)	150.34	8.58	166.82	18.75	5.65**	0.000
Lower socio economic status (n=100)	130.88	11.87	158.38	19.08	8.65**	0.000

** Highly Significant

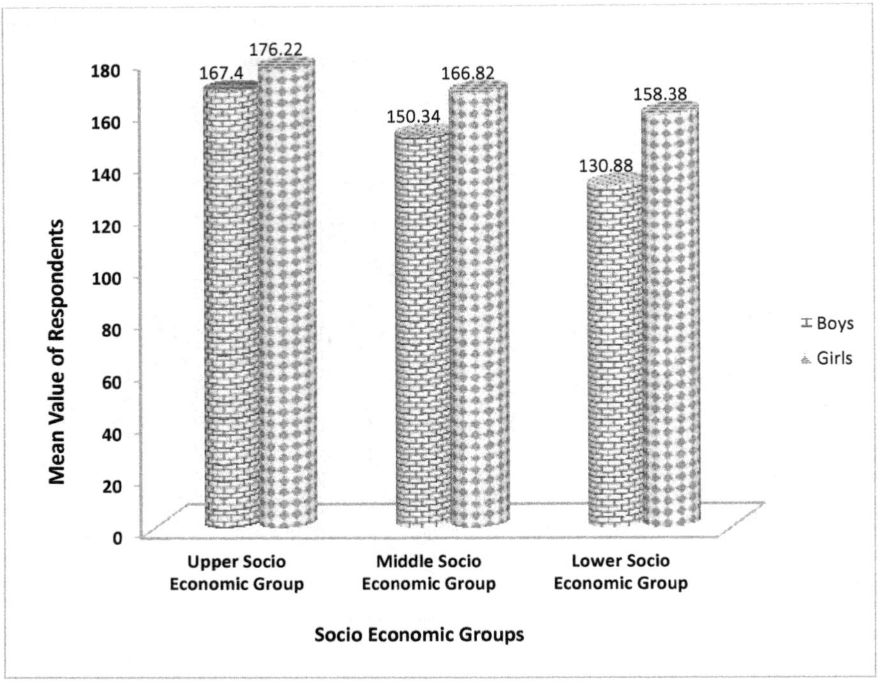

Fig 4.47 Comparison of boys and girls belonging to different socio economic groups based on their attitude towards modernization

Table 4.16 and **figure 4.47** shows the comparative analysis of urban and rural boys and girls belonging to various socio-economic classes on the basis of their respective characteristics attitude towards modernization. In case of respondents from the upper socio economic group it was evident from the table that there lies a strongly significant gender variance in modernization among the boys and girls were (t= 3.12, p= 0.002). The mean values further indicated that girls in this group had slightly better attitude towards modernization as compared to their male counterparts.

A highly significant gender variance regarding modernization was also evident among both boys and girls belonging to the middle socio economic group (t= 5.65, p= 0.000). The mean values further indicated that girls in lower socio economic group and middle socio economic group had better attitude towards modernization as compared to their male counterparts.

It is clear from the table that there is a rather important distinction among boys and girls belonging to lower socio economic group with regard to their attitude towards modernization as the t-value were found to be 8.65 and p-value 0.000.

Better education, understanding of government policies and empowerment programmes for women in this society that seeks to boost women's status is responsible for cultivating a positive attitude toward modernization. A research by **Chawla and Kang (2012)**, which also found that the attitude of males and females toward modernization differed considerably, yielded similar results. Males tended more to politics, women's status and marriage while women had a more liberal approach of education. Women are more informed, more self-employed and motivated in recent decades. They can take care of their families scientifically and comfortably comply with social standards and norms. They support their husband to earn money and they help women in household work to lead a decent life, thereby giving them a modern approach to the quality of their lives.

Table 4.17 Socio cultural differences among boys and girls with regard to their attitude towards modernization

Socio cultural setting	Boys n= 150		Girls n= 150		t-cal	p-value
	Mean	SD	Mean	SD		
Urban (n=150)	156.84	13.54	173.74	17.50	6.61**	0.000
Rural (n=150)	141.89	18.17	160.53	20.17	5.94**	0.000

** Highly Significant

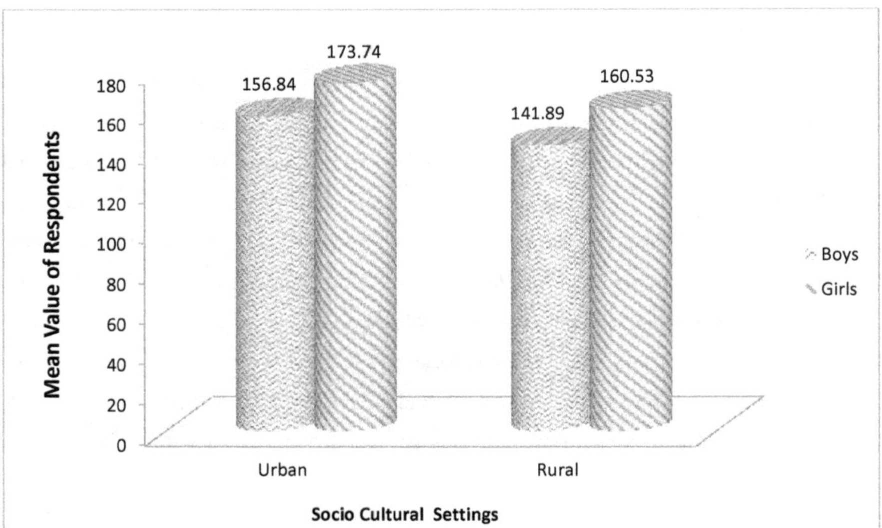

Fig 4.48 Socio cultural differences among boys and girls with regard to their attitude towards modernization

Table 4.17 and **figure 4.48** depicts the socio cultural differences among boys and girls with regard to their attitude towards modernization in which table indicates the mean, standard deviation, t' value and 'p' value. It is clear from the table that there is a rather important distinction among boys and girls in both urban and rural socio cultural settings with regard to their attitude towards modernization as the t-value was found to be 6.61 and p-value 0.000 in urban socio cultural setting. A highly significant difference in rural socio cultural setting was also observed with regard to their attitude towards modernization as the t-value was found to be 5.94 and p-value 0.000. The mean values further indicated that girls in both cultural setting had found more positive attitude towards modernization as compared to their male counterparts.

The development and improvements in gender roles have played a major part in education. There is now focus on education for women who have supported and motivated women economically, socially, politically and personally. Equality between men and women has come about as a result of modernization, with equal rights and opportunities. Modernization has weakened the existing gender disparities in traditional society. The study conducted by **Hussain *et al.*, (2015)** showed that the shift in gender roles has been substantially related to modernization, mass media, technology and education.

Table 4.18 Socio cultural differences among college going students with regard to their attitude towards modernization

College going students (n=300)					
Urban (n=150)		Rural (n=150)		t-cal	p-value
Mean	SD	Mean	SD		
165.20	17.78	151.21	21.29	6.169*	0.000

*Significant

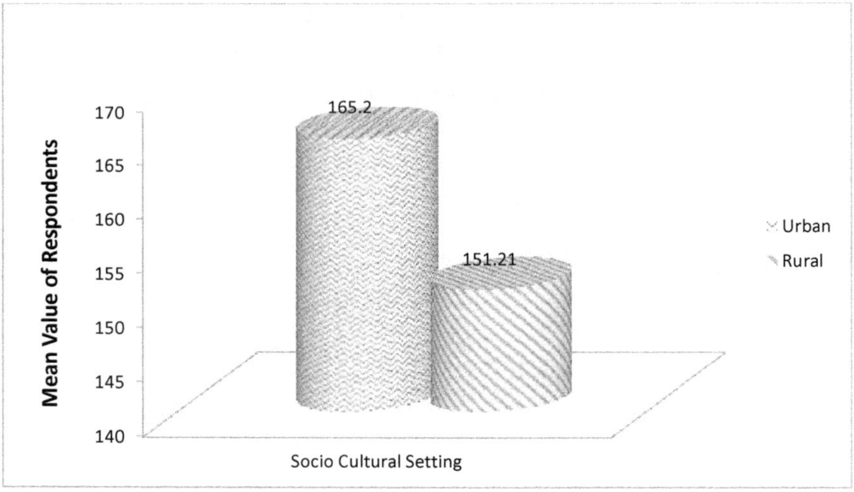

Fig 4.49 Socio cultural differences among college going students with regard to their attitude towards modernization

Table 4.18 and **figure 4.49** depicts the socio cultural differences among college going students with regard to their attitude towards modernization in which table indicates the mean, standard deviation, t' value and 'p' value. It is clear from the table that there is a rather important distinction in the urban and rural college going students with regard to their attitude towards modernization as the t-value was found to be 6.169 and p-value 0.000. The mean values further indicated that students from urban socio cultural setting had found more positive attitude towards modernization as compared to students from rural socio cultural setting. The school's education level and form of organizational environment are strongly connected with modernity. Students from urban schools encounter a lot more enriching compared to rural students, as available services are more accessible in urban areas in the form of better qualified teachers, enhanced facilities, emancipated environments etc. **Jelena (2007)** also found that rural school students and urban school pupils have a more positive view of modernization from a variety of points of view such as the environmental, parenthood style and education.

Table 4.19 Gender differences among college going students with regard to their attitude towards modernization

College going students (n=300)					
Boys (n=150)		Girls (n=150)		t-cal	p-value
Mean	SD	Mean	SD		
149.36	17.64	167.14	19.95	8.171*	0.000

*Significant

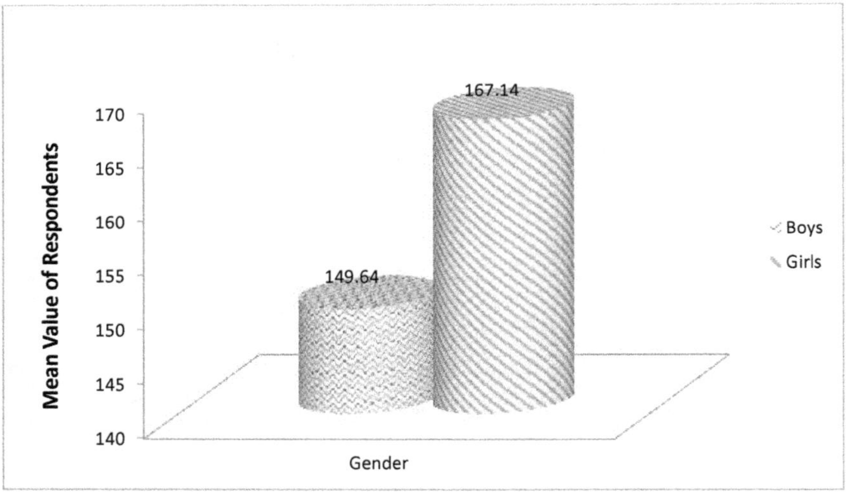

Fig 4.50 Gender differences among college going students with regard to their attitude towards modernization

Table 4.19 and **figure 4.50** depicts the gender differences among boys and girls with regard to their attitude towards modernization. The above table indicates the mean, standard deviation, t' value and 'p' value from which it is evident that there lies a highly significant difference among boys and girls with regard to their attitude towards modernization as the t-value was found to be 8.171 and p-value 0.000. The mean values further showed that, relative to their male counterparts, girls had a more optimistic approach to modernization. In terms of thought, dress, perception and attitudes, the idea of modernization is a phase in which the societal changes are fully accepted. **Hussain *et al.*, (2015)** concluded that women are stronger than men today and that women have greater freedom to participate at every social level, whether socially, professionally or politically. Modernization thus changed the role of gender and influenced decision-making. Students' optimistic attitudes to the various aspects of modernization were also seen at the study of **Adair et al. (2000).** In modernization, there was a major disparity between females and males.

Table 4.20 Frequency and percentage distribution of urban and rural respondents belonging to various socio-economic classes on the basis of financial stress before and after intervention

Level of Stress	Intervention	Urban Respondents (n=150)												Rural Respondents (n=150)											
		Upper socio economic group				Middle socio economic group				Lower socio economic group				Upper socio economic group				Middle socio economic group				Lower socio economic group			
		Boys (n=25)		Girls (n=25)		Boys (n=25)		Girls (n=25)		Boys (n=25)		Girls (n=25)		Boys (n=25)		Girls (n=25)		Boys (n=25)		Girls (n=25)		Boys (n=25)		Girls (n=25)	
		F	%	F	%	F	%	F	%	F	%	F	%	F	%	F	%	F	%	F	%	F	%	F	%
High (30-26)	Pre	10	40	07	28	05	20	13	52	00	00	01	04	04	16	15	60	11	44	08	32	08	32	12	48
	Post	07	28	03	12	02	08	10	40	00	00	00	00	01	04	08	32	09	36	07	28	08	32	11	44
Moderate (25-16)	Pre	15	60	18	72	20	80	12	48	25	100	24	96	21	84	9	36	14	56	16	64	17	68	11	44
	Post	18	72	15	60	18	72	14	56	16	64	22	44	20	80	12	48	14	56	16	64	10	40	13	52
Low (15-07)	Pre	00	00	00	00	00	00	00	00	00	00	00	00	00	00	01	04	00	00	01	04	00	00	02	08
	Post	00	00	07	21	05	20	01	04	09	36	03	12	04	16	05	20	02	08	03	12	07	28	01	04

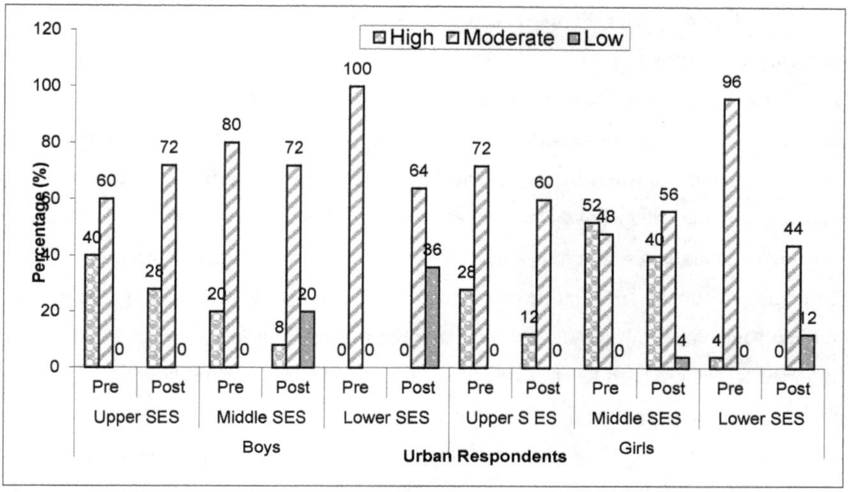

Fig 4.51 Percentage distribution of respondents belonging to different socio economic groups from urban socio cultural setting on the basis of financial stress before and after intervention

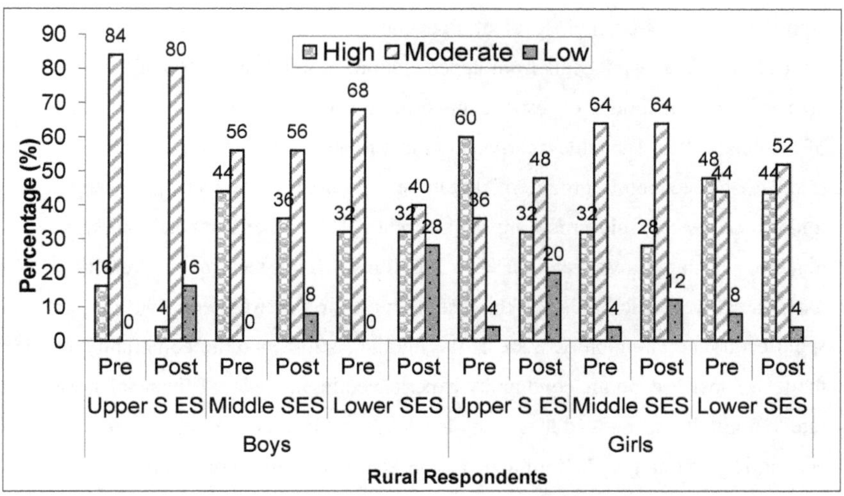

Fig 4.52 Percentage distribution of respondents belonging to different socio economic groups from rural socio cultural setting on the basis of financial stress before and after intervention

Table 4.20 and **Figures 4.51** and **Figure 4.52** highlights the frequency and percentage distribution of urban and rural respondents belonging to various socio-economic classes on the basis of financial stress. The table clearly shows that high level of financial stress was possessed by 40 percent urban boys belonging to upper socio economic group followed by 20 percent boys belonging to middle socio economic strata and none of the urban boys from lower socio economic status reported to possess high level of financial stress but after intervention, it was seen that only 28 percent urban boys belonging to upper socio economic group followed by 08 percent boys belonging to middle socio economic status and none of respondents from lower socio economic status reported to possess high level of financial stress. In the case of rural boys, it was seen that 16 percent from upper socio economic community, 44% of the middle socio-economic community and 32% of the lower socio-economic community possessed high level of financial stress whereas, after intervention, it was seen that only 04 percent from upper socio economic strata, 36 percent from middle and 32 percent respondents from lower socio economic group had high level of financial stress. In case of girls from urban socio cultural setting, it was seen that 28 percent from upper socio economic community, 52% of the middle socio-economic community and 04% of the lower socio-economic community possessed high level of financial stress whereas, after intervention, it was noticed that 12% respondents from upper socio-economic class, 40% of the middle socio-economic class and none of respondents from lower socio economic group had high level of financial stress. The table clearly shows that financial stress is more common among the middle socio economic group which can be attributed to the fact that respondents from middle socio economic group are capable enough to make a realistic appraisal of their objective economic resources and their liabilities making them more stressful about their anticipated economic hardships. In case of rural girls, it was seen that 60% from upper socio economic community, 32% of the middle socio-economic community and 48% of the lower socio-economic community experienced higher level of financial stress but after intervention, it was noticed that stress level was reduced i.e. 32 percent from upper socio economic community, 28% of the middle socio-economic community and 44% of the lower socio-economic community experienced higher level of financial stress among the rural girls. The results obtained is supported by the research findings which clearly state that in families belonging to lower social income classes, financial hardship is more generally seen, as they must often work hard in order to achieve their goals and resolve economic challenges at every turn of their lives. **Angel *et al.* (2003)** reported that inquiries from lower or higher sociopaths would likely feel financial burden or pressure more often.

The table also showed moderate level of financial stress was possessed by 60 percent urban boys belonging to upper socio economic status, 80 percent boys belonging to middle socio economic strata and 100 percent from lower socio economic group reported to possess moderate level of financial stress but after intervention, stress level was reduced and it was noticed that 72 percent boys belonging to upper and middle socio economic strata followed by 64 percent urban boys belonging to lower socio economic group had average level of financial stress. In the case of rural boys, it was seen that 84 percent boys from upper socio-economic class, 56% of the middle socio-economic class and 68% of boys from lower socio-economic class possessed average level of financial stress whereas, after intervention, it was seen that 80 percent boys from upper socio economic group, 56 per cent of boys from the middle socio-economic community and 40 per cent from the lower socio-economic community had moderate levels of financial stress. For girls from urban socio-cultural backgrounds, 72 percent of girls from the upper socio-economic community and 48 percent of girls from the middle socio-economic community are seen as girls from the upper socio-economic community and 96 percent girls from lower socio economic group possessed moderate level of financial stress but intervention showed that 60% of girls from upper socio economic community, 56% of girls from the middle socio-economic community and 44% of girls from the lower socio-economic community had moderate level of financial stress which is clearly shows that financial stress is more common among the lower socio economic group. In case of rural girls, it was seen that 36 percent girls from upper socio economic strata, 64 percent girls from middle socio economic group followed by 44 percent girls from lower socio economic group experienced moderate level of financial stress but after intervention, it was identified that 48 percent girls from upper socio economic strata, 64 percent girls from middle socio economic group followed by 52 percent girls from lower socio economic group experienced moderate level of financial stress. Students experience multiple causes of financial stress such as low family income, big families with more relatives, losses, personal health conditions, wide areas of growth, weak parental relationships, parent deaths, peer pressure, modern fashion trends, inadequate coping practice and higher education needs.

As far as low level of financial stress as concerned, none of boy respondents from urban as well as rural had low level of financial stress. They all were facing high level as well as average level of financial stress whereas after intervention, it was seen that none of urban boy respondents from upper socio economic group had low level of financial stress, 20 percent boys from middle socio economic group and 36 percent from lower socio economic group and in case of boys from rural socio cultural setting, 16 percent of respondents from upper socio economic community, 8 per cent of the middle socio-economic community and 24 per cent of the boys in the lower socio-economic community were facing low level of financial stress which clearly revealed that those urban as well as rural boys who were facing high and moderate level of stress started experiencing low stress as the result of intervention which proves the efficacy of the planned intervention in reducing stress among adolescents. None of urban girls from all socio economic groups had low stress. Urban girls were also facing high to average level of financial stress but after intervention, it was identified that number of respondents facing low stress level increased. Twenty one percent urban girls from upper socio economic group, 04 percent girls from middle and 12% of respondents from the lower socio-economic community faced low levels of stress whereas, in case of rural girls, it was seen that 04 percent girls from upper and middle socio economic strata and 08 percent girls from lower socio economic group experienced higher level of financial stress and after intervention, it was seen that 20 percent girls from upper socio economic group followed by 12 percent girls from middle socio economic group and 04 percents girls from lower socio economic strata experience low level of financial stress which proved that adolescents who experienced high and moderate level of stress started experiencing low level of stress after being a part of the intervention. Most respondents have been found financially stressed because students are not financially strong during this age and they experience a lot of academic and parental pressure. One must face the rising prices of all in this modern age. The costs for schooling, coaching, housing, entertainment, food and paper are all high and bring great financial stress to the young people.

Table 4.21 Frequency and percentage distribution of respondents belonging to different socio economic groups from urban and rural socio cultural setting on the basis of family stress before and after intervention

Level of Stress	Intervention	Urban Respondents (n=150)												Rural Respondents (n=150)											
		Upper socio economic group				Middle socio economic group				Lower socio economic group				Upper socio economic group				Middle socio economic group				Lower socio economic group			
		Boys (n=25)		Girls (n=25)		Boys (n=25)		Girls (n=25)		Boys (n=25)		Girls (n=25)		Boys (n=25)		Girls (n=25)		Boys (n=25)		Girls (n=25)		Boys (n=25)		Girls (n=25)	
		F	%	F	%	F	%	F	%	F	%	F	%	F	%	F	%	F	%	F	%	F	%	F	%
High	Pre	18	72	20	80	11	44	18	72	10	40	04	16	20	80	21	84	17	68	18	72	16	64	18	72
(56-40)	Post	03	12	18	72	05	20	15	60	04	16	01	04	17	68	19	76	10	40	12	48	06	24	10	40
Moderate	Pre	06	24	03	12	12	48	06	24	11	44	18	72	05	20	03	12	05	20	06	24	08	32	05	20
(39-23)	Post	15	60	06	24	18	72	09	36	11	44	12	48	07	28	04	16	13	52	12	48	15	60	10	40
Low	Pre	01	04	02	08	02	08	01	04	04	16	03	12	00	00	01	04	03	12	01	04	01	04	02	08
(22-07)	Pos	07	28	01	04	02	08	01	04	10	40	12	48	01	04	02	08	02	08	01	04	04	16	05	20

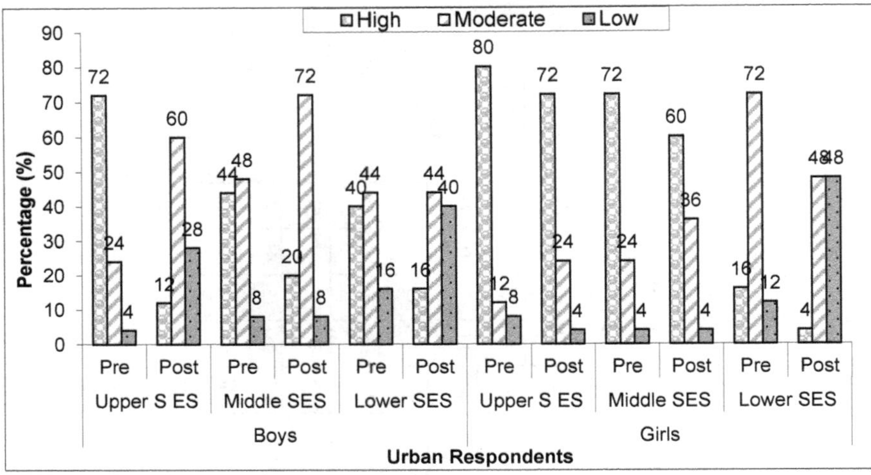

Fig 4.53 Percentage distribution of respondents belonging to different socio economic groups from urban socio cultural setting on the basis of family stress before and after intervention

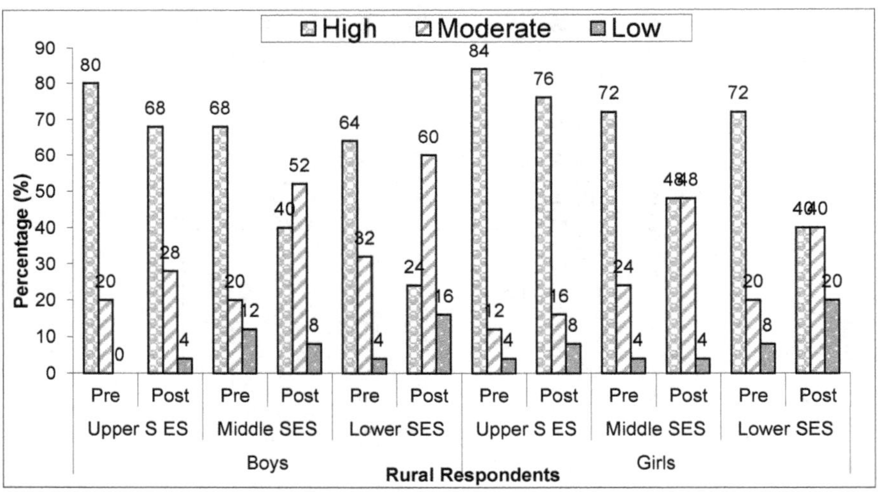

Fig 4.54 Percentage distribution of respondents belonging to different socio economic groups from rural socio cultural setting on the basis of family stress before and after intervention

Table 4.21 and **figures 4.53** and **4.54** shows the frequency and percentage distribution of respondents belonging to different socio economic groups belonging to urban as well as rural socio cultural setting regarding family stress. It is clear from the table that in case of urban boys, maximum percent i.e 72 percent of those belonging to upper socio economic group possessed high level of stress followed by 44 percent of boys belonging to middle socio economic group and 40 percent from lower socio economic group but after intervention, stress level was reduced i.e. 12 percent from upper socio economic group, 20 percent of those belonging to middle socio economic group followed by 16 percent of boys belonging to lower socio economic class possessed high level of stress. In the case of rural boys, 80% of the upper socio-economic class, 68% of the middle socio-economic class, and 64% of the lower socio-economic class had high levels of family stress whereas after intervention it was noticed that only 68 per cent of rural boys from the upper socio-economic class, 40 per cent from the middle socio-economic class and 24 per cent from the lower socio-economic class were found to have high levels of family stress. In the case of girls belonging to the urban environment, 80% of the upper socio-economic community were found to be from the urban environment, followed by 72 percent from middle socio economic group and 16 percent from lower socio economic strata had high level of family stress but intervention it was found that 72 percent urban girls from upper socio economic group, followed by 60 percent had a high degree of family tension from the middle socio-economic community and 04 percent from the lower socio-economic community. In the case of girls from rural backgrounds, 84 percent of the upper socio-economic community is observed and an equal percent i.e 72 percent girls from both middle as well as lower socio economic group possessed high level of family stress but after intervention it reduced to 76 percent from upper socio economic class, 48% of the middle socio-economic class and 40% of the lower socio-economic class had high level of family stress.

The table further highlights that moderate family stress was indicated by 24 percent urban boys from upper socio economic community, 48% of the middle socio-economic community and 44% of the lower socio-economic community. After the implementation of the intervention it was seen that 60 percent urban boys from upper socio class, 72% of the middle socio-economic class and 44% of the lower socio-economic class showed moderate level of family stress which clearly indicated that although there was a rise in number of urban boys suffering from moderate level of family stress but that rise was due to the fact that the respondents who were having high level of family stress before intervention moved on to having moderate level of stress after intervention which proved the efficacy of the intervention. In case of boys from rural background, it was seen that 20 percent from upper as well as middle socio economic group and 32 percent from lower socio economic strata displayed moderate level of family stress but after intervention, it was identified that 28% of the upper socio-economic community, 52% of the middle-economic community and 60% of rural boys from the lower socio-economic class reported a moderate level of family tension. In the case of urban girls, 12 percent of the upper socio-economic class, 24 percent of the middle socio-economic class and 72 percent of the lower socio-economic class displayed a moderate level of family stress, and 24 percent of the upper socio-economic group, 36 percent of the middle socio-economic class and 48 percent of urban girls from the lower socio-economic class were noted after intervention whereas, in case of girls from rural background, it was seen that 12 percent of the upper socio-economic class, 24 percent of the middle socio-economic class and 20 percent of the lower socio-economic class reflected moderate levels of family stress, but 16 percent of the upper socio-economic community, 48 percent of the middle socio-economic community and 40 percent of the lower socio-economic community were found after intervention, reflected moderate level of family stress showing that a great number of respondent benefitted from the intervention and their level of status reduced from high to moderate.

Low stress level was witnessed in very few respondents from both urban as well as rural cultural setting. In case of urban boys 4% from upper socio-economic category, 8% of the upper socio-economic category and 16% of the lower socio-economic category possessed low level of family stress whereas, after intervention, it was seen that 28 percent from upper socio economic class, 08 percent of the middle socio economic class and 40 per cent urban boys from lower socio economic class possessed low level of family stress. None of the rural boys from upper socio economic strata, 12 percent belonging to middle socio economic group and 04 percent from lower socio economic group possessed low level of family stress before intervention but after intervention, it was noticed that 04 percent from upper socio economic strata, 08 percent from middle socio economic group and 16 percent rural boys belonging to lower socio economic group possessed low level of family stress.

In case of urban girls, it was seen that pre intervention 08 percent of the upper socio economic class, 04 percent of the middle socio economic class and 12 percent of the lower socio economic class possessed low family stress but after implementing intervention program, it was noticed that 04 percent from upper and middle socio economic group and 48 percent from lower socio economic group possessed low family stress.

In case of rural girls, 04 percent each from upper as well as middle socio economic group and 08 percent rural girls from lower socio economic status were facing family stress pre intervention but after intervention, it was identified that 08 percent rural girls from upper socio economic group, 04 percent from middle and 20 percent lower socio economic group were facing low level of family stress. It is clearly reflected that maximum respondents both from rural as well as urban cultural setting possessed high level of family stress. As we all know that all families at one time or the other has to deal with stress. For various people and the whole family, the nature of stress can be various. The family today must deal with a high level of competition, high costs, busy schedules, higher life costs and much more. Psychological stress during puberty, when children are under tremendous physical stress, often contributes to difficulties in their family relations. Anything concerning the family may be likely to cause stress to the child, such as unreasonable expectations, strained sibling relationships, marital disparities between parents, family disorder and family funding. Family stress may also erupt as a result of the adolescents seeking independence and separation from their parents. Issues like difference in opinion, poor communication as well as discipline issues may also trigger stress in the family. The results are support with the study conducted by **Robert *et al.* (2018)** who found that family traumatic incidents, such as marital strife and parental divorce, are also circumstances that raise the family's stress burden dramatically and are linked to dysfunctional behaviour. Finding of the study coincides with the study conducted by **Miller *et al.* (1974)** who concluded that some traumatic events seem to affect the rural families' interpersonal environment, while urban families are connected to the society by the same stressors. The results also indicate that stress induced by cumulative changes in life would be recognized differently by urban and rural families on account of environmental influences. Specifically, stress may affect rural families' interpersonal relations to a greater extent than urban families.

Table 4.22 Frequency and percentage distribution of urban and rural respondents belonging to various socio-economic classes on the basis of social stress before and after intervention

Level of Stress	Intervention	Urban Respondents (n=150)												Rural Respondents (n=150)											
		Upper socio economic group				Middle socio economic group				Lower socio economic group				Upper socio economic group				Middle socio economic group				Lower socio economic group			
		Boys (n=25)		Girls (n=25)		Boys (n=25)		Girls (n=25)		Boys (n=25)		Girls (n=25)		Boys (n=25)		Girls (n=25)		Boys (n=25)		Girls (n=25)		Boys (n=25)		Girls (n=25)	
		F	%	F	%	F	%	F	%	F	%	F	%	F	%	F	%	F	%	F	%	F	%	F	%
High (56-40)	Pre	24	96	24	96	17	68	22	88	20	80	16	64	09	36	14	56	09	36	17	68	18	72	18	72
	Post	18	72	20	80	06	24	03	12	06	24	09	36	07	28	11	44	08	32	08	32	15	60	13	52
Moderate (39-23)	Pre	01	04	01	04	06	24	03	12	01	04	06	24	14	56	10	40	13	52	08	32	06	24	03	12
	Post	05	20	04	16	18	72	20	80	16	64	13	52	13	52	13	52	14	56	12	48	08	32	10	40
Low (22-07)	Pre	00	00	00	00	02	08	00	00	04	16	03	12	02	08	01	04	03	12	00	00	01	04	04	16
	Post	02	08	01	04	01	04	02	08	03	12	03	12	05	20	01	04	03	12	05	20	02	08	02	08

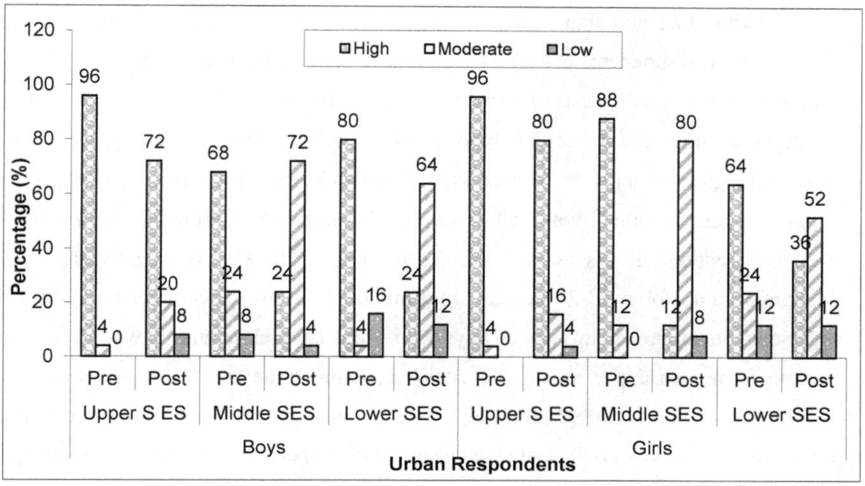

Fig 4.55 Percentage distribution of respondents belonging to different socio economic groups from urban socio cultural setting on the basis of social stress before and after intervention

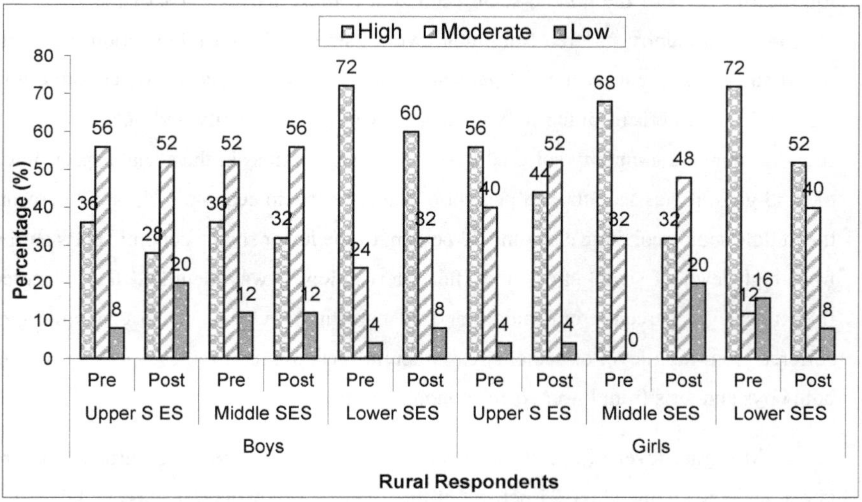

Fig 4.56 Percentage distribution of respondents belonging to different socio economic groups from rural socio cultural setting on the basis of social stress before and after intervention

Table 4.22 and **figures 4.55** and **4.56** highlights the frequency and percentage distribution of respondents belonging to different socio economic groups from urban and rural background on the basis of social stress. The table clearly shows that in case of boys belonging to urban cultural setting, high level of social stress is possessed by 96 percent of those belonging to upper socio economic group followed by 68 percent of the middle socio economic community and 80 percent of the lower socio economic community but after intervention, it was noticed that 72 percent of those belonging to upper socio economic group followed 24 percent from middle and lower socio economic strata had high level social stress. In case of boys from rural cultural setting, it was seen that 36 percent from both upper and middle socio economic strata and 72 percent from lower socio economic strata suffered from high level of social stress whereas, after intervention, it was reduced as only 28 percent respondents of the upper socio economic community, 32 percent of the middle socio economic community and 60 percent of the lower socio economic community suffered from high level of social stress. As far as girls were concerned, the table reflected that 96 percent urban girls from upper socio economic group followed by 88% of the middle socio economic community and 64% of the lower socio economic community suffered from high level of stress but after intervention the level of social stress was reduced i.e. 80 percent urban girls from upper socio economic group followed by 12 percent of the middle socio-economic community and 36% of the lower socio-economic community suffered from high level of stress in the social aspect. In case of rural girls, it was seen that 56 percent of the upper socio economic class, 68 percent of the middle socio economic class and 72 percent of the lower socio economic class suffered from high level of social stress and after intervention, it was identified that 44 percent from upper, 32 percent from middle and 52 percent from lower socio economic group suffered from high level of social stress wherein, maximum stress level was seen among both boys and girls from lower socio economic group.

Moderate level of social stress was seen among 04 percent of urban boys from upper socio economic class, 24 percent of the middle socio economic class and 04 percent of the lower socio economic class but after intervention, it was seen that 20% of the upper socio economic class, 72% of the urban boys of the middle socio economic class and 64% of the lower socio economic class possessed moderate level of social stress. Among rural boys moderate level of social stress was witnessed among 56 per cent of the upper socio-economic category, 52 per cent of the middle socio-economic category and 24 per cent of the lower socio-economic category , but after intervention, 52 per cent of the upper, 56 per cent of the middle and 32 per cent of the lower socio-economic group had moderate level of stress. Many respondents who suffered from high level of social stress before intervention were able to reach moderate level of stress after intervention showing the effectiveness of the intervention program in reducing stress among the respondents. In the case of girls from urban backgrounds, it was noticed that 04% of the upper socio-economic class, 12% of the middle socio-economic class and 24% of the lower socio-economic class possessed moderate level of social stress but after intervention, it was seen that 16 percent from upper socio economic group, 80 percent of the middle socio-economic category and 52 percent of the lower socio-economic category had a moderate level of social stress, while in the case of rural girls, it was noticed that 40 per cent of the upper socio-economic category and 32 percent of the middle socio-economic category and 12 percent from lower socio economic group were having moderate level of social stress but after receiving intervention, it was noticed that 52 percent from upper socio economic class, 48 percent of the middle socio economic class and 40 percent of the lower socio economic class possessed moderate level of social stress.

Very few respondents both from rural as well as urban cultural setting despite of their gender suffered low level of social stress. Before intervention none of the urban boy from upper socio-economic category, 8% of the upper socio-economic category and 16% of the lower socio-economic category were identified with low social stress but after intervention, it was seen that 08 percent from upper socio economic category, 04 percent of the middle socio economic category and 12 percent urban boys from lower socio economic group were identified with low level of social stress. For boys from rural cultural backgrounds, 08% from the upper socio-economic class, 12% from the middle and 04% from the lower socio-economic community had a low degree of social stress before intervention whereas after intervention, it was seen that 20 percent from upper, 12 percent from middle and 08 percent from lower socio economic group had low level of social stress. As far as urban girls were concerned, it was noticed that before intervention none of respondents from upper as well as middle socio economic group and only 12 percent from lower socio economic group possessed low level of social stress whereas, after intervention, it was noticed that 04 percent from upper socio-economic community, 8% of the middle socio-economic community and 12% of urban girls belonging to lower socio economic group possessed low level of social stress as the respondents who possessed higher levels of social before the implementation of the intervention package stared possessing lower levels of stress after the intervention. Intervention compressing of counseling, relaxation techniques, development of hobbies etc proved beneficial for the respondents in reducing their stress levels. On the whole it was seen that maximum number of respondents apart from their gender and socio cultural setting were laid down with high level of social stress. Social support is important for maintaining good physical and mental health of the human being. Positive social support of high quality can enhance resilience to stress, coping with stress and helps protect against developing psychological problems. In case of rural girls, before intervention it was seen that 04 percent from upper socio economic class, none of the middle socio economic class and 16 percent of the lower socio economic class possessed low level of stress but after intervention, it was identified that 04 percent from upper, 20 percent from middle and 08 percent from lower socio economic group possessed low level of social stress.

Table 4.23 Frequency and percentage distribution of urban and rural respondents belonging to various socio-economic classes on the basis of educational stress before and after intervention

Level of Stress	Intervention	Urban Respondents (n=150)												Rural Respondents (n=150)											
		Upper socio economic group				Middle socio economic group				Lower socio economic group				Upper socio economic group				Middle socio economic group				Lower socio economic group			
		Boys (n=25)		Girls (n=25)		Boys (n=25)		Girls (n=25)		Boys (n=25)		Girls (n=25)		Boys (n=25)		Girls (n=25)		Boys (n=25)		Girls (n=25)		Boys (n=25)		Girls (n=25)	
		F	%	F	%	F	%	F	%	F	%	F	%	F	%	F	%	F	%	F	%	F	%	F	%
High	Pre	03	12	06	24	04	16	17	68	10	40	14	56	20	80	22	88	15	60	17	68	12	48	11	44
(56-40)	Post	03	12	05	20	03	12	13	52	09	36	12	48	14	56	16	64	04	16	09	36	10	40	09	36
Moderate	Pre	20	80	15	60	18	72	06	24	14	56	11	44	5	20	02	08	09	36	08	32	10	40	13	52
(39-23)	Post	16	64	12	48	15	60	10	40	15	60	11	44	06	24	08	32	18	72	15	60	12	48	12	48
Low	Pre	02	08	04	16	03	12	02	08	01	04	00	00	00	00	01	04	01	04	00	00	03	12	01	04
(22-07)	Post	06	24	08	32	07	28	02	08	01	04	02	08	05	20	01	04	03	12	01	04	03	12	04	16

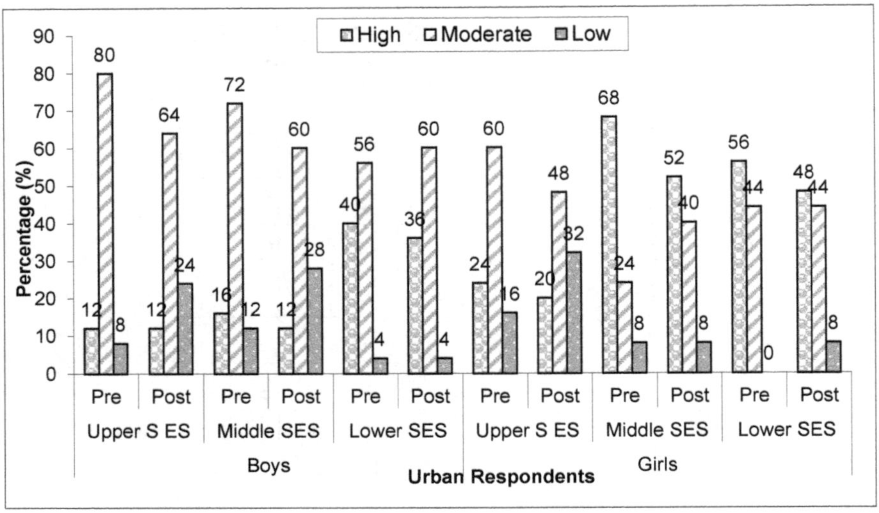

Fig 4.57 Percentage distribution of respondents belonging to different socio economic groups from urban socio cultural setting on the basis of education stress before and after intervention

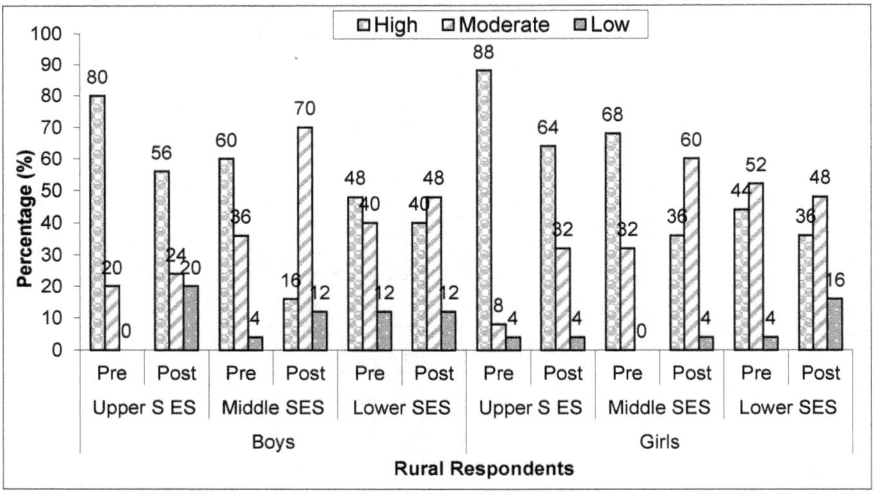

Fig 4.58 Percentage distribution of respondents belonging to different socio economic groups from rural socio cultural setting on the basis of education stress before and after intervention

Table 4.23 and illustrations in **figures 4.57** and **4.58** highlights the frequency and percentage distribution of urban and rural adolescents belonging to different socio economic groups (Lower, middle and upper socio economic group) on the basis of their educational stress. The data represented in the table indicates that in case of boys belonging to urban background, it was noticed that before intervention 12 percent from upper socio economic strata, 16 percent from middle and 40 percent belonging to lower socio economic group possessed high level of educational stress which after intervention was reduced to 12 percent from middle and upper socio economic strata and 36 percent from lower socio economic strata. Among their rural counterparts, it was seen that 80 percent boys from upper, 60 percent from middle and 48 percent from lower socio economic group suffered from high level of educational stress but after intervention, it was reduced that 56 percent from upper, 16 percent from middle and 40 percent from lower socio economic group suffered from high level of educational stress. The data clearly points out to the fact that in rural areas, educational facilities do not make teenagers nervous about their schooling and worried about their occupation in the coming years.

In the case of girls belonging to the urban cultural environment, it was seen that before intervention, 24% of the upper socio-economic class , 68% of the middle socio-economic class and 56% of the lower socio-economic class suffered from high levels of educational stress whereas, after intervention, it was reduced 20 percent from upper, 52 percent from middle and 48 percent from lower socio economic. With regard to girls from rural background, it was found that before intervention 88 percent from upper, 68 percent from middle and 44 percent from lower socio economic group faced high level of educational stress but after the implementation of intervention package, it was reduced to 64 percent from upper, 36 percent from middle and lower socio economic group faced high level of educational stress.

Moderate category of educational stress was seen among 80 percent urban boys from upper socio economic group, followed by 72 percent from middle and 56 percent from lower socio economic strata before intervention but after the implementation of intervention package, it was seen that 64 percent urban boys from upper socio economic group, followed by 60 percent boys from middle and lower socio economic strata possessed moderate level of educational stress which clearly indicates that those respondents who suffered from high level of stress before intervention where suffering from moderate level of educational stress after intervention. In case of rural boys, it was seen that before intervention moderate level of educational stress was possessed by 20 percent of respondents from the upper socio-economic community, 36 percent from the middle socio-economic community and 40 percent of boys from the lower socio-economic community, but after intervention, it was reported that 24 percent from the upper, 72 percent from the middle and 48 percent from the lower socio-economic community possessed moderate level of educational stress. As far as girls were concerned, it was noticed that before intervention, 60 percent urban girls from upper socio economic group, 24 percent from middle and 44 percent from lower socio economic strata possessed moderate level of educational stress whereas, after intervention, it was seen that 48 percent from upper socio economic group, 40 percent from middle and 44 percent from lower socio economic strata suffered from moderate level of educational stress. In case of rural girls the table highlights that before intervention 08 percent from upper socio economic strata, 32 percent from middle and 52 percent from lower socio economic strata had moderate level of educational stress whereas, after intervention, it was seen that 32 percent from upper, 60 percent from middle and 48 percent from lower socio economic strata had possessed moderate level of educational stress.

Very few respondents from both rural and urban cultural setting were found to have low educational stress. In case of urban boys it was seen that before intervention 08 percent from upper, 12 percent from middle and 04 percent from lower socio economic strata possessed low level of educational stress whereas, after intervention, it was seen that 24 percent from upper, 28 percent from middle and 04 percent from lower socio economic strata suffered from low level of educational stress which reflected the efficacy of the intervention program as the respondents who earlier were having high and moderate stress levels were having low stress levels after intervention. Among the rural boys, it was seen that before intervention none from upper socio economic level, 04 percent from middle and 12 percent from lower socio economic level suffered from low educational stress but after intervention, it was seen that 20 percent from upper socio economic group and 12 percent each from middle and lower socio economic level had low level of educational stress. As far as urban girls were concerned, it was noticed that before intervention 16 percent from upper socio economic strata, 08 percent from middle and none from lower socio economic group suffered from low level of educational stress whereas, after intervention, low stress level was seen among 32 percent from upper socio economic strata and 08 percent each from middle and lower socio economic group suffered from low level of educational stress. In case of rural girls, it was seen that before intervention only 04 percent rural girls belonging to upper socio economic level, none of respondents from middle socio economic level and 04 percent girls from lower socio economic group suffered from low level of stress but after intervention, it was noticed that 04 percent rural girls belonging to upper as well as middle socio economic group and 16 percent respondents from lower socio economic group had low level of stress related to educational pursuit. The table clearly highlights that high to moderate level of educational stress is present among the respondents which is quite understandable in this competitive era. Academic factors are the most important stressors, hence certain targeted measures need to be taken to decrease substantially the burden of stress caused by academics which requires that teaching techniques and college environments should be adapted to the needs of the students. The productive utilization of existing student welfare programs, development of more student friendly environment and regular periodic extracurricular activities with universal participation can prove to be useful stress busters. **Bartwal and Raj (2013)** conducted an investigation and found that in rural and urban teens, there was no gap showing that both girls and boys are under similar stress in schooling. Thus, in order to minimize educational stress that can cause low self-esteem and lead to many emotional problems, including depression and even suicide at the university, better teaching strategies are needed. The research by **Mathew and Jayan (2006)** has shown that both the males and the girls are similarly depressed and that there is no distinction between them.

Table 4.24 Frequency and percentage distribution of urban and rural respondents belonging to various socio-economic classes on the basis of ego threats stress before and after intervention

Level of Stress	Intervention	Urban Respondents (n=150)												Rural Respondents (n=150)											
		Upper socio economic group				Middle socio economic group				Lower socio economic group				Upper socio economic group				Middle socio economic group				Lower socio economic group			
		Boys (n=25)		Girls (n=25)		Boys (n=25)		Girls (n=25)		Boys (n=25)		Girls (n=25)		Boys (n=25)		Girls (n=25)		Boys (n=25)		Girls (n=25)		Boys (n=25)		Girls (n=25)	
		F	%	F	%	F	%	F	%	F	%	F	%	F	%	F	%	F	%	F	%	F	%	F	%
High (56-40)	Pre	13	52	14	56	10	40	20	80	17	68	19	76	16	64	20	80	17	68	15	60	10	40	12	48
	Post	10	40	11	44	08	32	17	68	12	48	08	32	07	28	10	40	04	16	07	28	14	56	10	40
Moderate (39-23)	Pre	12	48	11	44	12	48	03	12	07	28	03	12	08	32	05	20	06	24	09	36	15	60	10	40
	Post	13	52	11	44	15	60	05	20	08	32	14	56	16	64	11	44	15	60	15	60	09	36	10	40
Low (22-07)	Pre	00	00	00	00	03	12	02	08	01	04	03	12	01	04	00	00	02	08	01	04	00	00	03	12
	Post	02	08	03	12	02	08	03	12	05	20	03	12	02	08	04	16	06	24	03	12	02	08	05	20

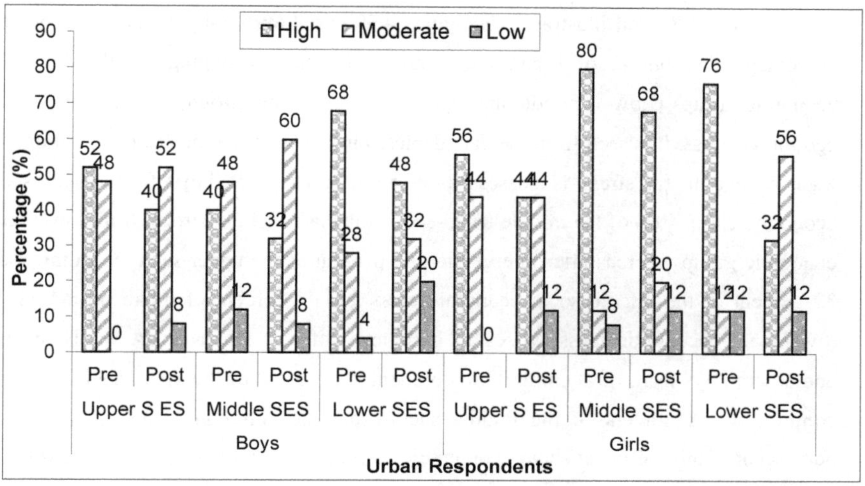

Fig 4.59 Percentage distribution of respondents belonging to different socio economic groups from urban socio cultural setting on the basis of ego threat stress before and after intervention

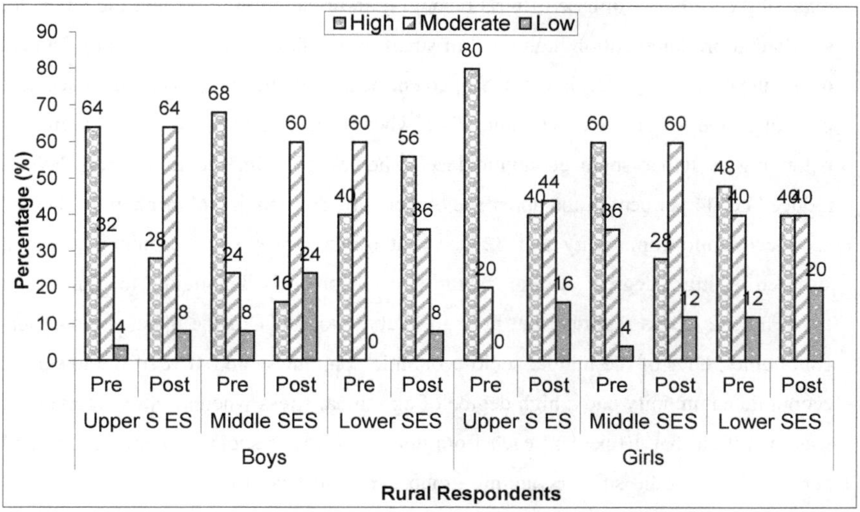

Fig 4.60 Percentage distribution of respondents belonging to different socio economic groups from rural socio cultural setting on the basis of ego threat stress before and after intervention

Table 4.24 and illustration in figures **4.59** and **4.60** highlights the frequency and percentage distribution of urban and rural adolescents belonging to different socio economic groups (Lower, middle and upper socio economic group) on the basis of their ego threat stress. It is seen from the data depicted in the table that before intervention high level of ego threat stress is possessed by 52 percent urban boys from upper socio-economic class, 40% of the middle socio-economic class and 68 percent from lower socio economic group whereas after intervention 40 percent of the upper socio economic class, 32 percent of the middle socio economic class and 48 percent of urban boys from the lower socio economic class possessed high level of ego threat stress. In the case of adolescent boys from rural cultural environment, 64 percent of the upper socio-economic community, 68 percent of the middle socio-economic community and 40 percent of adolescents from the lower socio-economic community had a high degree of stress before intervention, while after intervention, it was reported that 28 percent of the upper socio-economic group followed just 16 percent of respondents from the middle and 56 per cent adolescents of the lower socio economic community suffered from high level of stress regarding ego threat. In case of girls belonging to urban cultural setting, the table clearly shows that pre intervention high level of stress of ego threat was possessed by 56 percent of the upper socio economic class, 80 percent of the middle socio economic class and 76 percent of the lower socio economic class wherein maximum stress can be seen in girls belonging to upper socio economic level whereas after intervention, stress level was reduced i.e. 44 per cent of the upper socio-economic community, 68 per cent of the middle socio-economic community and 32 per cent of the lower socio-economic community suffered a high degree of ego threat stress. For girls belonging to rural cultural environment, it was reported that prior to intervention 80% of the upper socio-economic community, 60% of the middle socio-economic community and 48% of the lower socio-economic community had a high degree of ego threat stress whereas, after intervention, it was identified that 40 percent each from upper and lower socio economic group and 28 percent from middle socio economic group had high level of ego threat stress wherein, maximum ego threats stress could be seen in girls belonging to upper socio economic level.

Table also reveals that moderate level of ego threat stress before intervention was possessed by 48 percent urban boys from both upper and middle socio economic group and only 28 percent of urban boys belonging to lower socio economic group belonged to this category whereas, after intervention, 52 percent boys from upper socio economic group, 60 percent boys from middle socio economic group and 32 percent of urban boys belonging to lower socio economic group possessed moderate level of stress regarding ego threats which shows that respondents who were having higher stress level before the implementation of intervention were identified to have reduced levels of stress after intervention and hence more respondents possessed moderate levels of stress post intervention. In case of rural boys, it was seen that moderate ego threat stress pre intervention was possessed by 32 percent of the upper socio economic community, 24 percent of the in middle socio economic community and 60 percent of the lower socio economic community whereas after intervention, it was observed that 64 percent from upper socio economic group followed by 60 percent of the middle socio-economic community and 36% of the lower socio-economic community suffered from moderate level of stress regarding ego threats. Among girls belonging to urban background, it was witnessed that before intervention 44 percent from upper socio economic group followed by 12 percent each from middle and lower socio economic group had moderate level of ego threat whereas, post intervention, it was identified that 44 percent of the upper socio economic class, 20 percent of the middle socio economic class and 56 percent of the lower socio economic class possessed moderate level of ego threat stress. In case of rural girls, moderate ego threat was seen among 20 per cent from the upper socio-economic category, 36 per cent from the middle socio-economic category and 40 per cent from the lower socio-economic category before intervention and post intervention, it was reported that 44 per cent from the upper socio-economic category followed by 60 per cent from the middle socio-economic category and 40 per cent from the lower socio-economic category possessed moderate level of ego threat stress.

The table also indicated that before intervention none of urban boys from upper socio economic strata, 12 percent from middle and 04 percent from lower socio economic group possessed low level of ego threat stress whereas, after intervention, it was seen that an equal percent i.e. 08 percent from upper and middle socio economic strata and 20 percent urban boys from lower socio economic group suffered from low level of stress regarding ego threats. Low ego threat stress was witnessed pre intervention among only 04 percent and 08 percent rural boys belonging to upper and middle socio economic group respectively and none of respondents from lower socio economic group whereas after intervention low level of stress was seen among 24 percent rural boys belonging to middle and 8 percent each from upper and lower socio economic group. In case of girls from urban cultural setting, it was noticed that before intervention none of the girls from upper socio-economic community, 8% of the middle socio-economic community and 12% from lower socio economic group possessed low level of ego threat stress but after intervention, it was noticed that 12 percent each from upper, middle and lower socio economic group possessed low level of stress regarding ego threat. In case of rural girls, low level of ego threat was identified among none of the respondents from the upper socio-economic class, 04 per cent from the middle socio-economic class and 12 percent adolescents before intervention whereas after intervention, it was observed that 16 percent from the upper socio economic group, 12 percent respondents from the middle socio-economic community and 20% from the lower socio-economic community had low level of ego threat stress. It is clear from the table that both gender i.e boys and girls were suffering from high level of ego threat stress in both urban and rural socio cultural setting. Ego threat is a threat to a person's self esteem and self image. Several studies suggest that ego threat disturbs self-esteem threats with public image threats or less influence over negative incidents, resulting in the inability to differentiate between threats to the egos of individuals and threats to public images or feelings of power **(Leary *et al.* 2009).** In interpersonal decision-making the threat to ego and concomitant emotions are important during the adolescence period since decisions made during this time will have a major effect in the future. **Vohs and Heatherton (2003)** also revealed that moderate to low self-esteem men and women were more sensitive when they threatened themselves, while high self-esteem men were considered less likeable when they threatened themselves. Personality tests have shown that men and women, who are at highest level of self-esteem, i.e. false, disrespectful, disrespectful and uncooperative, have been highly antagonized.

Table 4.25 Frequency and percentage distribution of urban and rural respondents belonging to various socio-economic classes on the basis of bereavement stress before and after intervention

Level of Stress	Intervention	Urban Respondents (n=150)												Rural Respondents (n=150)											
		Upper socio economic group				Middle socio economic group				Lower socio economic group				Upper socio economic group				Middle socio economic group				Lower socio economic group			
		Boys (n=25)		Girls (n=25)		Boys (n=25)		Girls (n=25)		Boys (n=25)		Girls (n=25)		Boys (n=25)		Girls (n=25)		Boys (n=25)		Girls (n=25)		Boys (n=25)		Girls (n=25)	
		F	%	F	%	F	%	F	%	F	%	F	%	F	%	F	%	F	%	F	%	F	%	F	%
High	Pre	23	92	22	88	19	76	20	80	11	44	17	68	15	60	11	36	09	36	05	20	04	16	06	24
(56-40)	Post	11	44	13	52	03	12	07	28	08	32	12	48	11	44	09	36	03	12	02	08	04	16	01	04
Moderate	Pre	02	08	02	08	04	16	04	16	06	24	03	12	06	24	13	52	12	48	18	72	20	80	19	76
(39-23)	Post	10	56	09	36	16	64	14	56	06	24	06	24	10	40	11	44	13	52	14	56	17	68	13	52
Low	Pre	00	00	01	04	02	08	01	04	08	32	05	20	04	16	01	04	04	16	02	08	01	04	00	00
(22-07)	Post	04	16	03	12	06	24	04	16	11	44	07	28	04	16	05	20	09	36	09	36	04	16	11	44

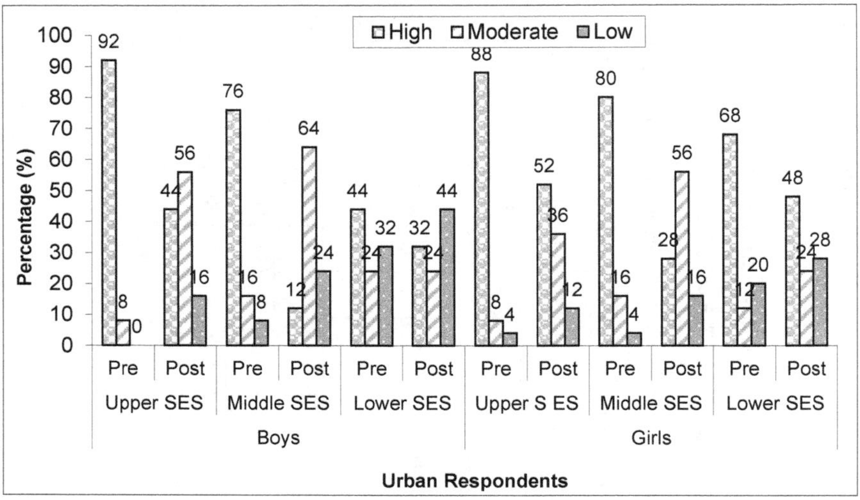

Fig 4.61 Percentage distribution of respondents belonging to different socio economic groups from urban socio cultural setting on the basis of bereavement stress before and after intervention

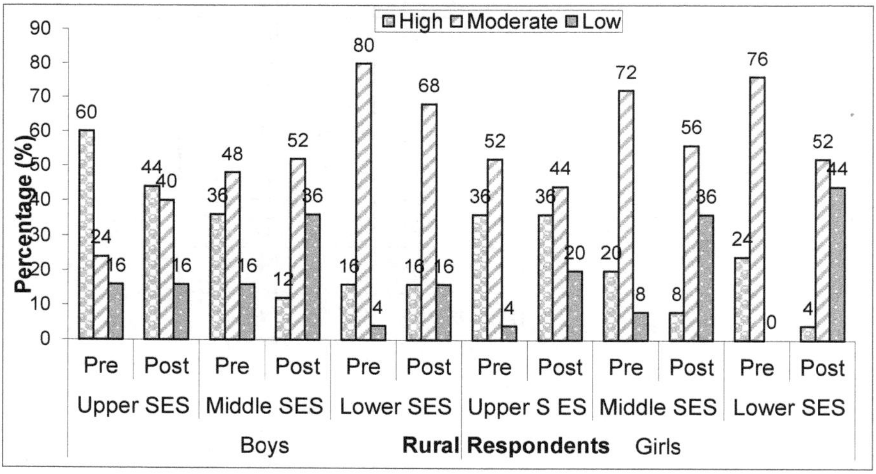

Fig 4.62 Percentage distribution of respondents belonging to different socio economic groups from rural socio cultural setting on the basis of bereavement stress before and after intervention

Table 4.25 and illustration depicted in figures **4.61** and **4.62** highlights the frequency and percentage distribution of respondents belonging to different socio economic groups from urban and rural background on the basis of bereavement stress. The table clearly showed that before intervention high level of bereavement stress was possessed by 92% of urban boys from the upper socio-economic class, 76% from the middle socio-economic class and 44% from the lower socio-economic class, while after intervention, it was reported that 44% of urban boys from the upper socio-economic class, 12% from the middle socio-economic class and 32 percent from the lower socio economic class suffered from high level of bereavement stress. In case of boys from rural cultural setting, it is clear from the data depicted in the table that high level of bereavement stress was possessed by 60 percent of respondents from the upper socio economic class, 36 percent from the middle socio economic class and 16 percent from the lower socio economic class before intervention whereas, after intervention, it was reported that 44 per cent adolescents from the upper socio-economic category, 12 per cent from the middle socio-economic category and 16 per cent from the lower socio-economic category had a high degree of bereavement stress. In the case of girls of urban cultural environment, maximum number of respondents in all socio-economic classes were found to have high stress levels before intervention i.e. 88 percent, 80 percent and 68 percent respondents from upper, middle and lower socio economic group respectively wherein, maximum bereavement stress can be seen among respondents belonging to upper socio economic group whereas, after intervention, it was identified that bereavement stress level was reduced i.e. 52 per cent, 28 per cent and 48 per cent of urban girls in upper, middle and lower socio-economic classes were affected by high levels of bereavement stress. In case of girls belonging to rural cultural environment it was reported that before intervention high bereavement stress levels was possessed by 36 percent, 20 percent and 24 percent respondents from upper, middle and lower socio economic group respectively whereas, after intervention, it was noted that 36 per cent of adolescents from the upper socio-economic class, 08 per cent of rural girls from the middle socio-economic class and 04 per cent from the lower socio-economic class had a high level of bereavement stress.

In case of urban boys it was seen that before intervention moderate degree of bereavement stress was 08 percent of the upper socio-economic class, 16 percent of the middle socio-economic class and 24 percent urban boys belonging to lower socio economic group whereas after intervention, it was witnessed that 56% of urban boys from the upper socio-economic class, 64% of boys from the middle socio-economic class, and 24% of boys from the lower socio-economic class had moderate levels of bereavement stress. In the case of boys of rural environment, it was witnessed that before intervention 24 percent, 48 percent and 80 percent respondents from upper, middle and lower socio economic groups respectively faced moderate level of bereavement stress while after intervention, it was identified that 40 percent, 52 percent and 68 percent respondents from upper, middle and lower socio economic groups respectively suffered from moderate level of bereavement stress. The intervention was thus successful in reducing the stress levels of the respondents as the ones suffering from high level of stress started experiencing moderate level of stress after participating in the prepared intervention program. In the case of urban-based girl respondents, it was reported that 08 per cent of the upper socio-economic category, 16 per cent of the middle socio-economic category followed by the 12 percent of the lower socio economic class possessed moderate level of bereavement stress before intervention whereas, after intervention, it was reported that 36 percent of participants from the upper socio-economic community led by 56 percent from the middle socio-economic community and 24% from the lower socio-economic community had moderate level of bereavement stress. Moderate bereavement stress was also seen in 52 per cent of rural girl adolescents from the upper socio-economic community, 72 per cent from the middle socio-economic community and 76 per cent from the lower socio-economic community before intervention, while after intervention, it was identified that 44 per cent from the upper socio-economic community, 56 per cent from the middle socio-economic community and 52 per cent students from lower socio economic community possessed moderate level of stress regarding bereavement.

Low level of bereavement stress before intervention was found in none of urban adolescent boys belonging to upper socio economic class, 08 percent of the middle socio economic class and 32 percent of the lower socio economic class but after intervention, among 16 percent of urban boys belonging to the upper socio-economic class, 24 percent from the middle socio-economic class, and 44 percent of urban adolescent boys from the lower socio-economic class, low stress levels were seen. In case of rural boys, it was noticed that before intervention low level of bereavement stress was possessed by 16 percent respondents each from upper socio economic and middle socio economic group and 04 percent boys from lower socio economic group whereas post intervention, it was seen that equal percent i.e. 16 percent each from upper socio economic and lower socio economic group and 36 percent from middle socio economic group possessed low level of bereavement stress. Table also highlights that in case of urban girls, 04 percent each from upper and middle socio economic group and 20 percent from lower socio economic group possessed low level of bereavement stress before intervention but after intervention, it was reported that 12 percent of the upper socio economic class, 16 percent of the middle and 28 percent of the lower socio economic class suffered from low level of bereavement stress whereas, in case of their rural counterparts, it was identified that before intervention 04% and 08% of respondents from the upper and middle socio-economic classes had low levels of bereavement stress, respectively, and none of the respondents from the lower socio-economic community had low bereavement stress but after intervention 20 percent from upper socio economic group, 36 percent respondents from middle and 44 percent respondents from lower socio economic group possessed low level of bereavement stress. Stress may occur when a loved one, such as a family member, near friend or an animal dies. Bereavement stress such as psychiatric depression, anxieties, persistent stress and panic syndromes can also result in a number of psychological disorders. High level of stress recorded by **Caserta and Lund (1992)** during their research. The results are consistent with evidence that resilience on the part of people who experienced a loss in the early stage is shown and the capacity to deal with the loss is often underestimated.

Bereavement stress is related to many issues, including sleep disorders, depression, migraine, anxiety, high blood pressure, cardiac disease and diabetes. Study conducted by **Jacob (1998)** also stated that up to a third of the most specifically affected individuals may experience adverse effects on physical or mental health or the two after a severe loss such as death of a spouse or infant. The risk of such bereavement stress raises the risk of death from heart disease, suicide and psychosomatic and mental conditions, or of contributing to them. Many factors, including how the person died, his support system, past experiences with death and their strengths and weakness, when coping with tension, hardship and high emotions, can affect a youth grieving.

Table 4.26 Frequency and percentage distribution of urban and rural respondents belonging to various socio-economic classes on the basis of separation stress before and after intervention

Level of Stress	Intervention	Urban Respondents (n=150)												Rural Respondents (n=150)											
		Upper socio economic group				Middle socio economic group				Lower socio economic group				Upper socio economic group				Middle socio economic group				Lower socio economic group			
		Boys (n=25)		Girls (n=25)		Boys (n=25)		Girls (n=25)		Boys (n=25)		Girls (n=25)		Boys (n=25)		Girls (n=25)		Boys (n=25)		Girls (n=25)		Boys (n=25)		Girls (n=25)	
		F	%	F	%	F	%	F	%	F	%	F	%	F	%	F	%	F	%	F	%	F	%	F	%
High	Pre	05	20	09	36	08	32	12	48	10	40	14	56	01	04	00	00	05	20	06	24	13	52	17	68
(56-40)	Post	02	08	06	24	06	24	07	28	08	32	08	32	00	00	00	00	04	16	03	12	09	36	13	52
Moderate	Pre	18	72	10	40	14	56	08	32	13	52	11	44	22	88	24	96	18	72	15	60	10	40	07	28
(39-23)	Post	20	80	12	48	16	64	14	56	15	60	16	64	18	72	20	80	15	60	14	56	11	44	09	36
Low	Pre	02	08	06	24	03	12	05	20	02	08	00	00	02	08	01	04	02	08	04	16	02	08	01	04
(22-07)	Post	03	12	07	28	03	12	04	16	02	08	01	04	07	28	05	20	06	24	08	32	05	20	03	12

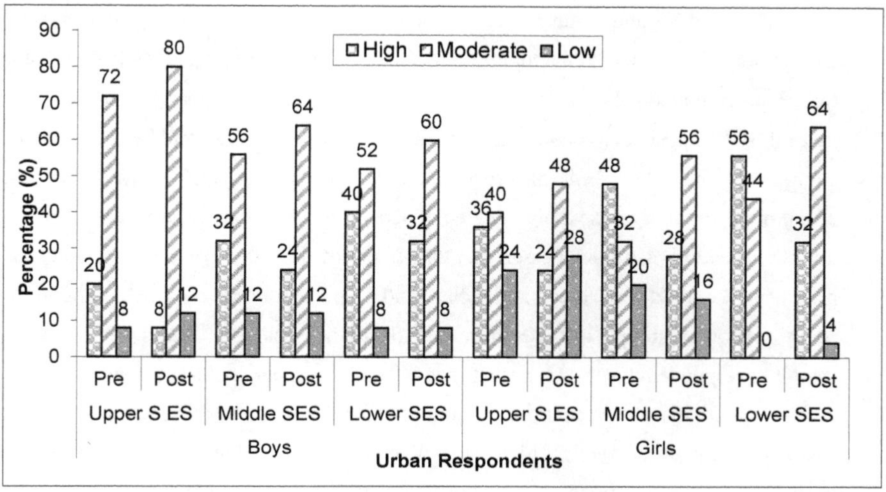

Fig 4.63 Percentage distribution of respondents belonging to different socio economic groups from urban socio cultural setting on the basis of separation stress before and after intervention

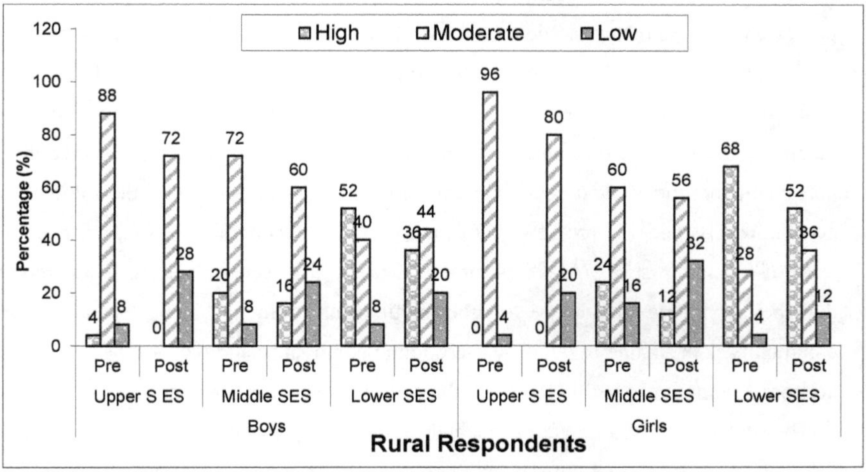

Fig 4.64 Percentage distribution of respondents belonging to different socio economic groups from rural socio cultural setting on the basis of separation stress before and after intervention

Table 4.26 and figures **4.63** and **4.64** highlights the frequency and percentage distribution of respondents belonging to different socio economic groups from urban and rural background on the basis of separation stress. The table clearly indicates that 20 percent of the upper socio-economic community, 32 percent of the middle socio-economic community and 40 percent of urban adolescent boys belonging to the lower socio-economic community have a high degree of separation stress before intervention whereas, after intervention, it was witnessed that 08 percent of the upper socio economic class, 24 percent of the middle socio economic class and 32 percent urban boys belonging to lower socio economic group suffered from high level of separation stress. In the case of rural boy respondents, it was reported that 44% of the upper socio-economic community, 20% of the middle socio-economic community and 52 percent of those belonging to lower socio economic group showed high level of separation stress but after intervention, stress level was reduced i.e. none of rural boys from upper socio economic group, 16 percent of the middle socio-economic community and 36% of the lower socio-economic community possessed high level of separation stress. In case of girls belonging to urban cultural setting, the table clearly shows that high level of stress regarding separation is possessed by 36% of urban adolescent girls from the upper socio-economic community, 48% from the middle socio-economic community and 56% from the lower socio-economic community before intervention wherein maximum stress could be seen in girls belonging to lower socio economic strata whereas, after intervention, it was noted that 24 percent of the upper socio economic class followed by 28 percent of the middle socio economic class and 32 percent girls of the lower socio economic class experienced high level of separation stress. As far as rural adolescent girls were concerned it was reported that before intervention none of the participants from the upper socio-economic community, 24% of the middle socio-economic community and 68% of the lower socio-economic community had high level of separation stress but after intervention the stress levels were reduced that none of respondents belonging to upper socio economic group followed by 12 percent from the middle socio economic group and 52 percent of those belonging to lower socio economic group suffered from high separation stress.

As far as moderate level of separation stress was concerned, it was witnessed that before intervention 72 percent of the urban boys from upper socio economic class, 56 percent of the middle socio economic class and 52 percent of the lower socio economic class experienced moderate level of stress while after intervention, it was reported that 80 percent of the upper socio economic class, 64 percent of the middle socio economic class and 60 percent of the urban boys from the lower socio economic class possessed moderate level of separation stress. The higher number of respondents experiencing moderate level of stress after intervention signifies that those experiencing higher level of stress earlier started experiencing moderate level of separation stress after the implementation of intervention program which is a clear indication of the efficacy of the planned and implemented intervention. Among the rural boys, moderate level of stress was possessed by 88 percent respondents from upper socio economic strata, 72 percent from middle and 40 percent among lower socio economic group before intervention whereas, after intervention, it was noticed that 72 percent from upper socio economic strata followed by 60 percent from middle and 44 percent were elicited among lower socio economic group who were experiencing moderate level of stress. Among the female respondents from urban background, it was witnessed that before intervention 40% of girls in the upper socio-economic community, 32% in the middle socio-economic community, and 44% in the lower socio-economic community had moderate level of separation stress whereas, after implanting the intervention package, it was observed that that 48% of the upper socio-economic category, 56% of the middle socio-economic category and 64% of the lower socio-economic category were found to experience moderate stress regarding separation. Among the rural girls moderate level of stress was noted among 96% of girls in the upper socio-economic class were followed by 60% in the middle socio-economic class and 28% in the lower socio-economic class before intervention but after intervention, it was identified that 80% of girls in the upper socio-economic class were followed by 56% of the middle socio-economic class and 36% of the lower socio-economic class possessed moderate level of separation stress.

As far as low level of separation stress was concerned it was noted that before intervention 08% of urban adolescent boys from the upper socio-economic community, 12% from the middle socio-economic community, and 08% of urban adolescent boys from the lower socio-economic community had low separate stress but after intervention, it was seen that 12 percent respondents both from upper as well as middle socio economic group and 08 percent urban boys from lower socio economic group suffered from low level of stress. As far as rural boys were concerned pre intervention data reveals that 08 percent respondents from all three socio economic group suffered from low level of separation stress, but after intervention, low stress level was witnessed among 28 percent respondents from upper socio economic group followed by 24 percent respondents from the middle socio-economic community and 20% from the lower socio-economic community. Among the urban girls low level of separate stress was seen among 24 percent girls belonging to upper socio economic group, followed by 20 percent from middle socio economic group and none of the respondents from lower socio economic strata suffered from low separate stress before intervention but after providing intervention, it was reported that 28% of girls from the upper socio-economic category were accompanied by 16% from the middle socio-economic category and 04% from the lower socio-economic category possessed low level of separation stress. Table also showed that before intervention 04 percent rural girls belonging to upper socio economic group, 16 percent belonging to middle socio economic group followed by 4 percent from lower socio economic group exhibited low separation stress whereas, after intervention, it was seen that 32 percent of rural girls belonging to middle socio economic group had low level of separation stress followed by 20 percent and 12 percent of the respondents exhibited separation stress in the upper and lower socio economic group respectively. Teenagers may experience separating stress through hospital shifts, school shifts, marriage, divorce of parents, transition etc. For stress reduction, it is necessary to follow effective strategies such as meditation, participation in hobbies, yoga, exercise and psychological therapy, in order to benefit from positive benefits.

The table clearly indicates that adolescents are subjected, regardless of sex, to both high and moderate levels of separation stress. Individuals with anxiety or worry over separation may be socially isolated or have intense sorrow or trouble separating from loved ones. The children are very concerned about their own protection and wellbeing and can experience somatic symptoms when they are separated. In its research, **Topolsky *et al.*, (1997)** found little self recognition to raise the risk of anxiety development in general. As a portable risk factor of separate anxiety **(Bernd *et al.*, 1989)** included age of the subject and low socioeconomic status.

Table 4.27 Frequency and percentage distribution of urban and rural respondents belonging to various socio-economic classes on the basis of personal setback stress before and after intervention

Level of Stress	Intervention	Urban Respondents (n=150)												Rural Respondents (n=150)											
		Upper socio economic group				Middle socio economic group				Lower socio economic group				Upper socio economic group				Middle socio economic group				Lower socio economic group			
		Boys (n=25)		Girls (n=25)		Boys (n=25)		Girls (n=25)		Boys (n=25)		Girls (n=25)		Boys (n=25)		Girls (n=25)		Boys (n=25)		Girls (n=25)		Boys (n=25)		Girls (n=25)	
		F	%	F	%	F	%	F	%	F	%	F	%	F	%	F	%	F	%	F	%	F	%	F	%
High (56-40)	Pre	17	68	22	88	11	44	14	56	04	16	11	44	10	40	06	24	14	56	14	56	07	28	02	08
	Post	14	56	17	68	06	24	05	20	02	08	02	08	08	32	02	08	07	28	06	24	04	16	01	04
Moderate (39-23)	Pre	07	28	03	12	12	48	08	32	18	72	09	36	11	44	18	72	05	20	11	44	17	68	21	84
	Post	09	36	07	28	16	64	17	68	16	64	19	76	12	48	22	88	13	52	16	64	18	72	19	76
Low (22-07)	Pre	01	04	00	00	02	08	03	12	03	12	05	20	04	16	01	04	06	24	00	00	01	04	02	08
	Post	02	08	01	04	03	12	03	12	07	28	04	16	05	20	01	04	05	20	03	12	03	12	05	20

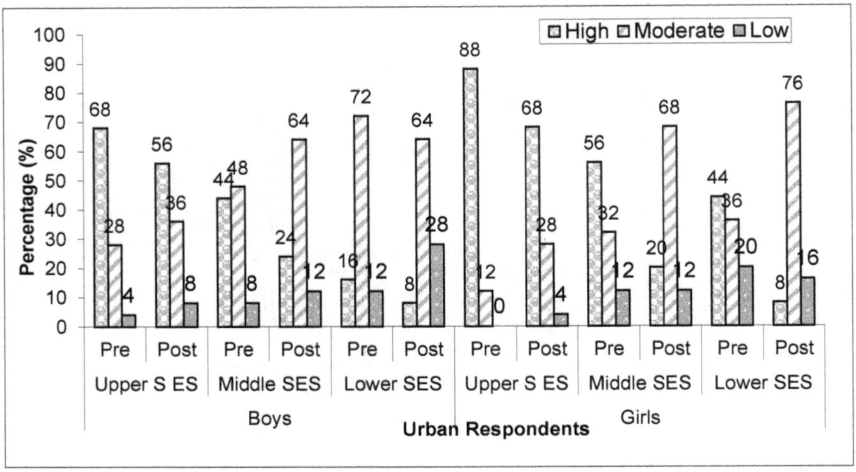

Fig 4.65 Percentage distribution of respondents belonging to different socio economic groups from urban socio cultural setting on the basis of personal setback stress before and after intervention

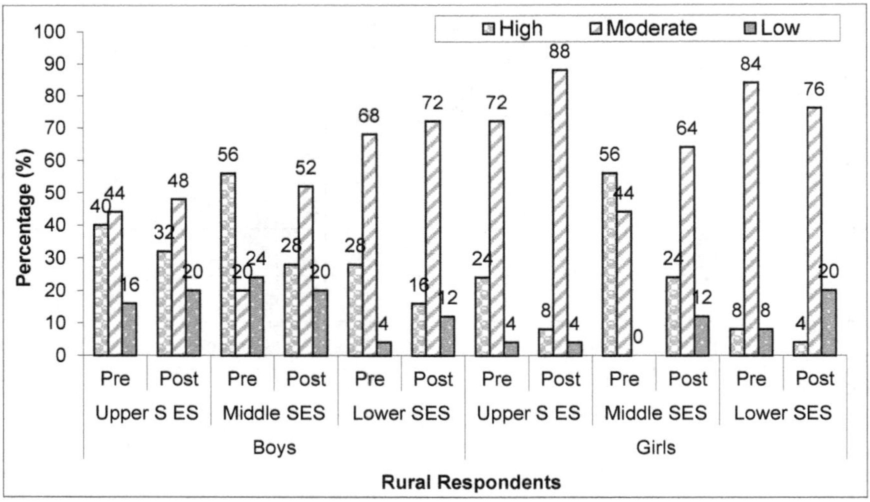

Fig 4.66 Percentage distribution of respondents belonging to different socio economic groups from rural socio cultural setting on the basis of personal setback stress before and after intervention

Table 4.27 and figures **4.65** and **4.66** highlights the frequency and percentage distribution of respondents belonging to different socio economic groups from urban and rural background on the basis of their personal setback stress. The table clearly showed that among the boys belonging to urban cultural setting 68 percent from the upper socio economic community, 44% of the middle socio-economic community and 16% of the lower socio-economic community possessed high level of personal setback stress before intervention whereas, after intervention, stress levels were reduced i.e. 56 percent from upper socio economic group, 24 percent in the middle socio-economic class and 08% in the lower socio-economic class suffered from higher level of personal setback stress. The table also revealed maximum personal setback among boys belonging to the upper socio economic status. In case of rural adolescent boys, in all the socio economic groups a number of respondents were identified with high stress level before intervention i.e. 40 percent, 56 percent and 28 percent from upper, middle and lower socio economic group respectively whereas after intervention, it was noticed that 32 percent, 28 percent and 16 percent from upper, middle and lower socio economic group respectively suffered from high personal setback stress. Among the urban adolescents girls, Maximum number of respondents in all socio-economic classes were found to have high setback stress before intervention i.e. 88 percent, 56 percent and 44 percent respectively from the upper, middle and lower socio economic group but after intervention, 68 percent, 20 percent and 08 percent urban girls from the upper, middle and lower socio economic group respectively possessed high level of personal setback stress. In case of rural girls, it was identified that before intervention 24 percent, 56 percent and 08 percent respondents from upper, middle and lower socio economic group had respectively high level of personal setback stress whereas, after providing intervention package, it was identified that 08 percent, 24 percent and 04 percent respondents from upper, middle and lower socio economic group respectively suffered from higher level of personal setback stress.

With regard to the moderate level of personal setback stress, it was witnessed that pre intervention 28 percent, 48 percent and 72 percent urban adolescent boys respectively from upper, middle and lower socio economic group respectively belonged to this category but after giving intervention, it was observed that 36 percent respondents from upper socio economic group and 64 percent boys each from middle and lower socio economic group had moderate level of stress regarding personal setbacks. A good numbers of rural boys were also found to be laid down with moderate stress level pre intervention i.e. 44 percent, 20 percent and 68 percent from upper, middle and lower socio economic group respectively whereas, after intervention, it was seen that 48 percent, 52 percent and 72 percent respectively from upper, middle and lower socio economic group possessed average level of personal setback stress. The reason for the increase in the percentage of respondents after intervention is due to the fact that many of those who were having high stress level before intervention were identified to have moderate level of stress after intervention as many of them moved from higher to moderate level of stress.

Moderate level of personal setback stress was possessed by 12 percent, 32 percent and 36 percent urban girls belonging to upper, middle and lower socio economic group respectively before intervention but after intervention, it was noticed that 28 percent, 68 percent and 76 percent urban girls belonging to upper, middle and lower socio economic group respectively suffered from moderate level of stress wherein, maximum stress could be seen in girls belonging to lower socio economic group. Seventy two percent rural girls belonging to upper Socio-economic group, 44% of the upper socio-economic community, 84% of the lower socio-economic community also showed moderate level of personal setback stress before intervention but after intervention, it was evident that 88 percent from upper socio economic group, 64 percent rural girls belonging to middle socio economic group and 76 percent from lower socio economic group possessed moderate level of personal setback stress wherein, maximum stress could be seen among rural girls from lower socio economic group.

Low levels of stress were reported by 04% of urban adolescent boys from the upper socio-economic class, 08 percent from the middle socio-economic class and 12 percent from the lower socio-economic class whereas, post study, low stress level were noticed among 08 percent urban boys from upper socio economic strata followed by 12 percent from middle socio economic group and 28 percent urban boys from lower socio economic group. In view of rural boys, it was seen that before intervention low stress levels regarding personal setbacks was identified among 16 percent respondents from upper socio economic group, 24 percent from middle socio economic group followed by and only 04 percent rural boys from lower socio economic strata whereas, after intervention, it was noted that 20 percent of the participants both from the upper and middle socio-economic class followed by 12 percent participants from the lower socio-economic class were having low level of personal setback stress. Table also reveals that before intervention none of urban girl respondents from upper socio economic group, 12 percent respondents from middle socio economic group and 20 percent urban girls from lower socio economic group were found to have low level of personal setback stress but after intervention, it was reflected that 04 percent urban girls from upper socio economic group followed by 12 percent respondents from middle socio economic group and 16 percent girl respondents from lower socio economic group possessed low level of personal setback stress. As far as rural girls were concerned, it was seen that before intervention low stress was possessed by 04 percent respondents from the upper, none of girl respondents in the middle socio-economic class and 08% in the lower socio-economic class whereas, after post intervention, it was reported that 04% of the upper socio-economic class, 12% of the middle socio-economic class, and 20% of the lower socio-economic class suffered from low level of stress regarding personal setback.

From the table it is clear that high level of personal setback stress is evident among majority of girls whereas moderate level of personal setback stress is seen among majority of boys in the urban socio cultural setting. Personal setback may arise due to the adolescent's failure to come up to their own expectations. Adolescents are very likely to be discouraged during these growing years. Changes take time and setbacks are part of the learning cycle. Adolescents need to learn from experience and plan to clear the hurdles to regain control of the situations. Stress is more likely to arise if proper strategies for handling setbacks are not adopted. The main reasons that generate personal setback stress are likely uncontrollable or unpredictable but there are several resources available like time management, personal awareness and sharing of feelings. Many times adolescents hesitate to share their personal setbacks with others which may lead to development of chronic stress. **Keinan and Perlberg (1986)** also argued that feelings of anger, anxiety, and depression can have a high level of stress. If coping mechanisms are not implemented, the overall performance of young people will be affected.

Table 4.28 Frequency and percentage distribution of urban and rural respondents belonging to various socio-economic classes on the basis of health of others stress before and after intervention

Level of Stress	Intervention	Urban Respondents (n=150)												Rural Respondents (n=150)											
		Upper socio economic group				Middle socio economic group				Lower socio economic group				Upper socio economic group				Middle socio economic group				Lower socio economic group			
		Boys (n=25)		Girls (n=25)		Boys (n=25)		Girls (n=25)		Boys (n=25)		Girls (n=25)		Boys (n=25)		Girls (n=25)		Boys (n=25)		Girls (n=25)		Boys (n=25)		Girls (n=25)	
		F	%	F	%	F	%	F	%	F	%	F	%	F	%	F	%	F	%	F	%	F	%	F	%
High (56-40)	Pre	09	36	13	52	18	72	16	64	13	52	17	68	03	12	18	72	11	44	12	48	13	52	10	40
	Post	06	24	09	36	16	64	13	52	09	36	12	48	02	08	13	52	06	24	07	28	12	48	08	32
Moderate (39-23)	Pre	12	48	11	44	04	16	05	20	11	44	08	32	15	60	05	20	9	36	10	40	08	32	14	56
	Post	14	56	09	36	04	16	11	44	15	60	10	40	13	52	08	32	15	60	13	52	07	28	16	64
Low (22-07)	Pre	04	16	01	04	03	12	04	16	01	04	00	00	07	28	02	08	05	20	03	12	04	16	01	04
	Post	05	20	07	28	05	20	01	04	01	04	03	12	10	40	04	16	04	16	05	20	06	24	01	04

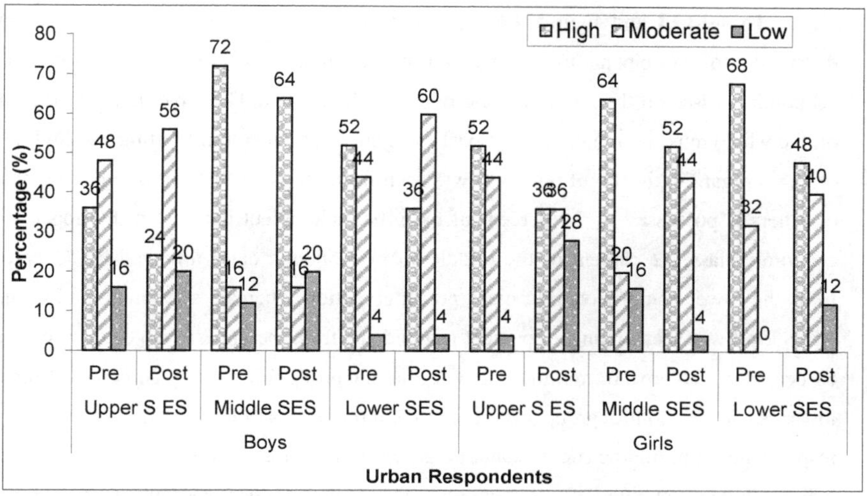

Fig 4.67 Percentage distribution of respondents belonging to different socio economic groups from urban socio cultural setting on the basis of health of others stress before and after intervention

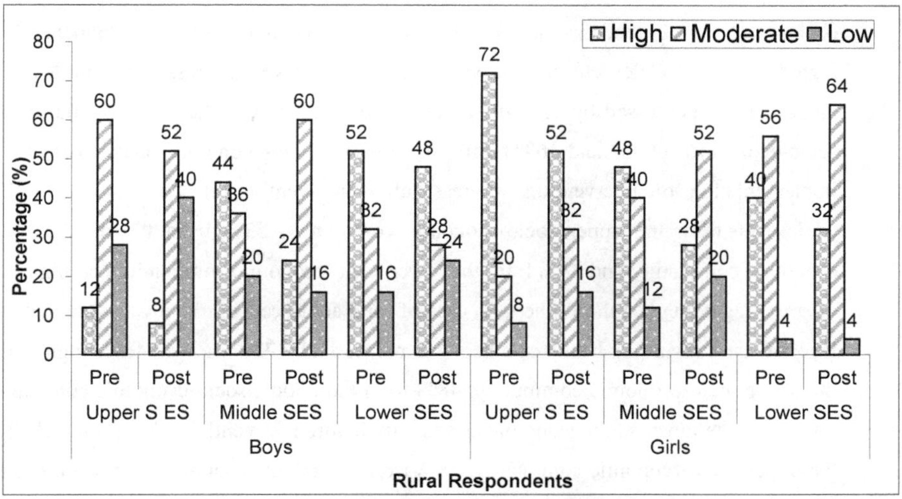

Fig 4.68 Percentage distribution of respondents belonging to different socio economic groups from rural socio cultural setting on the basis of health of others stress before and after intervention

Table 4.28 and figures **4.67** and **4.68** highlights the frequency and percentage distribution of participants from urban and rural communities belonging to various socio-economic classes on the basis of stress over health of other. The table made it clear that, on the whole maximum number of boys belonging to urban cultural setting had high level of stress regarding health of others. It was seen from the table that stress regarding health of others is possessed by 36 percent of the urban adolescent boys from the upper socio economic class, 72 percent of the middle socio economic class followed by 52 percent from the lower socio economic class pre intervention whereas, after intervention, high stress level was seen among 24 percent respondents from the upper socio economic group, 64 percent urban boys from middle socio economic group followed by 36 percent from the lower socio economic group wherein, maximum stress level could be seen in the respondents from middle socio economic group. In the case of rural boys, it was seen that before intervention high level of stress regarding health of others was possessed by 12% of the upper socio-economic category, 44% of the middle socio-economic category, and 52% of the lower socio-economic category but after post intervention, high stress level was noted among 08% of upper socio-economic group respondents, 24% of middle socio-economic group respondents, and 48% of lower socio-economic group respondents. With regards to urban adolescent girls, it was seen that high level of stress regarding health of others having possessed by 52% of the upper socio-economic class, 64% of the middle socio-economic class and 68% of the lower socio-economic class before the implementation of intervention whereas, after intervention, it was noted that 36% adolescents from the upper socio-economic community, 52% from the middle socio-economic community and 48% from the lower socio-economic community had high level of stress regarding health of others. In case of rural adolescents girls, it was seen that high level of stress regarding health of others was possessed by 72% rural adolescent girls from the upper socio-economic community, 48% from the middle socio-economic community, 40% from the lower socio-economic community before intervention, 52% rural girls from the upper socio-economic community, 28% from the middle socio-economic community, 32% from the lower socio-economic community suffered from high level of stress regarding health of others.

From the table it was also seen that moderate stress regarding health of others was exhibited by 48 percent of urban adolescent boys from the upper socio-economic class, 16 percent from the middle socio-economic class and 44 percent from the lower socio-economic class before intervention, while after post intervention, it was noted that 56 percent of urban boy respondents from the upper socio-economic class, 16 percent from the middle socio-economic class and 60 percent from the lower socio-economic class had moderate level of stress regarding health of others. In the case of rural boys, it was seen that before intervention moderate stress level regarding health of others was identified among 60 percent adolescents from the upper socio economic class followed by 36 percent of the middle socio economic class and 32 percent from the lower socio economic class whereas, after implementing the intervention package, it was identified that 52 percent respondents from upper socio economic group followed by 60 percent from middle socio economic group and 28 percent rural boys from lower socio economic group had moderate level of stress. Among the urban girls, it was seen that before intervention moderate stress level regarding health of others was identified among 44 percent of urban adolescent girls from the upper socio-economic community, 20 percent from the middle socio-economic community and 32 percent from the lower socio-economic community, but after post intervention, it was noted that 36 percent from the upper socio-economic community, 40 percent from the lower socio-economic community, and 44 percent from the lower socio-economic community possessed moderate level of stress regarding health of others. In case of their rural counterparts, moderate stress level was possessed by 20% of rural adolescent girls in the upper socio-economic class, 40% of the middle socio-economic category and 56% of participants in the lower socio-economic category before intervention whereas after intervention, it was seen that 32 percent rural girls from the upper socio economic strata, 52 percent girls from middle socio economic group and 64 percent girl respondents from lower socio economic group still suffered from moderate level of stress regarding health of others.

Among urban boys low level of stress regarding health of others was seen among 16 percent, 12 percent and 04 percent urban boys from upper, middle and lower socio economic group respectively before intervention whereas, after intervention, low stress level was seen among 20 percent respondents both from upper and middle socio economic group and 04 percent boys from lower socio economic group. Among rural boys, low level of stress regarding health of others was noted among 28% of adolescent boys from the upper socio-economic class followed 20% from the middle socio-economic class and 16% from the lower socio-economic class before intervention, while post intervention, 40 percent of rural adolescent boys from the upper socio-economic class followed 16% from the upper socio-economic class and 24% from the lower socio-economic class possessed low level of stress. Among female respondents from urban cultural setting, it was seen that before intervention low level of stress regarding health of others was possessed by 04 percent and 16 percent girls from upper and middle socio economic group respectively and none of respondents were found facing this type of stress among the lower socio economic group but after intervention, it was noticed that 28 percent of upper adolescent girls, 04 percent of middle socio-economic category girls and 12 percent of lower socio-economic category respondents had low level of stress regarding health of others whereas, among the girls from rural cultural background, it was found that before intervention low level of stress regarding health of others was possessed by 08 percent, 12 percent and 04 percent respondents from upper, middle and lower socio economic group respectively whereas, after providing the intervention package, it was seen that low stress level was possessed by 16 percent, 20 percent and 04 percent respondents from upper, middle and lower socio economic group respectively.

Stress can be witnessed in a person when family member is ill, admitted in hospital, develop serious disease or chronic disease. Stress does not directly causes ill-health to a person. Adolescents may develop concerns and even stress regarding the health of the their loved ones especially their parents in case of an acute, chronic or terminal health condition, frequent hospitalization, home safety concerns, fear of falling, weight loss or gain, mobility issues, need of assistance with household chores and also regarding isolation of their parents when children are not around. Having too much stress regarding the health of others may give rise to problems like anxiety and depression among the adolescents. Long term stresses have a major influence upon mood, sense of well-being, behaviour and health. **Schneiderman *et al.* (2005)** stated that the long-term effects of stressors can harm health, particularly in older or unhealthy people. The connation between psycho-social stressors and disease is influenced by the existence, number and persistence of stressors, the biological vulnerability and the psychosocial resources of the person and the learning of how to cope.

Table 4.29 Frequency and percentage distribution of urban and rural respondents belonging to various socio-economic classes on the basis of stress before and after intervention

Level of Stress	Intervention	Urban Respondents (n=150)												Rural Respondents (n=150)											
		Upper socio economic group				Middle socio economic group				Lower socio economic group				Upper socio economic group				Middle socio economic group				Lower socio economic group			
		Boys (n=25)		Girls (n=25)		Boys (n=25)		Girls (n=25)		Boys (n=25)		Girls (n=25)		Boys (n=25)		Girls (n=25)		Boys (n=25)		Girls (n=25)		Boys (n=25)		Girls (n=25)	
		F	%	F	%	F	%	F	%	F	%	F	%	F	%	F	%	F	%	F	%	F	%	F	%
High	Pre	24	96	23	92	21	84	23	92	18	72	19	76	19	76	21	84	19	76	17	68	13	52	15	60
(56-40)	Post	09	36	15	60	11	44	16	64	14	56	10	40	09	36	19	76	10	40	06	24	08	32	13	52
Moderate	Pre	01	04	02	08	04	16	02	08	07	28	06	24	05	20	04	16	06	24	08	32	09	36	09	36
(39-23)	Post	13	52	09	36	12	48	08	32	08	32	15	60	14	56	05	20	11	44	18	72	12	48	10	40
Low	Pre	00	00	00	00	00	00	00	00	00	00	00	00	01	04	00	00	00	00	00	00	03	12	01	04
(22-07)	Post	03	12	01	04	02	08	01	04	03	12	00	00	02	08	01	04	04	16	01	04	05	20	02	08

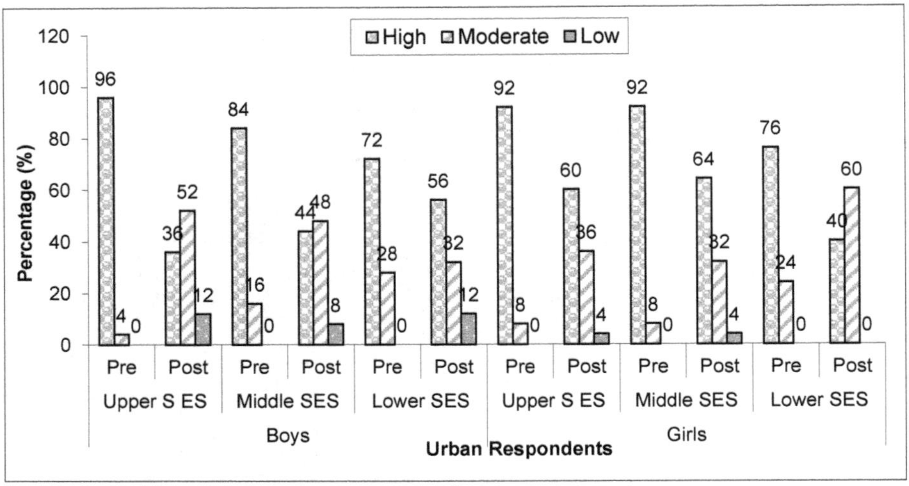

Fig 4.69 Percentage distribution of respondents belonging to different socio economic groups from urban socio cultural setting towards stress before and after intervention

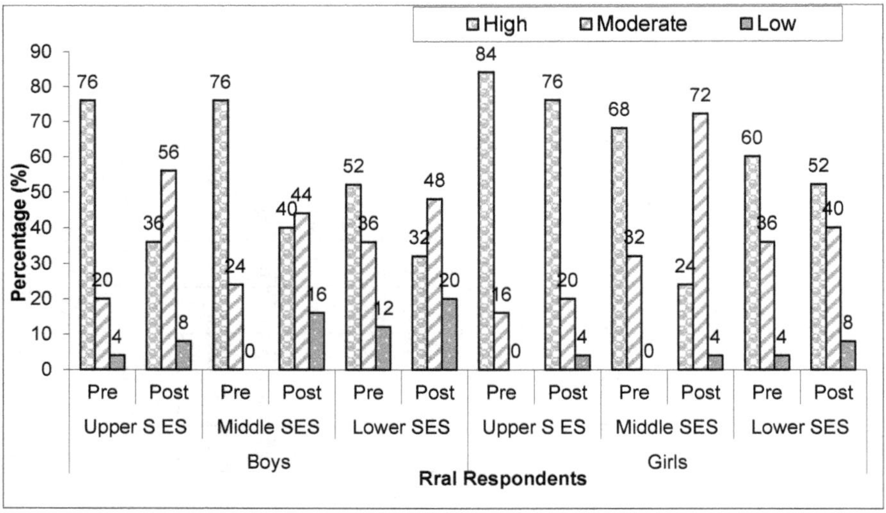

Fig 4.70 Percentage distribution of respondents belonging to different socio economic groups from rural socio cultural setting towards stress before and after intervention

Table 4.29 and figures **4.69** to **4.70** highlights the frequency and percentage distribution of respondents belonging to different socio economic groups belonging to urban as well as rural socio cultural setting towards their cumulative stress. It is clear from the table that in case of urban boys, maximum percent i.e. 96 percent of those belonging to upper socio economic group possessed high level of stress before intervention followed by 84 percent of boys belonging to middle socio economic group and 72 percent from lower socio economic group whereas, after providing intervention the percentage of respondents facing high stress level was reduced and it was noticed that 36 percent from upper socio economic group followed by 44 percent of urban boys from middle socio economic group and 56 percent of those belonging to lower socio economic group had high level of stress. In case of rural boys, it was witnessed that before intervention 76 percent from both upper and middle socio economic group and 52 percent from lower socio economic group possessed high level of stress but after intervention the respondents reporting high level of stress were reduced i.e. 36% of the upper socio-economic class, 40% of the middle socio-economic class, and 32% of the lower socio-economic class suffered from high level of stress. In the case of girls belonging to urban settings, it was noticed that before intervention 92 percent from both upper and middle socio economic group and 76 percent from lower socio economic strata were facing high level of stress whereas, after intervention, high level of stress were present in 60 percent of the upper socio-economic community, 64 percent of the middle socio-economic community and 40 percent of the lower socio-economic community. In the case of adolescent girls from rural environment, 84 percent of the upper socio-economic community, 68 percent of the middle socio-economic community and 60 percent of the lower socio-economic community had high stress levels before intervention, but after post intervention, 76 percent of the upper socio-economic community, 24 percent of the middle socio-economic community and 52 percent of the lower socio-economic community possessed high level of stress.

The table further highlighted that before intervention moderate level of stress was indicated by only 04 percent urban boys from upper socio economic group, 16 percent belonging to middle socio economic group and 28 percent from lower socio economic group whereas, after intervention, it was seen that 52 percent urban boys from upper socio economic group, 48 percent belonging to middle socio economic group and 32% of boys from the lower socio-economic community had moderate level of stress. Adolescent boys from rural environment, it was noted before intervention that 20% from the upper socio-economic class, 24% from the middle and 36% from the lower socio-economic community displayed moderate level of stress but after intervention, it was seen that 56 percent from upper socio economic strata and 44 percent from middle and 48 percent boys from lower socio economic group possessed moderate level of stress. The higher percentage of respondents signifies that after intervention the ones who were facing higher level of stress moved on the category of moderate stress level. In case of urban girls, it was seen that before intervention an 08 percent each from upper and middle socio economic group, 24 percent from lower socio economic group highlighted moderate level of stress and after implementing intervention, it was noted that 36 per cent of the upper socio-economic category had moderate stress, followed by 32 per cent of adolescent girls from the middle socio-economic category and 60 per cent from the lower socio-economic category. In the case of rural adolescent girls, 16 per cent of the upper socio-economic category, 32 per cent of the middle socio-economic category and 36 per cent of the lower socio-economic community represented moderate levels of stress prior to intervention whereas, after post intervention, it was identified that 20 percent of the upper socio economic community, 72 percent from the middle socio-economic community and 40% from the lower socio-economic community possessed moderate level of stress.

Before intervention low stress level was witnessed in none of urban boys from all three socio economic groups but after intervention, low stress level was noticed among 12 percent respondents each from upper and lower socio economic group and 08 percent boys from middle socio economic group had low level of stress. Among rural boys it was seen that before intervention 04% of rural adolescent boys belonging to the upper socio-economic class, none from the middle socio-economic class and 12% from the lower socio-economic class had low stress levels, while after post intervention, it was reported that 08% of rural adolescent boys belonging to the upper socio-economic community, 16% from the middle socio-economic community and 20% from the lower socio-economic community possessed low level of stress. In case of urban girls, it was noticed that before intervention none of respondents from all three socio economic groups possessed low level of stress but after intervention, it was identified that 04 percent girls, each from upper and middle socio economic group and none of respondents from lower socio economic group suffered from low level of stress. In case of rural girls it was seen that before intervention none of respondents from upper and middle socio economic group and 04 percent rural girls from lower socio economic status possessed low level of stress but after intervention, it was seen that low stress was possessed by 04 percent rural girls both from upper and middle socio economic status and 08 percent respondents from lower socio economic group possessed low level of stress.

It is clearly reflected that maximum respondents both from rural as well as urban cultural setting possessed high level of stress. Similarly a study conducted **Bhargava & Trivedi (2018)** clearly showed in their study that young people were stressed. Relationship stress, family, economical, social and psychological stress were the key causes of stress among the young. It was concluded that young people must follow some techniques for coping with stress, such as meditation, yoga, ample sleep and go out and speak to their friends and parents.

Table 4.30 Comparison of urban and rural boys and girls belonging to different socio economic groups based on their financial stress

Socio economic Status	Socio cultural setting	Boys n=150		Girls n=150		t-cal	p-value
		Mean	Standard Deviation	Mean	Standard Deviation		
Upper socio economic status (n=100)	Urban (n=50)	24.24	4.49	27.28	3.33	2.71*	0.008
	Rural (n=50)	20.64	3.13	25.28	3.39	5.01**	0.000
Middle socio economic status (n=100)	Urban (n=50)	19.24	2.99	23.36	2.74	0.88NS	0.381
	Rural (n=50)	22.68	3.19	21.64	3.67	1.06NS	0.292
Lower socio economic status (n=100)	Urban (n=50)	19.24	2.99	18.52	2.74	0.88NS	0.381
	Rural (n=50)	21.96	4.55	20.72	3.33	1.09NS	0.279

**Highly Significant

*Significant

NS Non Significant

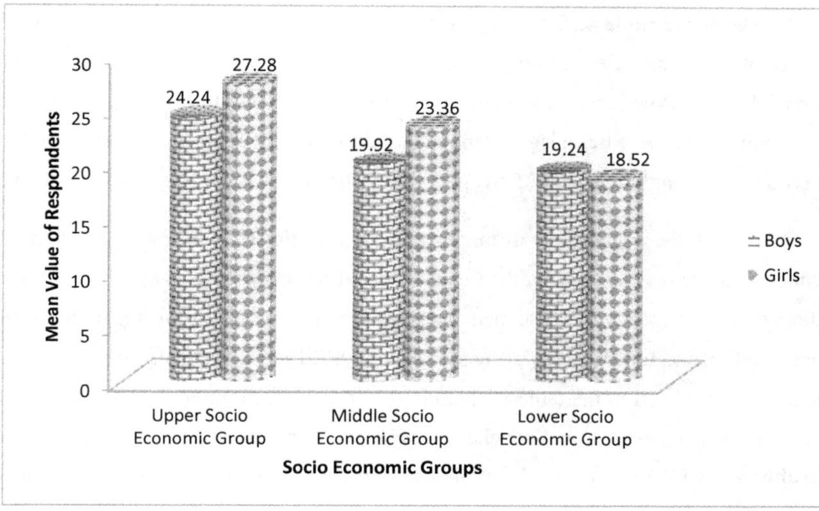

Fig 4.71 Financial stress of urban adolescents across three socio economic groups

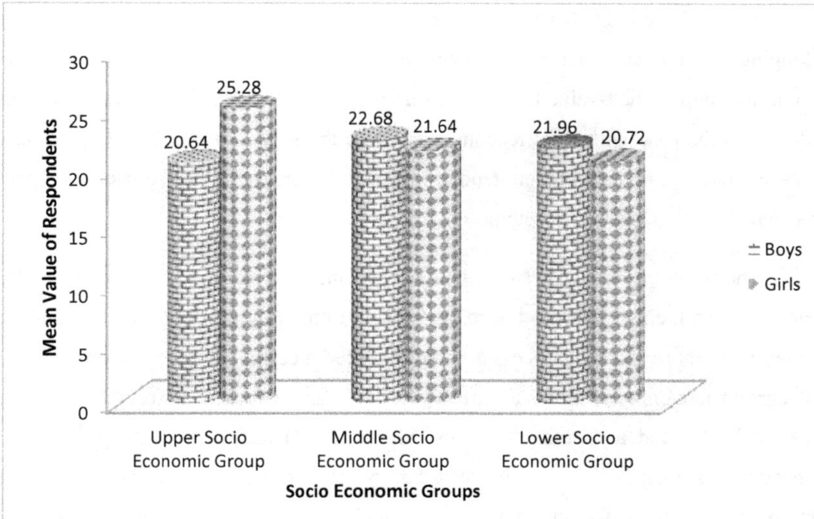

Fig 4.72 Financial stress of rural adolescents across three socio economic groups

The above **table 4.30** and **figure 4.71** and **4.72** indicates the comparison of urban and rural boys and girls belonging to different socio economic group based on the financial stress experienced by them. In case of respondents belonging to upper socio economic group, there lies a significant gender difference both among the urban and rural masses (t= 2.71, p=0.008 and t= 5.01, p= 0.000 respectively) regarding financial stress.

Among the respondents of middle socio economic strata in also a non significant gender variance is noted both in the urban and rural respondents (t= 0.88, p= 0.381 and t= 1.06, p= 0.292 respectively). The mean value further depicted that boys had more financial stress both in the urban and rural masses as compared to their female counterparts. The mean value depicted in the table further clarifies that boys in the middle and lower socio economic strata have more financial stress as compared to their female counterparts. **Ibrahim *et al.* (2013)** concluded that Students from low-income families and parental jobs appear to be overwhelming and nervous. More importantly, students and their families' financial difficulties have a detrimental influence on student stress. **(Andrews** and **Wilding, 2004).**

The table reflects that there is a non significant difference among boys and girls belonging to both urban and rural background among the respondents from lower socio economic group as the t-value for urban group was found to be 0.88 and p value was 0.381 and so was the case with rural respondents where the t-value was 1.09 and p value was 0.279 signifying a non significant gender difference among both the groups with regard to financial stress experienced by them.

The results revealed that financially boys and girls are much stressed as it affects their study and their demand and need also. **Brougham *et al.* (2009)** found that university women were more likely than college men to experience financial stress. They also said that current university students are deeply worried about financial stress and its related negative health and academic outcomes. **Sinha (2013)** suggested that by using stress management strategies, handle jobs, take care of friends and mentors students can easily cope with their stress. Parents may also help their teens to overcome depression through support and attention.

Table 4.31 Comparison of urban and rural boys and girls belonging to different socio economic groups based on family stress

Socio economic Status	Socio cultural setting	Boys n=150		Girls n=150		t-cal	p-value
		Mean	Standard Deviation	Mean	Standard Deviation		
Upper socio economic status (n=100)	Urban (n=50)	40.60	7.44	45.28	6.32	2.39*	0.019
	Rural (n=50)	34.56	9.53	32.40	9.42	0.80NS	0.426
Middle socio economic status (n=100)	Urban (n=50)	39.76	8.53	43.28	4.94	1.78NS	0.079
	Rural (n=50)	41.64	6.80	41.48	6.44	0.08NS	0.936
Lower socio economic status (n=100)	Urban (n=50)	36.20	6.75	31.00	7.21	2.63*	0.010
	Rural (n=50)	30.24	5.62	33.12	3.59	2.15*	0.348

*Significant

NS Non Significant

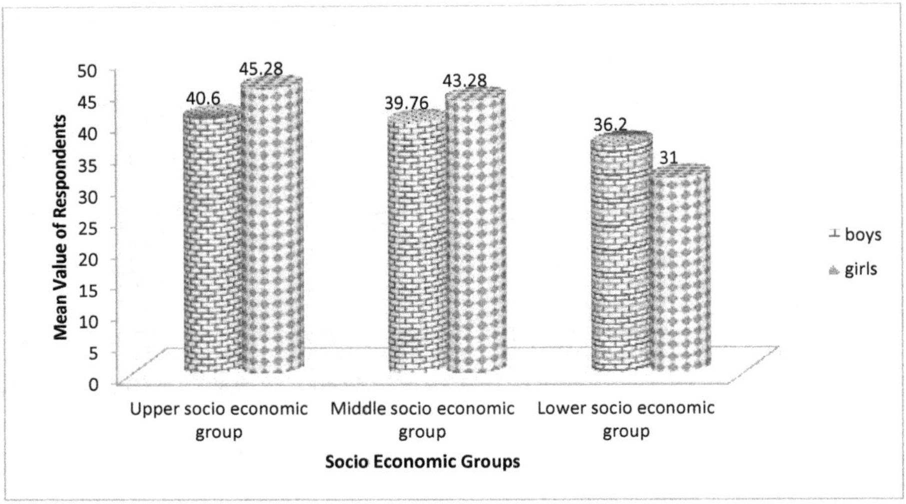

Fig 4.73 Family stress in urban adolescents across three socio economic groups

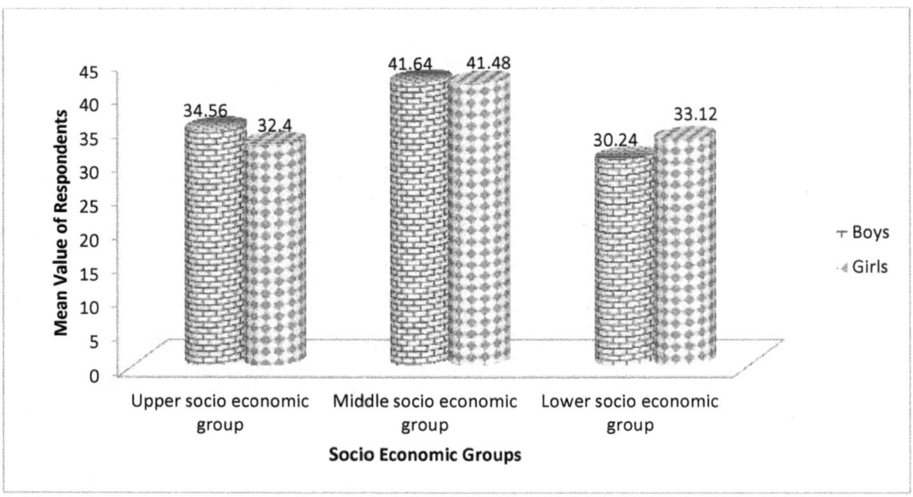

Fig 4.74 Family stress in rural adolescents across three socio economic groups

Table 4.31 and **figure 4.73** and **4.74** shows the comparative study of adolescent boys and girls from various social classes in urban and rural areas on the basis of family stress experienced by them. In case of respondents from the upper socio economic group it was evident from the table that there lies a significant gender variance in family stress among the urban masses (t=2.39, p= 0.019) whereas a non significant gender variance was noticed among the rural masses (t= 0.80, p= 0.426) although the mean values indicated that urban girls in this group possessed a slightly greater family stress as compared to their male counterparts.

A non significant gender variance regarding family stress was also evident among both the urban and rural masses belonging to the middle socio economic group (t=1.78, p= 0.079 and t= 0.08, p= 0.936 for both the urban and rural category. Urban girls in this group were found to have highly family stress as compared to the boys and in rural cultural setting both boys and girl possessed almost similar stress levels regarding family.

From the table it was also evident that there lies a significant difference among boys and girls both from urban and rural background belonging to lower socio economic group with regard to family stress as the t-value was found to be 2.63 and p-value 0.010 for the urban respondents and t-value 2.15 and p-value 0.348 for the rural masses indicating a significant gender variance. The mean values further indicated that boys from urban background and girls from the rural background possessed higher family stress as compared to their counterparts. **Shamsuddin *et al.* (2013)** reported that the socioeconomic background of families in rural areas is frequently diminished. It could also be clarified that some rural students move away from school and abandon their families, which may lead to problems for some students and tension during their college era. **Christie et al., (2002)** found that the risk of depression is lower for students living at home with their families because families are more supportive and shield themselves from academic stress. **Steinberg and Silk (2002), Grusec (2011)** reported that girls have greater conflicts with their parents than boys and experience more tension, even though it has been found that disputes with parents are often related to child violence. In addition, the girls have been tracked closer than the boys. These findings must be interpreted with respect to the adolescence period, which is defined for example by ambitions for freedom and independence.

Table 4.32 Comparison of urban and rural boys and girls belonging to different socio economic groups based on social stress

Socio economic Status	Socio cultural setting	Boys n=150		Girls n=150		t-cal	p-value
		Mean	Standard Deviation	Mean	Standard Deviation		
Upper socio economic status (n=100)	Urban (n=50)	24.40	2.94	22.36	3.49	2.23*	0.028
	Rural (n=50)	18.40	4.76	21.64	3.20	2.82*	0.006
Middle socio economic status (n=100)	Urban (n=50)	20.72	4.98	21.08	3.36	0.29NS	0.772
	Rural (n=50)	15.84	4.81	20.32	3.03	3.93*	0.000
Lower socio economic status (n=100)	Urban (n=50)	21.80	3.90	19.68	3.66	1.98*	0.051
	Rural (n=50)	23.04	4.23	20.76	2.53	2.30*	0.024

*Significant

NS Non Significant

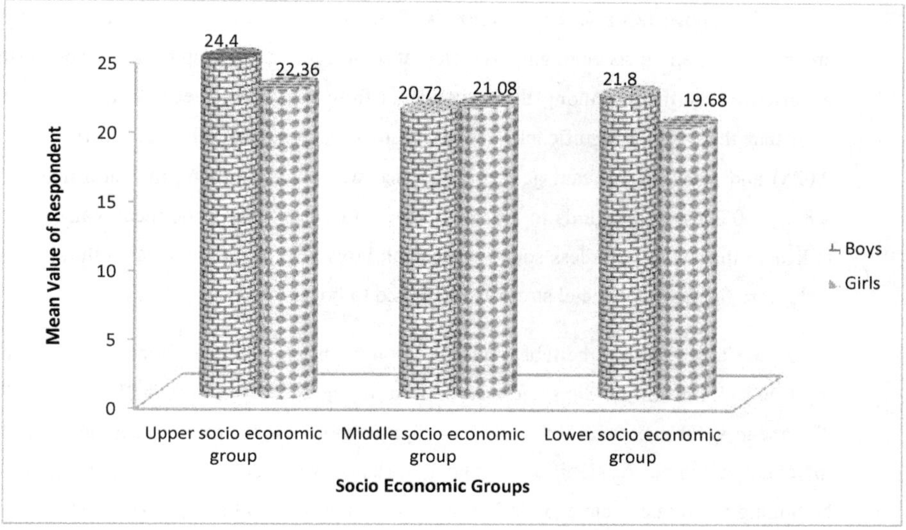

Fig 4.75 Social stress in urban adolescents across three socio economic groups

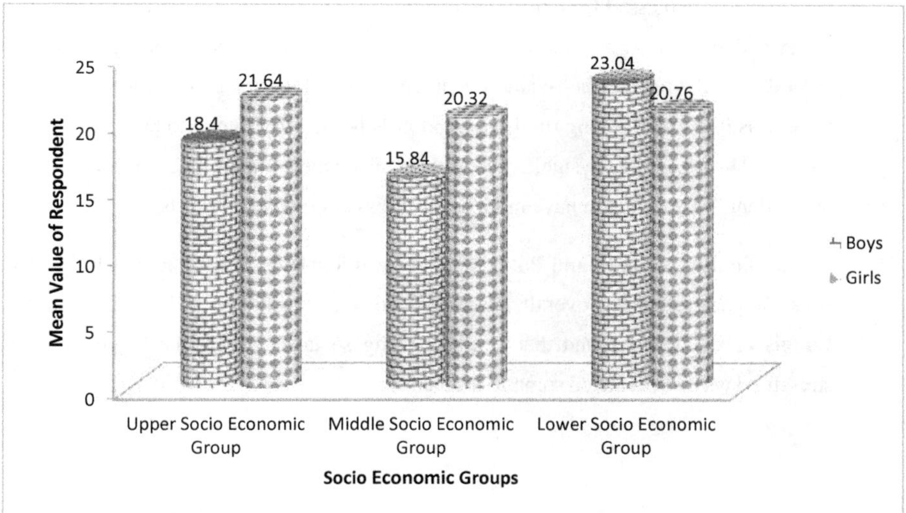

Fig 4.76 Social stress in rural adolescents across three socio economic groups

The above **table 4.32** and **figure 4.75** and **4.76** indicates the comparison of urban and rural boys and girls belonging to different socio economic group based on social stress experienced by them. Among the respondents from upper socio economic strata it was seen that there lies a significant gender difference among the urban group (t= 2.23, p= 0.028) and also a significant gender difference was evident among the rural masses (t= 2.82, p= 0.006) with regards to the social stress faced by them. The mean values further indicated that urban girls less social stress than boys whereas in the rural cultural settings girls were facing more social stress as compared to boys.

Data depicted in the table showed a non-significant gender variance among urban boys and girls from middle socio economic group as the t-value was 0.29 and p= 0.772. The mean value indicated that girls had slightly more social stress as compared to their male counterparts. A significant gender variance was seen among the rural masses belonging to middle socio economic status as t-value was 3.93 and p= 0.000 wherein girls were found to possess greater social stress as compared to their male counterparts.

It was witnessed from the table that their lies a significant gender difference among urban and rural boys and girls belonging to lower socio economic strata with concern towards social stress as the t-value for urban boys and girls was found to be 1.98 and p-value was 0.051 and among rural boys and girls t-value was found to be 2.30 and p-value was 0.024 indicating a significant gender difference among the respondents. Male respondents were found to have more social stress as compared to girls.

Similarly **George and Patrick (2017)** also found same result in which showed that stress impacts students' overall academic and social well-being. In their analysis **De Longis et al. (1988)** found that non-supporting social ties were the biggest burden on stressful days that predicted somatic problems.

Table 4.33 Comparison of urban and rural boys and girls belonging to different socio economic groups based on educational stress

Socio economic Status	Socio cultural setting	Boys n=150		Girls n=150		t-cal	p-value
		Mean	Standard Deviation	Mean	Standard Deviation		
Upper socio economic status (n=100)	Urban (n=50)	105.28	17.08	116.20	14.21	2.45*	0.016
	Rural (n=50)	103.88	12.49	113.92	11.66	2.93*	0.004
Middle socio economic status (n=100)	Urban (n=50)	107.16	18.40	113.16	12.35	1.35*	0.181
	Rural (n=50)	97.08	20.33	109.36	10.16	2.70*	0.008
Lower socio economic status (n=100)	Urban (n=50)	91.72	16.84	107.84	8.57	4.26*	0.000
	Rural (n=50)	107.56	18.70	106.48	12.17	0.24NS	0.810

*Significant

NS Non Significant

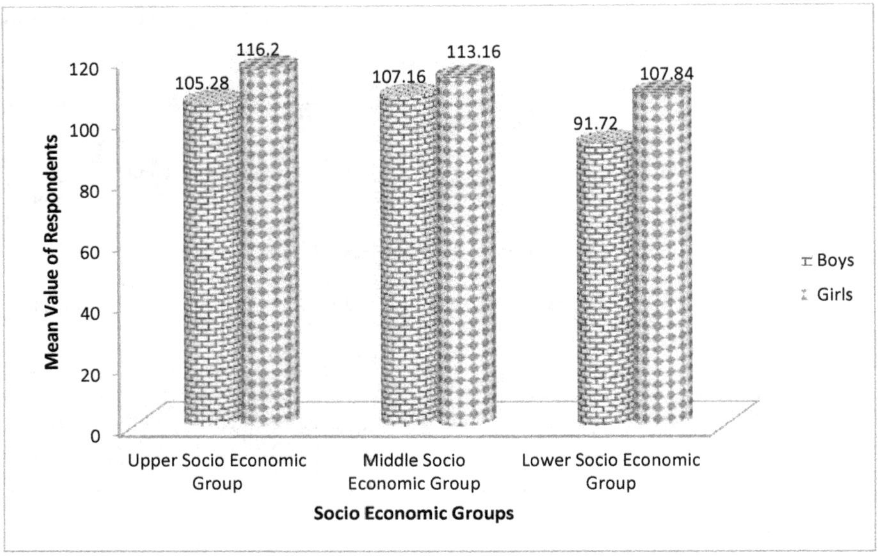

Fig 4.77 Educational stress in urban adolescents across three socio economic groups

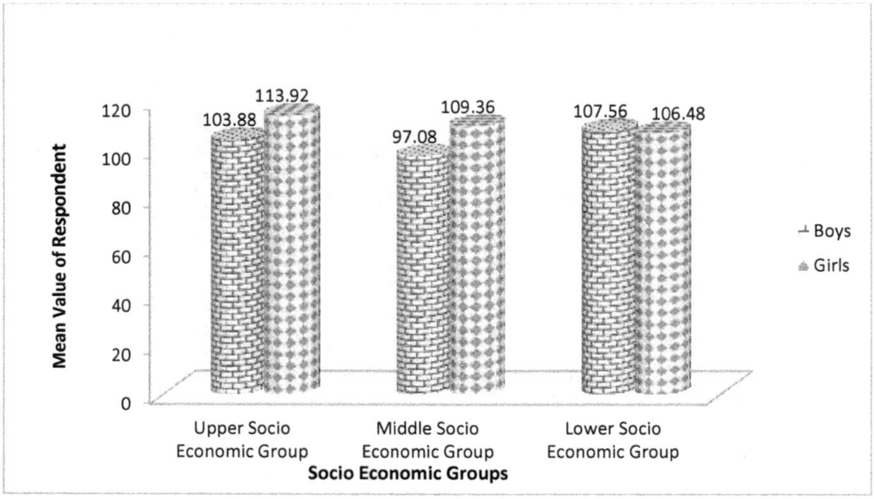

Fig 4.78 Education in rural adolescents across three socio economic groups

The above **table 4.33** and **figure 4.77** and **4.78** shows the comparative study of adolescent boys and girls from various social classes in urban and rural areas regarding educational stress. In case of respondents from the upper socio economic group it was evident from the table that there lies a significant gender variance in educational stress among the urban masses (t= 2.45, p= 0.016) as well as rural masses (t= 2.93, p= 0.004). The mean values indicated that girls in both the groups possessed a highly educational stress as compared to their male counterparts. The stress levels between men and women were different **(Amr, *et al.*, 2008).**

A significant gender variance regarding educational stress was also evident among both the urban and rural masses belonging to the middle socio economic group (t=1.35, p= 0.181 and t= 2.70, p= 0.008) for both urban and rural category. Girls in this group were also found to have highly educational stress as compared to boys.

Table also revealed a significant difference among boys and girls from urban background belonging to lower socio economic group regarding educational stress as the t-value was found to be 4.26 and p-value 0.000. a non significant gender variance was seen among the rural masses wherein t value was 0.24 and p value 0.810. The mean values further indicated that girls in the urban group had higher educational stress as compared to their male counterparts.

It's also seen that imposing too much pressure on girls by asking girls to do multiple jobs almost always might be one of the reasons for girls' stress. Because of their aspirations, both at home and in the academic arena, it would be difficult to meet demands because they cannot perform according to potential.

Stress impact on women in academic professions in particular. It was also important to note that the understanding of male and female students about stressors was substantially different. **Waghachavare *et al.* (2013)** suggested that measures to provide stress management in the educational curriculum should be taken. **Bartwal and Singh (2014)** suggested that in order to make adolescents stress free, effective teaching-learning approaches need to be implemented. **Dixit and Singh (2015)** also suggested that the instructor should consider psychology of the child and not surpass the children's standards.

Table 4.34 Comparison of urban and rural boys and girls belonging to different socio economic groups based on ego threat

Socio economic Status	Socio cultural setting	Boys n=150		Girls n=150		t-cal	p-value
		Mean	Standard Deviation	Mean	Standard Deviation		
Upper socio economic status (n=100)	Urban (n=50)	44.04	10.05	53.20	5.93	3.92*	0.000
	Rural (n=50)	44.40	8.25	38.96	8.90	2.24*	0.028
Middle socio economic status (n=100)	Urban (n=50)	51.84	5.28	47.40	7.38	2.44*	0.017
	Rural (n=50)	35.80	5.41	39.00	6.14	1.95*	0.054
Lower socio economic status (n=100)	Urban (n=50)	45.60	5.87	42.44	5.62	1.94*	0.056
	Rural (n=50)	35.80	5.41	39.00	6.14	1.95*	0.054

*Significant

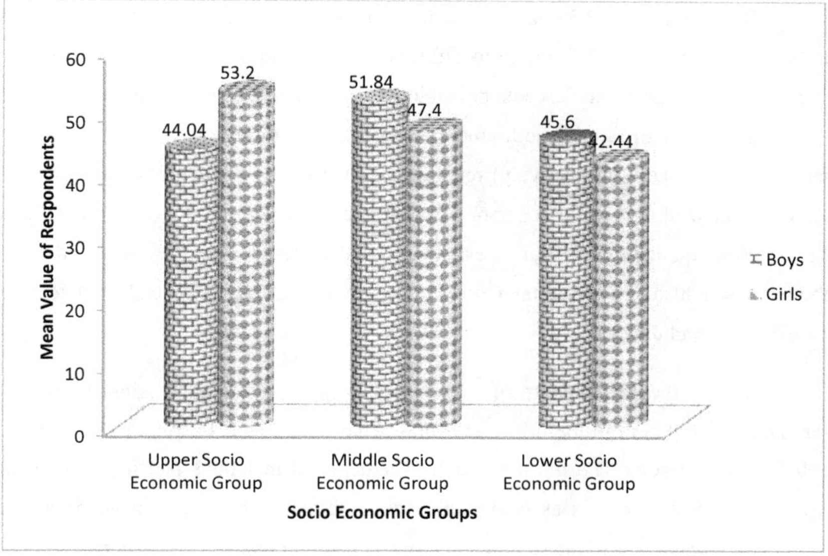

Fig 4.79 Ego threat in urban adolescents across three socio economic groups

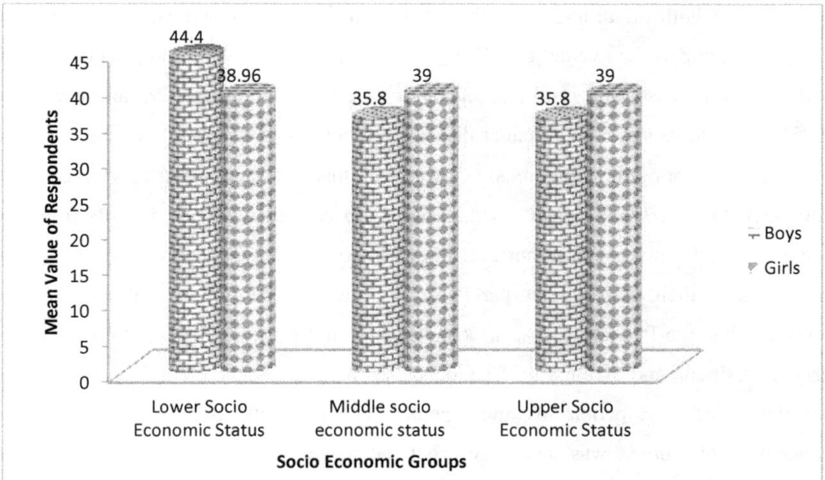

Fig 4.80 Ego threat in rural adolescents across three socio economic groups

The above **table 4.34** and **figure 4.79** and **4.80** indicates the comparison of urban and rural boys and girls belonging to different socio economic group based on their ego threat stress. In case of adolescents belonging to upper socio economic group, there lies a significant gender difference both among the urban and rural masses (t= 3.92, p= 0.000 and t= 2.24, p= 0.028 respectively) regarding their poor ego threat stress. Ego threat can be conceptualized as threat to a person's self image or self esteem. It is often seen that ego threats occur quiet often in our lives. Events that undermine ones beliefs and feelings about oneself also proves to taint ones image in others eyes and lead to a feeling of insufficiency and disgust.

Among the respondents of middle socio economic strata a significant gender variance is noted both in the urban and rural respondents, t= 2.44, p= 0.017 and t= 1.95, p=0.054 respectively. The mean value further depicted that boys had higher ego threat stress in the urban masses as compared to their female counterparts whereas girls had higher ego threat stress in the rural masses as compared to their male counterparts.

The table reflects that there is a significant difference among boys and girls belonging to both urban and rural background among the respondents from lower socio economic group as the t value for urban group was found to be 1.94 and p-value was 0.056 and so was the case with rural respondents where the t-value was 1.95 and p-value was 0.054 signifying a significant gender difference among both the groups with regard to ego threat stress. Among the urban masses it was seen that boys had higher ego threat stress as compared to their female counterparts whereas in case of rural respondents from lower socio economic group it was noticed that girls possessed higher ego threat stress when compared to their male counterparts. Study conducted by **Singh and Anand (2015)** revealed that ego-friendly people lack motivation and trust, while ego strong people are driven, resilient and willing to face obstacles by trusting in themselves and in their abilities. Gradually, people are incompetent. The research also showed that the self-conception of women was higher and that the power of the self was not dramatically different between women and men.

Table 4.35 Comparison of urban and rural boys and girls belonging to different socio economic groups based on bereavement stress

Socio economic Status	Socio cultural setting	Boys n=150		Girls n=150		t-cal	p-value
		Mean	Standard Deviation	Mean	Standard Deviation		
Upper socio economic status (n=100)	Urban (n=50)	22.96	3.31	22.56	3.93	0.38NS	0.705
	Rural (n=50)	20.60	2.53	21.12	3.12	0.64NS	0.524
Middle socio economic status (n=100)	Urban (n=50)	20.80	5.13	20.24	2.84	0.47NS	0.639
	Rural (n=50)	17.00	3.18	18.48	4.19	1.40NS	0.165
Lower socio economic status (n=100)	Urban (n=50)	21.56	3.39	19.24	2.81	2.63*	0.010
	Rural (n=50)	17.64	2.66	20.68	2.81	3.92*	0.000

*Significant

NS Non Significant

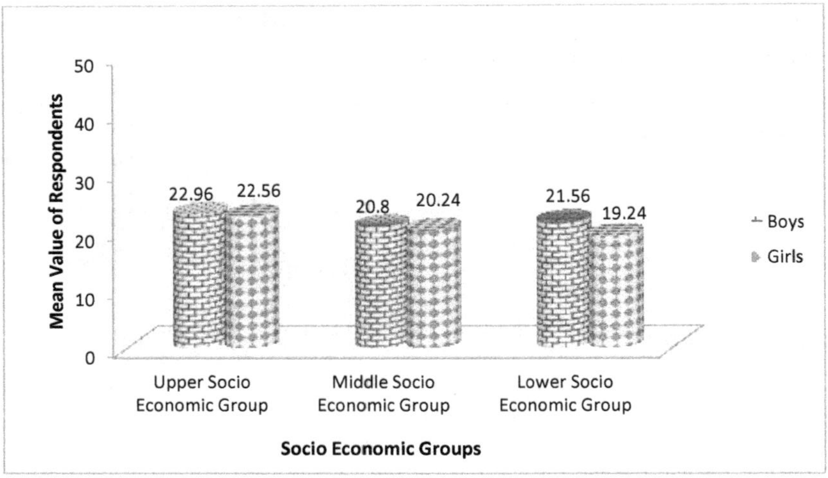

Fig 4.81 Bereavement stress in urban adolescents across three socio economic groups

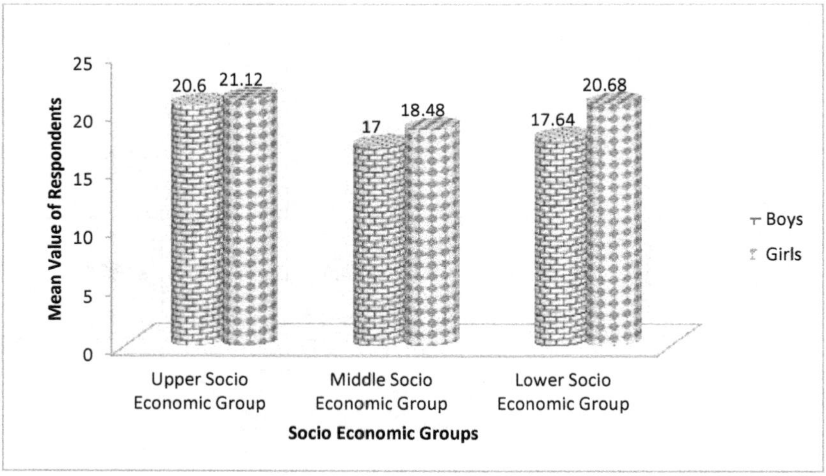

Fig 4.82 Bereavement stress in rural adolescents across three socio economic groups

Table 4.35 and **figure 4.81** and **4.82** shows the comparative study of adolescent boys and girls from various social classes in urban and rural areas on the basis of bereavement stress. In case of respondents from the upper socio economic group it was evident from the table that there lies a non significant gender variance in bereavement stress among the urban masses (t= 0.38, p= 0.705) as well as rural masses (t= 0.64, p= 0.524).

A non significant gender variance regarding bereavement stress was also evident among both the urban and rural masses belonging to the middle socio economic group (t= 0.47, p= 0.639 and t= 1.40, p= 0.165 for urban and rural category. Both boys and girls in this group were found to have almost equal bereavement stress.

From the table it is evident that there lies a significant differences among boys and girls both from urban and rural background belonging to lower socio economic group with regard to bereavement stress as the t-value was found to be 2.63 and p-value 0.010 for the urban respondents and t-value 3.92 and p-value 0.000 for the rural masses indicating a significant gender variance. The mean values further indicated that boys in urban group had higher bereavement stress as compared to their female counterparts whereas girls in rural group had higher bereavement stress as compared to their male counterparts.

Results revealed that boys and girls both are equally facing stress regarding bereavement. **Servaty and Hamilton (2006)** noted that bereavement stress causes tension among students, since the deplorable grades of students have fallen markedly. Given that low degrees are affecting the suffered and the effect of poor academic performance on students' graduation and career pursuits, timely institutional reactions to meet those academic needs are justified and in line with the university's mission to promote the advancement of students. **Balk and Vesta (1998)** also reported that bereavement also affects both physically and mentally students at universities. Grief may impede the resolution of normal developmental tasks such as the formation of autonomous lives, the creation of a clear sense of guidance and enduring interpersonal relationships.

Table 4.36 Comparison of urban and rural boys and girls belonging to different socio economic groups based on separation stress

Socio economic Status	Socio cultural setting	Boys n=150		Girls n=150		t-cal	p-value
		Mean	Standard Deviation	Mean	Standard Deviation		
Upper socio economic status (n=100)	Urban (n=50)	15.00	4.23	18.44	2.25	3.58*	0.000
	Rural (n=50)	14.60	3.83	17.24	2.53	2.87*	0.005
Middle socio economic status (n=100)	Urban (n=50)	17.04	2.16	16.32	2.75	1.02*	0.311
	Rural (n=50)	14.36	2.78	16.12	2.27	2.44*	0.017
Lower socio economic status (n=100)	Urban (n=50)	15.68	3.21	16.16	2.59	0.58NS	0.563
	Rural (n=50)	16.76	2.84	16.40	3.02	0.43NS	0.668

*Significant

NS Non Significant

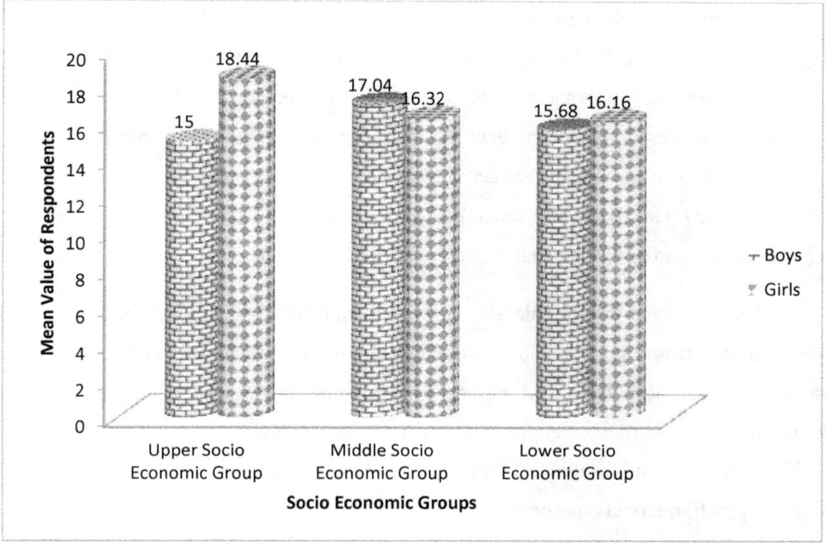

Fig 4.83 Separation stress in urban adolescents across three socio economic groups

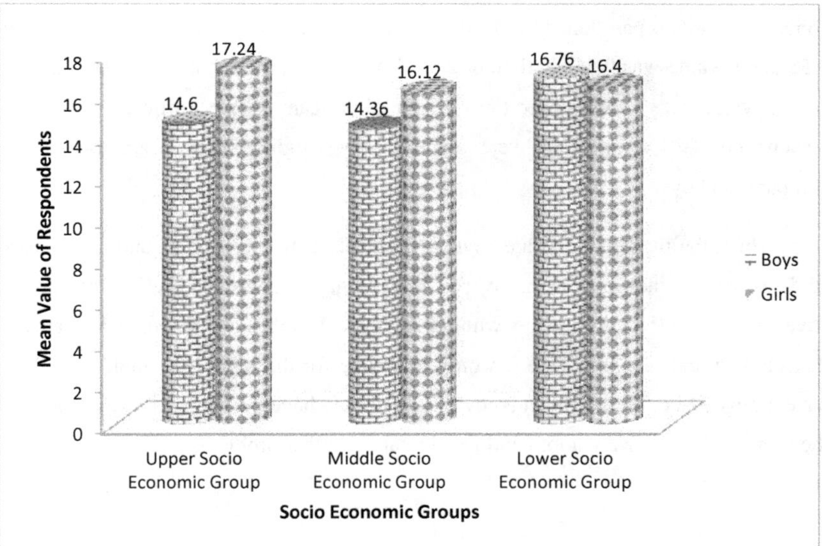

Fig 4.84 Separation stress in rural adolescents across three socio economic groups

The above **table 4.36** and **figure 4.83** and **4.84** indicates the comparison of urban and rural boys and girls belonging to different socio economic group based on stress regarding separation. Among the respondents from upper socio economic strata it was seen that there lies a significant gender difference among the urban group (t= 3.58, p= 0.000) as well as a significant gender difference was evident among the rural masses (t= 2.87, p= 0.005) with regards to separation stress wherein it was seen that girls had higher separation stress in both the group as compared to boys.

Data depicted in the table also showed a significant gender variance among urban boys and girls from middle socio economic group as t-value was 1.02 and p= 0.311. Mean values indicated that boys had higher separation stress as compared to their female counterparts. A significant gender variance was seen among the rural masses belonging to middle socio economic status as t-value was 2.44 and p-value was 0.017 wherein girls had higher separation anxiety as compared to boys.

It is witnessed from the table that their lies a non significant gender difference among urban and rural boys and girls belonging to lower socio economic strata with concern towards separation stress as the t-value for urban boys and girls was found to be 0.58 and p-value was 0.563 and among rural boys and girls t-value was found to be 0.43 and p value was 0.668 indicating a non significant gender difference among the respondents. Girl respondents were found to have slightly more separation anxiety as compared to boys.

In a family unit there are several problems that can lead to building tension in students. Events like separation, divorce, remarriage, sickness and high expectations may have a negative effect on students within the family. **Woolfolk (2007)** revealed same study that divorce and separation are not only traumatic for the involved couple but may also have a huge effect on the students involved and may have problems at school, changes in the routine of sleep, weight loss and weight gain, or other problems.

Table 4.37 Comparison of urban and rural boys and girls belonging to different socio economic groups based on personal setback stress

Socio economic Status	Socio cultural setting	Boys n=150		Girls n=150		t-cal	p-value
		Mean	Standard Deviation	Mean	Standard Deviation		
Upper socio economic status (n=100)	Urban (n=50)	40.48	5.33	37.04	6.17	2.10*	0.039
	Rural (n=50)	38.52	6.60	34.44	3.92	2.65*	0.009
Middle socio economic status (n=100)	Urban (n=50)	32.32	11.23	37.64	2.79	2.29*	0.024
	Rural (n=50)	29.52	5.84	33.88	3.80	3.12*	0.002
Lower socio economic status (n=100)	Urban (n=50)	33.64	5.42	35.40	3.76	1.33*	0.187
	Rural (n=50)	27.92	4.94	31.32	4.05	2.65*	0.009

*Significant

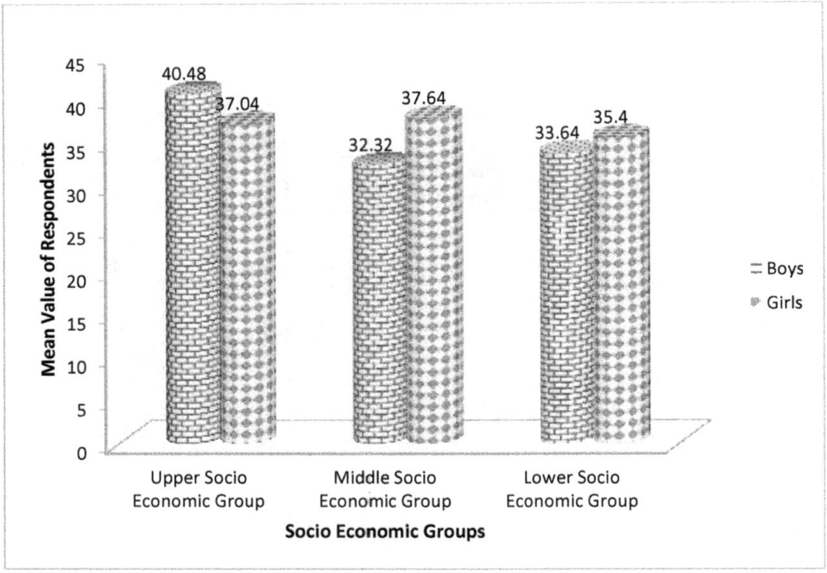

Fig 4.85 Personal setback stress in urban adolescents across three socio economic groups

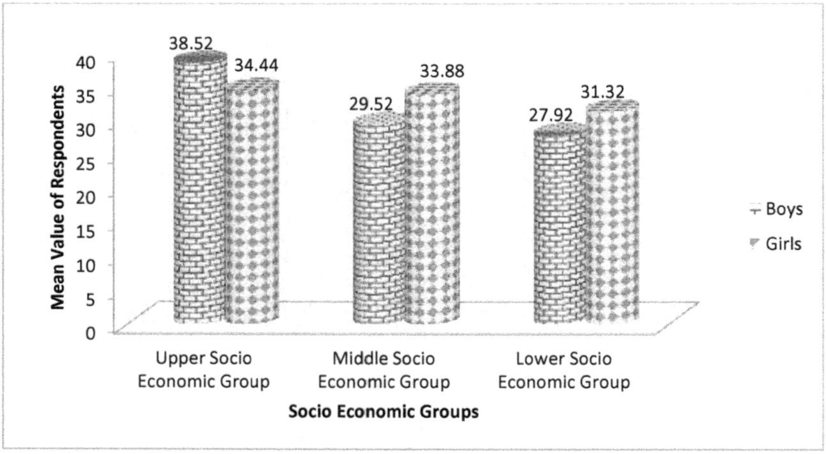

Fig 4.86 Personal setback stress in rural adolescents across three socio economic groups

The above **table 4.37** and **figure 4.85** and **4.86** indicates the comparison of urban and rural boys and girls belonging to different socio economic group based on their personal setback stress. In case of respondents belonging to upper socio economic group, there lies a significant gender difference both among the urban and rural masses (t= 2.10, p=0.039 and t= 2.65, p= 0.009 respectively) regarding personal setback stress. The mean value depicted in the table further clarifies that boys in the upper socio economic strata had poor attitude towards personal setback as compared to their female counterparts.

Similar results are evident among the respondents of middle socio economic strata wherein a significant gender variance is noted both in the urban and rural respondents (t= 2.29, p= 0.024 and t= 3.12, p= 0.002 respectively). The mean value further depicted that girls had higher personal setback stress both in the urban and rural masses as compared to their male counterparts.

The table reflects that there is a significant difference among boys and girls belonging to both urban and rural background among the respondents from lower socio economic group as the t-value for urban group was found to be 1.33 and p-value was 0.187 and so was the case with rural respondents where the t-value was 2.65 and p-value was 0.009 signifying a significant gender difference among both the groups with regard to their personal setback stress. Among the urban and rural masses it was seen that girls possessed higher stress regarding personal setback as compared to their male counterparts.

Results showed that personal setback stress is different in every socio-economic category and differs between boys and girls as well. The inescapable and unavoidable aspects of life are personal retrogression. One still faces difficulties, problems and temporary setbacks as a person. A happy individual understands that temporary deceptions and losses are inevitable and embraces them as a normal and necessary part of life. You do anything to prevent problems, but when problems arise, people without stress respond in a constructive way, learn from them and step on with their goals. **Christopher (2001)** also conducted the research in which reported that Personal strain is seen as tension, anxiety and depression with a life-added restlessness, heavy drinking, smoking, retirement and unable to focus. The effect of stress on individuals at each point needs to be taken care to encourage work.

Table 4.38 Comparison of urban and rural boys and girls belonging to different socio economic groups based on stress regarding health of others

Socio economic Status	Socio cultural setting	Boys n=150		Girls n=150		t-cal	p-value
		Mean	Standard Deviation	Mean	Standard Deviation		
Upper socio economic status (n=100)	Urban (n=50)	24.16	4.23	26.96	4.15	2.36*	0.020
	Rural (n=50)	19.72	3.02	23.52	3.80	3.90*	0.000
Middle socio economic status (n=100)	Urban (n=50)	19.36	5.88	22.48	3.25	2.32*	0.023
	Rural (n=50)	20.04	3.08	20.76	2.00	0.97NS	0.335
Lower socio economic status (n=100)	Urban (n=50)	23.64	2.73	22.04	3.72	1.73*	0.087
	Rural (n=50)	20.64	4.47	17.88	4.83	2.09*	0.040

*Significant, NS=Non Significant

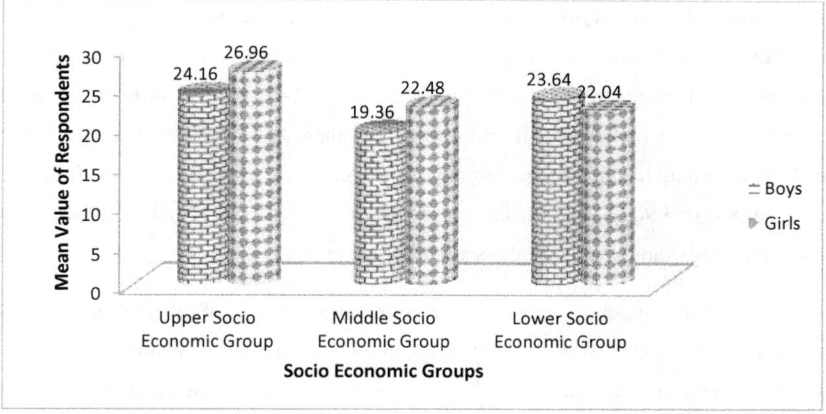

Fig 4.87 Stress regarding health of others in urban adolescents across three socio economic groups

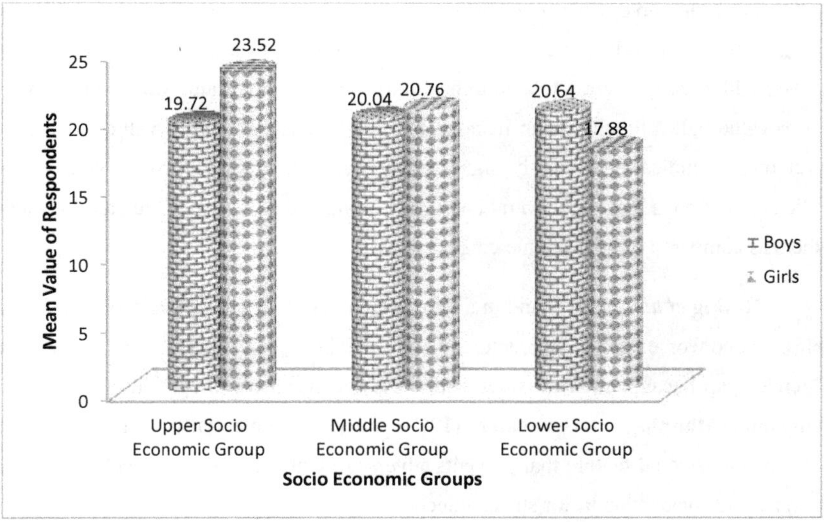

Fig 4.88 Stress regarding health of others in rural adolescents across three socio economic groups

Table 4.38 and **figure 4.87** and **4.88** shows the comparative analysis of urban and rural boys and girls belonging to various socio-economic classes on the basis of their respective characteristics stress regarding health of others. In case of respondents from the upper socio economic group it was evident from the table that there lies a significant gender variance in stress regarding health of others among the urban masses (t= 2.36, p= 0.020) as well as rural masses (t= 3.90, p= 0.000). The mean value of boys and girls indicated that girls had more stress regarding health of others as compared to boys.

A significant gender variance in stress regarding health of others was also evident among the urban and rural masses belonging to the middle socio economic group (t= 2.32, p= 0.023 and a non significant gender difference was seen among rural masses as the t value was 0.97, p= 0.335 signifying that both boys and girls possessed almost equal levels of stress regarding health of others.

From the table it was evident that there lies a significant differences among boys and girls both from urban and rural background belonging to lower socio economic group as well with regard to stress related to health of others as the t-value was found to be 1.73 and p-value 0.087 for the urban respondents and t-value 2.09 and p-value 0.040 for the rural masses indicating a highly significant gender variance. The mean values further indicated that boys in both the rural and urban group had higher stress related to health of others as compared to their female counterparts.

Ruthig *et al.* (2011) found in their research that Women showed more tension, less self-care and worse healthcare practices than men. The researchers proposed that there was a gender gap because men consider stress less social than women. The negative health symptoms **Manning and Fusilier (1999)** identified potentially from stress. They described a personal feature that prevents adverse effects. This research included strength, exercise and social support for stress reduction.

Table 4.39 Comparison of boys and girls belonging to different socio economic groups based on their total stress levels

Socio economic Status	Boys n=150		Girls n=150		t-cal	p-value
	Mean	SD	Mean	SD		
Upper socio economic status (n=100)	328.22	26.46	346.10	28.27	3.81**	0.000
Middle socio economic status (n=100)	314.10	28.43	332.20	21.12	3.61**	0.000
Lower socio economic status (n=100)	302.54	27.60	310.8	16.50	1.81*	0.072

**Highly Significant

*Significant

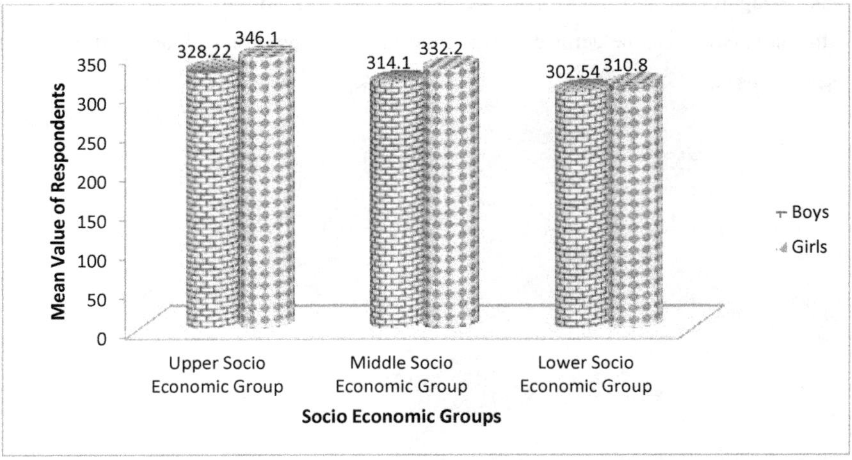

Fig 4.89 Comparison of boys and girls belonging to different socio economic groups based on their stress levels

Table 4.39 and **figure 4.89** shows the comparative analysis of urban and rural boys and girls belonging to various socio-economic classes on the basis of their respective characteristics stress level. In case of respondents from the upper socio economic group it was evident from the table that there lies a highly significant gender variance in stress among the boys and girls (t= 3.81, p= 0.000). The mean values further indicated that girls in this group had higher level of stress as compared to their male counterparts.

A highly significant gender variance regarding stress was also evident among boys and girls belonging to the middle socio economic group (t= 3.61, p= 0.000). The mean values further indicated that girls from middle socio economic group had higher stress as compared to their male counterparts.

The table also reveals a significant difference among boys and girls belonging to lower socio economic group with regard to their stress level as the t-value were found to be 1.81 and p-value 0.072. The stress level of girls in this group was found to be more than boys. **Mathew (2017)** revealed students suffer from multiple strains and do not follow appropriate recovery methods. Time problems, economic problems and other academic stress factors in students are the biggest burden for the students. The study found that the stressed individuals and weak coping strategies using successful coping strategies have had a significant influence on university students. **Goodman (1993)** also noted that student stressors can be defined as academic, financial, time-related, or health-related and self-imposed.

Table 4.40 Socio cultural differences among boys and girls with regard to their attitude towards stress

Socio cultural setting	Boys n=150		Girls n=150		t-cal	p-value
	Mean	SD	Mean	SD		
Urban (n=150)	326.45	27.46	342.24	30.06	3.35**	0.001
Rural (n=150)	303.45	26.54	319.21	18.20	4.24**	0.000

**Highly Significant

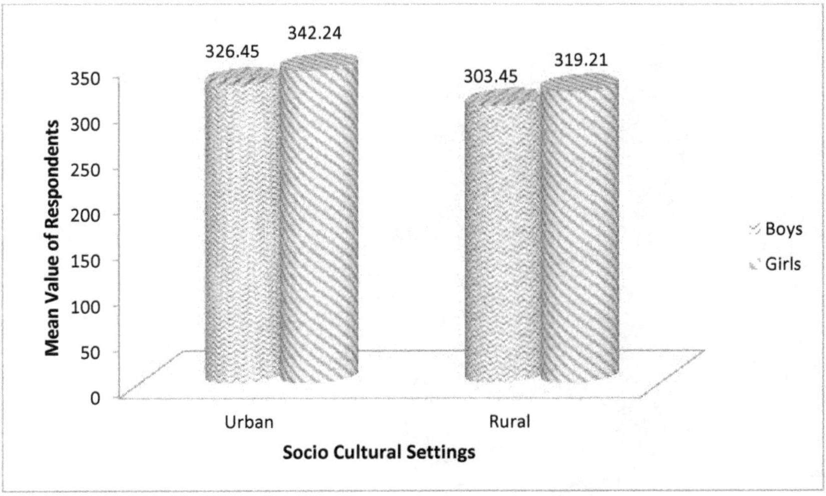

Fig 4.90 Socio cultural differences among boys and girls with regard to their attitude towards stress

Table 4.40 and **figure 4.90** depicts the socio cultural differences among boys and girls with regard to their attitude towards stress. The table denoted the mean, standard deviation, t' value and 'p' value. It is clear from the table that there is a rather important distinction among boys and adolescent girls belonging to urban cultural background with regard to their level of stress as the t-value was found to be 3.35 and p-value 0.001. A highly significant difference among boys and girls also in existed among the rural respondents with regard to their stress level as the t-value was found to be 4.24 and p-value 0.000. The mean values further indicated that girls in both the cultural settings had higher level of stress as compared to their male counterparts.

Kumar and Bhukar (2013) also reported that girls were stressed higher than boys, as girls have more difficulties in observing Indian Orthodox customs in society. **Kumar *et al.*, (2011)** indicated that since the stress level varies between the genders and the coping mechanisms for boys and girls cannot be the same and thus should not rely on any other basis but should be focused on stress factors.

Table 4.41 Socio cultural differences in stress among total college going students

Total college going students (n=300)					
Urban (n=150)		Rural (n=150)		t-cal	p-value
Mean	SD	Mean	SD		
334.34	29.77	311.38	24.01	7.35	0.000

*Significant

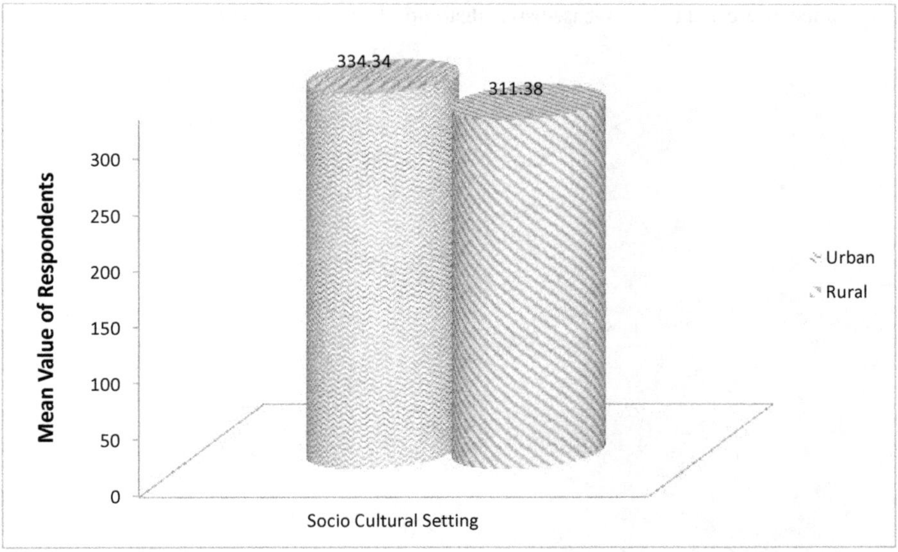

Fig 4.91 Socio cultural differences among total college going students with regard to their attitude towards stress

Table 4.41 and **figure 4.91** depicts the socio cultural differences in stress among total college going students. The table indicates the mean, standard deviation, t' value and 'p' value. It is clear from the table that there is a rather important distinction in socio cultural background with regard to the level of stress as the t-value was found to be 7.35 and p-value 0.000. The mean values further indicated that students from urban cultural settings had higher level of stress as compared to respondents from rural socio cultural setting. The results of the stud are in accordance with the findings of **Shaikh *et al.*, (2018)** who stated that in the city of Pune, urban students were considerably stress higher than in the rural areas. Stress was significantly related to dysfunctional communities, strict parents, and previous experience with adverse events, negative perceptions of academic performance and use of tobacco. **Sulaiman *et al.*, (2009)** also explored substantial variations in the degree of stress between students. It was also shown that several factors affect the stress of students, such as the education history of parents, the student atmosphere and a family-based style that impacts the lives of students.

Table 4.42 Gender differences in stress among the respondents stress

Total college going students (n=300)					
Boys (n=150)		Girls (n=150)		t-cal	p-value
Mean	SD	Mean	SD		
315.02	29.29	332.74	26.69	5.66*	0.000

*Significant

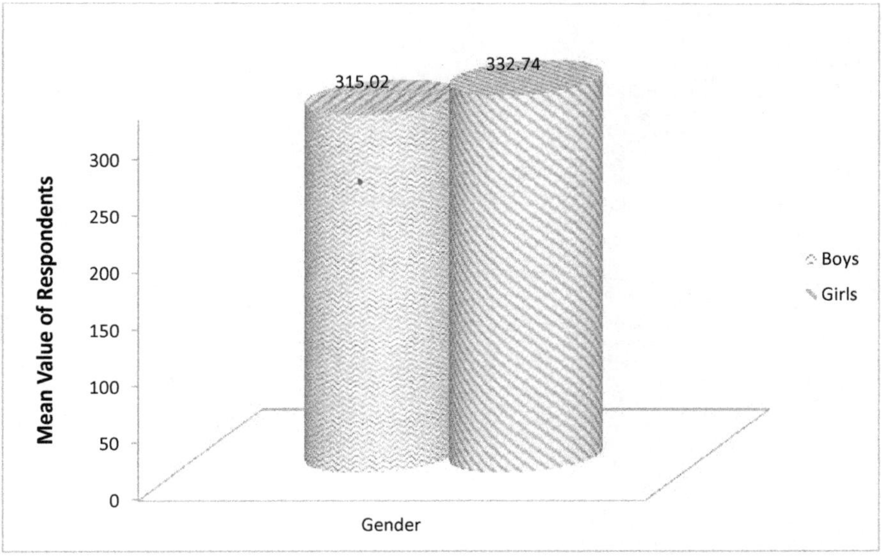

Fig 4.92 Gender differences in stress among the respondents stress

Table 4.42 and **figure 4.92** depicts the gender differences among respondents with regard to stress. Table indicates the mean, standard deviation, t' value and 'p' value. It is clear from the table that there is a rather important distinction among boys and girls with regard to their attitude towards stress as the t-value was found to be 5.66 and p-value 0.000. The mean values further indicated that girls had higher level of stress as compared to their male counterparts. It might be due to the fact that girls reveal their stress and often talk about the stressors in their life. Study conducted by **Calvarese (2015)** indicated that in consequences to stress, more females have been depressed, irritated and anxious than their males. More women have also been shown to display frustration in response to stress than men. **Vacek *et al.,* (2010)** have agreed that gender disparities in girls are more stressful than boys. The analysis also revealed that it was also likely that boys were under the same burden.

Table 4.43.1 Socio economic variance in different dimension of modernization

Source of Variance	Degree of freedom	Sum of Square	Mean sum of square	f cal	f tab (5%)
SES variance in modernization in education	2	851.13	425.56	60.36*	2.84
SES variance in modernization in parent child relationship	2	790.29	395.14	34.57*	2.84
SES variance in modernization in politics	2	600.83	300.41	32.54*	2.84
SES variance in modernization in Status of women	2	601.81	300.90	55.92*	2.84
SES variance in modernization in marriage	2	624.05	312.02	52.52*	2.84
SES variance in modernization in faith in God	2	757.22	378.61	33.89*	2.84
SES variance in modernization in socio cultural factors	2	652.58	332.61	60.39*	2.84
SES variance in total modernization	2	36250.33	18125.16	183.12**	2.84

*=Significant,

**=Highly Significant

Table 4.39 shows the socio economic variance in different aspects of modernization. The table clearly depicts a significant socio economic variance in all dimensions of modernization i.e. modernization in education (f=60.36), parent child relationship (f=34.57), politics (f=32.54), status of women (f=55.92), marriage (f=52.52), faith in God (f=33.89), socio cultural factors (f=60.39) and total modernization (f=183.12) as the estimated value of f was found to be significantly higher than the tabulated value of f at a 5 percent probability stage. **Marks (2009)** argues as societies become industrial and continue to grow, their impact on educational and socioeconomic outcome decreases with social context and other characteristics, while achievement is becoming more relevant in the educational system. The results of the analysis contradict **Marks (2009),** who found that socioeconomic context has an impact on schooling, job performance and earnings. Training has had a greater influence than women on occupational achievement.

Table 4.43.2 CD values and mean values among different socio economic groups on the basis of their attitude towards modernization in education

	USES= 24.43	MSES= 22.18	Critical Difference (CD) (5%)
LSES= 20.31	4.12*	1.87*	0.33
MSES= 22.18	2.25*		

***Significant**

As the ANOVA table provides significant result due to socio economic status on the basis of their attitude towards modernization in education hence the value of critical difference (CD) was also computed which was obtained 0.33.

The above table reveals that there was significant difference modernization in education among all the three socio economic statuses. The lowest modernization was seen in respondents from lower socio economic status followed by middle and upper socio economic class.

Table 4.43.3 CD values and mean values among different socio economic groups on the basis of their attitude towards modernization in parents child relationship

	USES= 24.56	MSES= 22.13	Critical Difference (CD) (5%)
LSES= 20.62	3.94*	1.51*	0.43
MSES= 22.13	2.43*		

***Significant**

The ANOVA table provides significant result due to socio economic status on the basis of their attitude towards modernization in parents child relationship hence the value of critical difference (CD) was also computed which was obtained 0.43.

The above table reveals that there was significant difference modernization in parents child relationship among all the three socio economic statuses. The lowest modernization was seen in respondents from lower socio economic status followed by middle and upper socio economic class.

Table 4.43.4 CD values and mean values among different socio economic groups on the basis of their attitude towards modernization in politics

	USES= 24.28	MSES= 22.08	Critical Difference (CD) (5%)
LSES= 20.86	3.42*	1.14*	0.39
MSES= 22.08	2.20*		

***Significant**

As the ANOVA table provides significant result due to socio economic status on the basis of their attitude towards modernization in politics hence the value of critical difference (CD) was also computed which was obtained 0.39.

The above table reveals that there was significant difference modernization in politics among all the three socio economic statuses. The lowest modernization was seen in respondents from lower socio economic status followed by middle and upper socio economic class.

Table 4.43.5 CD values and mean values among different socio economic groups on the basis of their attitude towards modernization in status of women

	USES= 24.22	MSES= 22.71	Critical Difference (CD) (5%)
LSES= 20.76	3.46*	1.95*	0.27
MSES= 22.71	1.51*		

*significant

The ANOVA table provides significant result due to socio economic status on the basis of their attitude towards modernization in status of women hence the value of critical difference (CD) was also computed which was obtained 0.27.

The above table reveals that there was significant difference modernization in status of women among all the three socio economic statuses. The lowest modernization was seen in respondents from lower socio economic status followed by middle and upper socio economic class.

Table 4.43.6 CD values and mean values among different socio economic groups on the basis of their attitude towards modernization in marriage

	USES= 24.13	MSES= 22.86	Critical Difference (CD) (5%)
LSES= 20.64	3.49*	2.22*	0.29
MSES= 22.86	1.44*		

*Significant

The ANOVA table provides significant result due to socio economic status on the basis of their attitude towards modernization in marriage hence the value of critical difference (CD) was also computed which was obtained 0.29.

The above table reveals that there was significant difference modernization in marriage among all the three socio economic statuses. The lowest modernization was seen in respondents from lower socio economic status followed by middle and upper socio economic class.

Table 4.43.7 CD values and mean values among different socio economic groups on the basis of their attitude towards modernization in faith in God

	USES= 24.97	MSES= 23.84	Critical Difference (CD) (5%)
LSES= 21.18	3.79*	2.66*	0.43
MSES= 23.84	1.13*		

***Significant**

As the ANOVA table provides significant result due to socio economic status on the basis of their attitude towards modernization in faith in God hence the value of critical difference (CD) was also computed which was obtained 0.43.

The above table reveals that there was significant difference modernization in faith in God among all the three socio economic statuses. The lowest modernization was seen in respondents from lower socio economic status followed by middle and upper socio economic class.

Table 4.43.8 CD values and mean values among different socio economic groups on the basis of their attitude towards modernization in socio cultural factor

	USES= 24.98	MSES= 22.78	Critical Difference (CD) (5%)
LSES= 20.26	4.72*	2.52*	0.44
MSES= 22.78	2.2*		

***Significant**

The ANOVA table provides significant result due to socio economic status on the basis of their attitude towards modernization in socio cultural factor hence the value of critical difference (CD) was also computed which was obtained 0.44.

The above table reveals that there was significant difference modernization in socio cultural factor among all the three socio economic statuses. The lowest modernization was seen in respondents from lower socio economic status followed by middle and upper socio economic class.

Table 4.43.9 CD values and mean values among different socio economic groups on the basis of their attitude towards modernization

	USES= 171.55	MSES= 158.58	Critical Difference (CD) (5%)
LSES= 144.63	26.82*	13.29*	13.19
MSES= 158.58	13.95*		

*Significant

As the ANOVA table provides significant result due to socio economic status on the basis of their attitude towards modernization hence the value of critical difference (CD) was also computed which was obtained 13.19.

The above table reveals that there was significant difference modernization among all the three socio economic statuses. The lowest modernization was seen in respondents from lower socio economic status followed by middle and upper socio economic class.

Table 4.44 Socio cultural variance in different dimension of modernization

Source of Variance	Degree of freedom	Sum of Square	Mean sum of square	f cal	f tab (5%)
Socio cultural variance in modernization in education	1	547.46	547.46	77.65*	3.69
Socio cultural variance in modernization in parent child relationship	1	252.08	252.08	22.05*	3.69
Socio cultural variance in modernization in politics	1	320.33	320.33	34.70*	3.69
Socio cultural variance in modernization in Status of women	1	286.16	286.16	53.18*	3.69
Socio cultural variance in modernization in marriage	1	302.00	302.00	50.84*	3.69
Socio cultural variance in modernization in faith in God	1	318.27	318.27	28.49*	3.69
Socio cultural variance in modernization in socio cultural factors	1	179.41	179.41	17.57*	3.69
Socio cultural variance in total modernization	1	14868.48	14868.48	150.21**	3.69

*=Significant,

**=Highly Significant

Table 4.44 shows the socio cultural variance in different aspects of modernization. The table clearly explained a significant variance in all dimensions of modernization i.e. modernization in education (f=77.65), parent child relationship (f=22.05), politics (f=34.70), status of women (f=53.18), marriage (f=50.84), faith in God (f=28.49), socio cultural factors (f=17.57) and total modernization (f=150.21) as the estimated value of f was found to be significantly higher than the tabulated value of f at a 5 percent probability stage. Modernization brings changes in gender roles and shift greater change in socio cultural settings. The main source of modernization is education, parent child relationship, politics, status of women, marriage, faith in God and socio cultural factors. Modernization, technology and education have played an important role to change gender roles in both socio cultural setting i.e. urban and rural. **Hussain *et al.* (2015)** researched that women today are more influential than men, the equality of women is greater than ever, women have complete freedom to participate in all campaigns and elections and top-level woman management is reduced even by domestic violence.

Table 4.45 Gender variance in different dimension of modernization

Source of Variance	Degree of freedom	Sum of Square	Mean sum of square	f cal	f tab (5%)
Gender variance in modernization in education	1	633.65	633.65	89.87*	3.69
Gender variance in modernization in parent child relationship	1	504.40	504.40	44.12*	3.69
Gender variance in modernization in politics	1	215.05	215.05	23.29*	3.69
Gender variance in modernization in status of women	1	401.36	401.36	74.60*	3.69
Gender variance in modernization in marriage	1	420.08	420.08	70.72*	3.69
Gender variance in modernization in faith in God	1	317.47	317.47	38.57*	3.69
Gender variance in modernization in socio cultural factors	1	316.21	316.21	30.97*	3.69
Gender variance in total modernization	1	23691.85	23691.85	239.38**	3.69

*=Significant,

**=Highly Significant

Table 4.45 shows the gender variance in different aspects of modernization. The table clearly reflected a significant variance in all dimensions of modernization i.e. modernization in education (f=89.87), parent child relationship (f=44.12), politics (f=23.29), status of women (f=74.60), marriage (f=70.72), faith in God (f=38.57), socio cultural factors (f=30.97) and total modernization (f=239.38) as the estimated value of f was found to be significantly higher than the tabulated value of f at a 5 percent probability stage. Female are more involve in social norms and values, societal activities, social rituals than males in both rural and urban socio cultural settings as well as in different socio economic group. Women have better frame of mind for their community. Similarly **Reddy (2017)** explained that women were traditionally home-builders and house-based workers, but in recent decades, the right education and knowledge and the living costs led women to pursue education and professions that have driven women across the world. **Kadam (2015)** also found that young people had higher and better education than their elderly women. In general, it has been reported that girls spend more time on their homework, spend more time with family and show less alarming behaviour, as they are able to learn faster than boys.

Table 4.46.1 Socio economic variance in different dimension of stress

Source of Variance	Degree of freedom	Sum of Square	Mean sum of square	f cal	f tab (5%)
Due to financial stress	2	902.58	642.29	27.46*	2.84
Due to family stress	2	249.53	124.76	4.92*	2.84
Due to social stress	2	279.25	139.62	8.12*	2.84
Due to educational stress	2	370.56	197.28	11.67*	2.84
Due to ego threat stress	2	297.34	154.49	9.07*	2.84
Due to bereavement stress	2	419.66	209.83	18.04*	2.84
Due to separation stress	2	9.15	4.57	1.01NS	2.84
Due to personal setback stress	2	427.25	225.10	15.05*	2.84
Due to health of others stress	2	524.69	262.34	16.02*	2.84
Due to total stress	2	51158.45	25579.22	7.42*	2.84

*=Significant,

**=Highly Significant,

NS=Non Significant

The above **Table 4.46.1** shows the socio economic variance in different dimension of stress. The table clearly reveals a significant variance in socio economic status with regard to financial stress (f=27.46), family stress (f=4.92), social stress (f=8.12), educational stress (f=11.6), ego threat stress (f=9.07), bereavement stress (f=18.04), personal setback stress (f=15.05), stress regarding health of others (f=16.02) as well as total stress (f=7.42) as the estimated value of f is higher than the tabulated value of f at 5 percent of the probability stage, a variance in stress based on the socio economic status of the respondents. The table also indicates a non-significant variation in separation stress depending on the respondents' socio-economic position, as the estimated value of f is reported to be 1.01 and the critical difference is reported to be 1.23, which is lower than the tabulated value of f at 5% probability level, respectively which indicates that irrespective of the socio economic status separation anxiety and stress is seen in all the respondents. **Koreti *et al.* (2018)** examined that educational stress and age, gender, social status, tests, expectations of parents and peers have influenced college students, and adolescents have also shown to use various coping mechanisms to cope with stress in the education field. **Sonali (2016)** concluded that the socio-economic status has a major influence on academic stress, as it eventually affects society as a whole, due to its low socio-economic status and its associations such as lower education, poverty and poor health.

Table 4.46.2 CD values and mean values among different socio economic groups on the basis of financial stress

	USES= 24.36	MSES= 21.90	Critical Difference (CD) (5%)
LSES= 20.13	4.23*	1.77*	0.51
MSES= 21.90	2.46*		

*Significant

The ANOVA table provides significant result due to socio economic status on the basis of financial stress hence the value of critical difference (CD) was also computed which was obtained 0.51.

The above table reveals that there was significant difference in financial stress among all the three socio economic statuses. The highest stress was seen in respondents from upper socio economic status followed by middle and lower socio economic class.

Table 4.46.3 CD values and mean values among different socio economic groups on the basis of family stress

	USES= 38.15	MSES= 41.54	Critical Difference (CD) (5%)
LSES= 32.63	5.52 *	8.91 *	0.33
MSES= 41.54	3.39*		

*Significant

The ANOVA table provides significant result due to socio economic status on the basis of family stress hence the value of critical difference (CD) was also computed which was obtained 0.33.

The above table reveals that there was significant difference in family stress among all the three socio economic statuses. The highest stress was seen in respondents from middle socio economic status followed by upper and lower socio economic class.

Table 4.46.4 CD values and mean values among different socio economic groups on the basis of social stress

	USES= 21.70	LSES= 21.32	Critical Difference (CD) (5%)
MSES= 19.49	2.21*	1.83*	0.55
LSES= 21.32	0.68*		

*Significant

The ANOVA table provides significant result due to socio economic status on the basis of social stress hence the value of critical difference (CD) was also computed which was obtained 0.55.

The above table reveals that there was significant difference in social stress among all the three socio economic statuses. The highest stress was seen in respondents from upper socio economic status followed by middle and lower socio economic class.

Table 4.46.5 CD values and mean values among different socio economic groups on the basis of educational stress

	USES= 10.98	MSES= 10.66	Critical Difference (CD) (5%)
LSES= 10.27	0.71*	0.39NS	0.49
MSES= 10.66	0.32NS		

*Significant

The ANOVA table provides significant result due to socio economic status on the basis of educational stress hence the value of critical difference (CD) was also computed which was obtained 0.49.

The above table reveals that there was significant difference in educational stress among all the three socio economic statuses. The highest stress was seen in respondents from upper socio economic status followed by middle and lower socio economic class.

Table 4.46.6 CD values and mean values among different socio economic groups on the basis of ego threat stress

	USES= 45.15	MSES= 44.54	Critical Difference (CD) (5%)
LSES= 40.71	4.44*	3.83*	0.98
MSES= 44.54	0.61NS		

*Significant

The ANOVA table provides significant result due to socio economic status on the basis of ego threat stress hence the value of critical difference (CD) was also computed which was obtained 0.98.

The above table reveals that there was significant difference in ego threat stress among all the three socio economic statuses. The highest stress was seen in respondents from upper socio economic status followed by middle and lower socio economic class.

Table 4.46.7 CD values and mean values among different socio economic groups on the basis of bereavement stress

	USES= 21.90	MSES= 19.13	Critical Difference (CD) (5%)
LSES= 19.78	2.12*	0.65*	0.43
MSES= 19.13	2.77*		

*Significant

The ANOVA table provides significant result due to socio economic status on the basis of bereavement stress hence the value of critical difference (CD) was also computed which was obtained 0.43.

The above table reveals that there was significant difference in bereavement stress among all the three socio economic statuses. The highest stress was seen in respondents from upper socio economic status followed by middle and lower socio economic class.

Table 4.46.8 CD values and mean values among different socio economic groups on the basis of separation stress

	USES= 16.32	MSES= 15.96	Critical Difference (CD) (5%)
LSES= 13.34	2.98*	2.62*	0.27
MSES= 15.96	0.36*		

*Significant

The ANOVA table provides significant result due to socio economic status on the basis of separation stress hence the value of critical difference (CD) was also computed which was obtained 0.27.

The above table reveals that there was significant difference in separation stress among all the three socio economic statuses. The highest stress was seen in respondents from upper socio economic status followed by middle and lower socio economic class.

Table 4.46.9 CD values and mean values among different socio economic groups on the basis of personal setback stress

	USES= 37.62	MSES= 33.34	Critical Difference (CD) (5%)
LSES= 32.01	5.61*	1.33*	0.80
MSES= 33.34	4.28*		

*Significant

The ANOVA table provides significant result due to socio economic status on the basis of personal setback stress hence the value of critical difference (CD) was also computed which was obtained 0.80.

The above table reveals that there was significant difference in personal setback stress among all the three socio economic statuses. The highest stress was seen in respondents from upper socio economic status followed by middle and lower socio economic class.

Table 4.46.10 CD values and mean values among different socio economic groups on the basis of stress regarding health of others

	USES= 23.64	MSES= 20.66	Critical Difference (CD) (5%)
LSES= 21.05	2.59*	0.39NS	0.54
MSES= 20.66	2.98*		

*Significant

The ANOVA table provides significant result due to socio economic status on the basis of stress regarding health of others hence the value of critical difference (CD) was also computed which was obtained 0.54.

The above table reveals that there was significant difference in stress regarding health of others among all the three socio economic statuses. The highest stress was seen in respondents from upper socio economic status followed by middle and lower socio economic class.

Table 4.46.11 CD values and mean values among different socio economic groups on the basis of total stress

	LSES= 306.68	MSES= 323.25	Critical Difference (CD) (5%)
USES= 338.66	31.98*	15.41*	8.30
MSES= 323.25	16.57*		

*Significant

The ANOVA table provides significant result due to socio economic status on the basis of total stress hence the value of critical difference (CD) was also computed which was obtained 8.30. The above table reveals that there was significant difference in total stress among all the three socio economic statuses. The highest stress was seen in respondents from upper socio economic status followed by middle and lower socio economic class.

Table 4.47 Socio cultural variance in different dimension of stress

Source of Variance	Degree of freedom	Sum of Square	Mean sum of square	f cal	f tab (5%)
Due to financial stress	1	23.40	23.40	0.02NS	3.69
Due to family stress	1	260.25	260.25	14.91*	3.69
Due to social stress	1	210.00	210.00	12.22*	3.69
Due to educational stress	1	72.03	72.03	0.28NS	3.69
Due to ego threat stress	1	417.52	417.52	29.16*	3.69
Due to bereavement stress	1	310.08	310.08	26.66*	3.69
Due to separation stress	1	16.33	16.33	3.72*	3.69
Due to personal setback stress	1	890.96	890.96	24.91*	3.69
Due to health of others stress	1	552.16	552.16	33.72*	3.69
Due to total stress	1	39560.08	39560.08	11.47*	3.69

*=Significant,

**=Highly Significant,

NS=Non Significant

The above **Table 4.47** shows the socio cultural variance in different dimension of stress. The table clearly reveals a significant variance in socio cultural setting with regard to family stress (f=14.91), social stress (f=12.22), ego threat stress (f=29.16), bereavement stress (f=26.66), separation stress (f=3.72), personal setback stress (f=24.91), stress regarding health of others (f=33.72) and total stress (f=11.47) as the estimated value of f is higher than the tabulated value of f at 5 percent of the probability stage,a variance in stress based on the socio cultural setting of the respondents. The table demonstrates a non-significant difference in financial stress and educational stress depending on the respondents' socio-cultural environment, as the measured value of f is found to be 0.02 and 0.28, respectively, which is lower than the tabulated value of f at the 5 percent probability scale, suggesting that irrespective of the financial and educational socio-cultural environment was seen in all participation. The results indicated that the socio cultural settings have non-significant differences because financial and educational stress was very common among both socio cultural settings i.e. rural and urban. **Pullokaran (2018)** also revealed in study that studies, financial challenges, parental pressure and unreasonable expectations were pressuring college students. In urban and rural cultural environments, education stress is common; it can have adverse effects on performance and health.

Table 4.48 Gender variance in different dimension of stress

Source of Variance	Degree of freedom	Sum of Square	Mean sum of square	f cal	f tab (5%)
Due to financial stress	1	140.08	140.08	9.27*	3.69
Due to family stress	1	30.72	30.72	4.61*	3.69
Due to social stress	1	5.6	5.6	0.32NS	3.69
Due to educational stress	1	542.25	542.25	28.08*	3.69
Due to ego threat stress	1	480.32	480.32	19.36*	3.69
Due to bereavement stress	1	179.65	179.65	14.52*	3.69
Due to separation stress	1	523.10	523.10	25.67*	3.69
Due to personal setback stress	1	104.43	104.43	3.92*	3.69
Due to health of others stress	1	270.75	270.75	16.53*	3.69
Due to total stress	1	18455.36	18455.36	5.35*	3.69

*=Significant,

**=Highly Significant,

NS=Non Significant

The above **Table 4.48** shows the gender variance in different dimension of stress. The table clearly reveals a significant variance in gender with regard to financial stress (f=9.27), family stress (f=4.61), educational stress (f=28.08), ego threat stress (f=19.36), bereavement stress (f=14.52), separation stress (f=25.67), personal setback stress (f=3.92), stress regarding health of others (f=16.53) as well as total stress (f=5.35) as the estimated value of f is higher than the tabulated value of f at 5 percent of the probability stage, a variance in stress based on the gender of the respondents. The table also reveals a non-significant difference in social stress depending on the gender of the adolescents, as the estimated value of f is found to be 0.32, which is less than the tabulated value of f at the 5 percent probability scale. Stress could affect the quality of student's academic performance as well as affects both students' physical and mental functioning. A non-significant gender variance was also noticed which may be due to the reason that girls and boys both gender had equal social stress in our society. Similarly **Huli (1991)** also explained in their study that dysfunctional personality such as antisocial can trigger high stress in adolescences. **Jha *et al.*, (2016)** have noted that there have been major gender gaps in stress levels.

Table 4.49 Correlation matrix between various dimensions of modernization and stress of urban respondents

-	Edu	P C R	Pol	S W	Mar	F G	S C F	Total	Fin	Fam	Soc	Edu	Ego	Ber	Sep	P S	H O	Total
Edu	1	0.45*	0.43*	0.39*	0.23*	0.41*	0.35*	0.70*	0.28*	0.32*	0.37*	0.28*	0.15*	0.60*	0.26*	0.18*	0.21*	0.33*
P C R		1	0.45*	0.29*	0.31*	0.31*	0.32*	0.66*	0.33*	0.34*	0.16*	0.47*	0.08NS	0.44*	0.35*	0.09NS	0.54*	0.28*
Pol			1	0.30*	0.27*	0.27*	0.25*	0.63*	0.22*	0.21*	0.23*	0.49*	0.01NS	0.32*	0.73*	0.08NS	0.13NS	0.20*
S W				1	0.51*	0.45*	0.46*	0.71*	0.35*	0.40*	0.52*	0.30*	0.31*	0.28*	0.70*	0.24*	0.17*	0.35*
Mar					1	0.36*	0.26*	0.61*	0.30*	0.65*	0.60*	0.20*	0.11NS	0.27*	0.18*	0.44*	0.62*	0.28*
F G						1	0.45*	0.71*	0.32*	0.16*	0.29*	0.34*	0.17*	0.39*	0.65*	0.29*	0.50*	0.34*
S C F							1	0.66*	0.39*	0.17*	0.31*	0.37*	0.16*	0.03NS	0.37*	0.20*	0.47*	0.44*
Total Moder								1	0.47*	0.42*	0.60*	0.38*	0.71*	0.62*	0.53*	0.42*	0.59*	0.48*
Fin									1	0.24*	0.25*	0.24*	0.28*	0.23*	0.09NS	0.25*	0.30*	0.54*
Fam										1	0.39*	0.40*	0.21*	0.73*	0.18*	0.36*	0.25*	0.48*
Soc											1	0.03NS	0.22*	0.12NS	0.40*	0.35*	0.17*	0.24*
Edu												1	0.49*	0.18*	0.48*	0.09NS	0.38*	0.69*
Ego													1	0.33*	0.25*	0.48*	0.02NS	0.43*
Ber														1	0.27*	0.63*	0.23*	0.347*
Sep															1	0.24*	0.19*	0.37*
P S																1	0.22*	0.40*
H O																	1	0.43*
Total Stress																		1

The above **table 4.49** indicates the correlation matrix between various dimensions of modernization and stress among the urban adolescents. Table shows a significant positive correlation between modernization and all aspects of stress. As the correlation between modernization and stress was found to be 0.48 which it can be deduced that both the variables are positively correlated with each other i.e. as the modernization level increases so does the stress levels. Urban adolescents perceived greater overall stress. They were often found in frightening, abusive, depressing, threatening, competitive and confusing situations because of the new technologies and environment. The percentage of suicides were more among the urban college students compared to the others and these suicides were mostly associated with academic failure or under achievement. Similarly, **Yung *et al.* (2012)** also found the urban residents have high levels of stress. Studies suggested that social status, income, schooling, marriage, form of profession, computer culture, family relationship and religion were correlated with different levels of stress. Government and local health authorities were crucial to work together to create and enforce a combination of policies and services aimed at dramatically reducing urban stress.

Table 4.50 Correlation matrix between various dimensions of modernization and stress of rural respondents

	Ed	P C R	Pol	S W	M	F G	S C F	Total	Fin	Fam	Soc	Edu	Ego	Ber	Sep	P S	H O	Total
Ed	1	0.61*	0.43*	0.34*	0.36*	0.46*	0.47*	0.71*	0.10NS	0.37*	0.52*	0.24*	0.19*	0.22*	0.42*	0.31*	0.35*	0.62*
P C R		1	0.52*	0.47*	0.49*	0.45*	0.52*	0.78*	0.31*	0.30*	0.49*	0.32*	0.07NS	0.26*	0.26*	0.34*	0.34*	0.57*
Pol			1	0.57*	0.48*	0.50*	0.40*	0.74*	0.38*	0.46*	0.48*	0.39*	0.22*	0.16*	0.28*	0.29*	0.16*	0.30*
S W				1	0.54*	0.50*	0.41*	0.73*	0.44*	0.05NS	0.16*	0.25*	0.34*	0.26*	0.23*	0.24*	0.25*	0.48*
M					1	0.56*	0.46*	0.75*	0.38*	0.28*	0.24*	0.36*	0.39*	0.25*	0.31*	0.24*	0.20*	0.52*
F G						1	0.49*	0.77*	0.08NS	0.36*	0.31*	0.43*	0.38*	0.20*	0.26*	0.20*	0.31*	0.79*
S C F							1	0.71*	0.18*	0.42*	0.29*	0.52*	0.33*	0.14NS	0.36*	0.22*	0.33*	0.48*
Total Moder								1	0.44*	0.56*	0.59*	0.73*	0.67*	0.79*	0.71*	0.65*	0.78*	0.53*
Fin									1	0.07NS	0.24*	0.36*	0.15*	0.02NS	0.49*	0.57*	0.39*	0.66*
Fam										1	0.22*	0.29*	0.60*	0.25*	0.22*	0.38*	0.40*	0.44*
Soc											1	0.16*	0.35*	0.31*	0.23*	0.41*	0.43*	0.76*
Edu												1	0.04NS	0.23*	0.03NS	0.22*	0.29*	0.52*
Ego													1	0.19*	0.17*	0.19*	0.48*	0.54*
Ber														1	0.20*	0.29*	0.20*	0.51*
Sep															1	0.32*	0.16*	0.49*
P S																1	0.33*	0.45*
H O																	1	0.49*
Total Stress																		1

Table 4.50 indicated the correlation matrix between various dimensions of modernization and stress among the rural respondents. Table shows a significant positive correlation of modernization with education (0.71), parents child relationship (0.78), politics (0.74), status of women (0.73), marriage (0.75), faith in God (0.77) and socio cultural factor (0.71) which was significant at 0.5 percent level of significance. A significant positive correlation was also seen of stress with finance (0.44), family (0.56), social (0.59), education (0.73), ego threats (0.67), bereavement (0.79), separation (0.71), personal setback (0.65), health of others (0.78) and total stress (0.53) which was also significant at 0.5 percent level of significance. Table showed a significant positive correlation between modernization and stress as the correlation was found to be 0.53 which indicated that both are positively correlated with each other as the modernization level increases so does the stress levels. Rural adolescents were often influenced by a high level of stress because they were not aware of emerging technology or were deprived of their money compared with others in certain areas of their lives, for example. A number of environmental problems in rural India affect adolescents such as lack of fuel, absence of a better shelter, lack of good academic atmosphere, absence of awareness of and lack of trust in modern technologies, these factors directly or indirectly affect young people's personalities and their quality of life, causing stress in all aspects of life. Similar results were obtained by a study carried out by **Shaikh *et al.* (2018)** which revealed that students from rural areas faced substantially higher stress levels. Stress was strongly correlated with higher levels of troubled families, rough parenthood, cultural interferences, early marriage, previous adverse incidents and negative academic feelings. Results showed that these students' mental health status is worrying that immediate action is needed.

Table 4.51 Correlation matrix between various dimensions of modernization and stress among boys

-	Edu	P C R	Pol	S W	Mar	F G	S C F	Total	Fin	Fam	Soc	Edu	Ego	Ber	Sep	P S	H O	Total
Edu	1	0.41*	0.42*	0.41*	0.21*	0.34*	0.48*	0.65*	0.34*	0.53*	0.42*	0.16*	0.30*	0.19*	0.19*	0.32*	0.25*	0.52*
P C R		1	0.42*	0.39*	0.47*	0.36*	0.50*	0.72*	0.43*	0.28*	0.41*	0.35*	0.33*	0.36*	0.29*	0.36*	0.17*	0.55*
Pol			1	0.39*	0.37*	0.38*	0.33*	0.68*	0.39*	0.27*	0.50*	0.31*	0.24*	0.17*	0.34*	0.36*	0.16*	0.67*
S W				1	0.50*	0.52*	0.46*	0.74*	0.52*	0.16*	0.43*	0.42*	0.29*	0.27*	0.37*	0.45*	0.30*	0.41*
Mar					1	0.45*	0.41*	0.69*	0.52*	0.16*	0.39*	0.55*	0.20*	0.18*	0.33*	0.34*	0.13NS	0.41*
F G						1	0.45*	0.71*	0.33*	0.17*	0.39*	0.53*	0.18*	0.24*	0.39*	0.23*	0.16*	0.37*
S C F							1	0.72*	0.39*	0.56*	0.48*	0.18*	0.18*	0.17*	0.41*	0.37*	0.11NS	0.45*
Total Moder								1	0.68*	0.74*	0.79*	0.61*	0.35*	0.42*	0.58*	0.49*	0.56*	0.46*
Fin									1	0.19*	0.29*	0.33*	0.17*	0.21*	0.34*	0.39*	0.39*	0.45*
Fam										1	0.34*	0.26*	0.19*	0.36*	0.22*	0.40*	0.42*	0.34*
Soc											1	0.37*	0.32*	0.21*	0.37*	0.37*	0.29*	0.29*
Edu												1	0.31*	0.34*	0.42*	0.25*	0.39*	0.69*
Ego													1	0.21*	0.24*	0.41*	0.30*	0.41*
Ber														1	0.09NS	0.26*	0.26*	0.37*
Sep															1	0.32*	0.35*	0.29*
P S																1	0.17*	0.47*
H O																	1	0.32*
Total Stress																		1

Table 4.51 indicates the correlation matrix between various dimensions of modernization and stress among boys. Table showed a significant positive correlation of modernization with education (0.65), parents child relationships (0.72), politics (0.68), status of women (0.74), marriage (0.69), faith in God (0.71) and socio cultural factor (0.72) which was significant at 0.5 percent level of significance. A significant positive correlation of stress with finance (0.68), family (0.74), social (0.79), education (0.61), ego threats (0.35), bereavement (0.42), separation (0.58), personal setback (0.49), health of others (0.56) and total stress (0.46) was also found to be significant at 0.5 level of significance. Table showed a significant positive correlation between modernization and stress as the correlation was found to be 0.46 which denoted that both are positively correlated with each other as modernization level increases so does the stress levels.

The key elements of stress for young children were financial instability by developing a new social network, computer activities, online apps, separation from home, family involvement and less parental support, living with a roommate, working with friends or working part time and coping with the demands of young adults. These stressing factors are a result of a modern age that emphasizes the characteristics of individuality, economic freedom and creation of identities. **Pastey and Aminbhavi (2006)** said the boys appeared to be more stressful. **Laursen and Collins (1994)** also explained that strong association between stress and external behaviour, was shown by males. In the case of precipitation of external psychopathology, clinical studies have shown the impact of family and peer stress and rejection. Students in unfamiliar environments experience relative increased stress **Yumba (2008).**

Table 4.52 Correlation matrix between various dimensions of modernization and stress among girls

-	Edu	P C R	Pol	S W	Mar	F G	S C F	Total	Fin	Fam	Soc	Edu	Ego	Ber	Sep	P S	H O	Total
Edu	1	0.60*	0.48*	0.31*	0.34*	0.44*	0.35*	0.74*	0.27*	0.42*	0.19*	0.19*	0.18*	0.14NS	0.29*	0.29*	0.32*	0.36*
P C R		1	0.54*	0.33*	0.32*	0.31*	0.33*	0.71*	0.26*	0.35*	0.16*	0.39*	0.39*	0.29*	0.33*	0.29*	0.32*	0.22*
Pol			1	0.50*	0.41*	0.38*	0.32*	0.73*	0.29*	0.40*	0.35*	0.42*	0.28*	0.35*	0.45*	0.30*	0.29*	0.23*
S W				1	0.52*	0.36*	0.40*	0.68*	0.23*	0.43*	0.44*	0.28*	0.48*	0.39*	0.45*	0.39*	0.42*	0.23*
Mar					1	0.41*	0.31*	0.67*	0.21*	0.53*	0.49*	0.36*	0.44*	0.49*	0.50*	0.36*	0.49*	0.22*
F G						1	0.45*	0.70*	0.18*	0.20*	0.45*	0.29*	0.36*	0.51*	0.52*	0.26*	0.21*	0.26*
S C F							1	0.65*	0.35*	0.36*	0.33*	0.38*	0.39*	0.52*	0.39*	0.42*	0.28*	0.32*
Total Moder								1	0.47*	0.66*	0.72*	0.59*	0.62*	0.70*	0.78*	0.66*	0.54*	0.78*
Fin									1	0.26*	0.65*	0.25*	0.36*	0.26*	0.30*	0.22*	0.32*	0.53*
Fam										1	0.26*	0.03NS	0.21*	0.55*	0.31*	0.45*	0.12NS	0.50*
Soc											1	0.46*	0.24*	0.56*	0.21*	0.27*	0.16*	0.27*
Edu												1	0.19*	0.21*	0.36*	0.16 *	0.40*	0.64*
Ego													1	0.25*	0.51*	0.26*	0.29*	0.63*
Ber														1	0.28*	0.39*	0.39*	0.40*
Sep															1	0.09NS	0.28*	0.28*
P S																1	0.25*	0.47*
H O																	1	0.48*
Total Stress																		1

Table 4.52 indicates the correlation matrix between various dimensions of modernization and stress among the female respondents. Table highlights a significant positive correlation of modernization with education (0.74), parents child relationships (0.71), politics (0.73), status of women (0.68), marriage (0.67), faith in God (0.70) and socio cultural factor (0.65) which are significant at 0.5 level of significance. A significant positive correlation of stress with finance (0.47), family (0.66), social (0.72), education (0.59), ego threats (0.62), bereavement (0.70), separation (0.78), personal setback (0.66), health of others (0.54) and total stress (0.78) was also evident which significant at 0.5 level of significance. Table showed a significant positive correlation between modernization and stress as the correlation was found to be 0.78 which showed that both variables are positively correlated with each other, as modernization level increases so does the stress levels. Female students were overwhelming. They were more under pressure from the society and the cultural practices, beliefs, aspirations of the parents and marriage were under control. In general, girls are more susceptible to stress due to academic life and job aspects. With advance mechanization and telecommunication, they drop more tension. **Melinda *et al.*, (2008)** revealed that women students with a higher level of stress may include women as the caretaker of the family and as effective students.

urban adolescents.

Table 4.53 Correlation matrix between various dimensions of modernization and stress among the total sample

-	Edu	P C R	Pol	S W	Mar	F G	S C F	Total	Fin	Fam	Soc	Edu	Ego	Ber	Sep	P S	H O	Total
Edu	1	0.58*	0.49*	0.42*	0.36*	0.48*	0.45*	0.74*	0.47*	0.29*	0.44*	0.21*	0.20*	0.17*	0.43*	0.29*	0.33*	0.39*
P C R		1	0.52*	0.42*	0.44*	0.42*	0.45*	0.75*	0.45*	0.28*	0.48*	0.24*	0.27*	0.23*	0.36*	0.26*	0.29*	0.34*
Pol			1	0.48*	0.43*	0.43*	0.36*	0.72*	0.33*	0.36*	0.36*	0.29*	0.48*	0.41*	0.03NS	0.24*	0.21*	0.30*
S W				1	0.56*	0.50*	0.47*	0.74*	0.49*	0.35*	0.36*	0.39*	0.39*	0.35*	0.26*	0.29*	0.27*	0.38*
Mar					1	0.50*	0.41*	0.71*	0.44*	0.43*	0.47*	0.34*	0.35*	0.36*	0.37*	0.24*	0.21*	0.32*
F G						1	0.50*	0.76*	0.32*	0.38*	0.32*	0.20*	0.33*	0.31*	0.27*	0.21*	0.25*	0.34*
S C F							1	0.70*	0.27*	0.22*	0.21*	0.24*	0.17*	0.23*	0.22*	0.26*	0.24*	0.38*
Total Moder								1	0.52*	0.58*	0.45NS	0.54*	0.53*	0.71*	0.52*	0.55*	0.55*	0.48*
Fin									1	0.29*	0.01NS	0.39*	0.26*	0.42*	0.33*	0.30*	0.33*	0.11*
Fam										1	0.25*	0.42*	0.33*	0.44*	0.36*	0.26*	0.35*	0.39*
Soc											1	0.46*	0.27*	0.31*	0.42*	0.28*	0.32*	0.28*
Edu												1	0.29*	0.10NS	0.02NS	0.29*	0.08NS	0.69*
Ego													1	0.23*	0.28*	0.17*	0.1*5	0.49*
Ber														1	0.37*	0.19*	0.28*	0.38*
Sep															1	0.08NS	0.36*	0.55*
P S																1	0.21*	0.46*
H O																	1	0.43*
Total Stress																		1

Table 4.53 indicates the correlation matrix between various dimensions of modernization and stress among all respondents. Table reflects a significant positive correlation of modernization with education (0.74), parents child relationship (0.75), politics (0.72), status of women (0.74), marriage (0.71), faith in God (0.76) and socio cultural factor (0.70) which was significant at 0.5 level of significance. A significant positive correlation of stress with finance (0.52), family (0.58), social (0.45), education (0.54), ego threats (0.53), bereavement (0.71), separation (0.52), personal setback (0.55), health of others (0.55) and total stress (0.48) was also found to be significant at 0.5 level of significance. Table showed a significant positive correlation between modernization and stress as the correlation was found to be 0.48 which showed that both are positively correlated with each other, as modernization level increases so does the stress levels. The undergraduate students experienced highest stress levels due to the increased class workload, smart classes followed by the pressure of family, society and having many hours of studies, marriage and financial difficulties and occasionally stressed by computer related problems which are the manifestation of keeping in pace with the modern era. The gender difference exists only with regard to a handful stressor. Female students experience higher degree of stress than males due to the increased class work overload, having pressure for marriage, pressure of parent expectations, financial difficulties, fear of separation, lack of social support, lack of university support, missing some lectures, lack of vacations or breaks and health problems. The results of the study are in accordance with the study conducted by **Plans (2018)** which stated modernization and stress were positively connected to the student's academic success. **Dey *et al.* (2014)** also revealed that the stress was more than rural for urban teenagers. The stress of the young women was more pronounced than the men. Results also showed that depression in young people is positively linked to success and change around the world. The diverse tasks and expectations of university students face higher stress levels. Female students were also more vulnerable to higher stress, which was highly likely to impact the health and academic performance of students **Magill (2017).**

Table 4.54 Comparison of urban and rural boys and girls belonging to different socio economic groups based on financial stress before and after intervention

Socio economic group	Gender	Socio cultural setting	Intervention	Mean	SD	t-cal	p-value
Upper socio economic group (n=100)	Boys (n=50)	Urban (n=25)	Pre	24.24	4.49	4.542*	0.000
			Post	18.88	5.29		
		Rural (n=25)	Pre	25.44	5.14	3.664*	0.000
			Post	20.64	3.13		
	Girls (n=50)	Urban (n=25)	Pre	27.28	3.33	2.201*	0.032
			Post	25.60	5.72		
		Rural (n=25)	Pre	26.40	3.80	2.967*	0.004
			Post	22.88	4.18		
Middle socio economic group (n=100)	Boys (n=50)	Urban (n=25)	Pre	19.92	4.20	2.259*	0.028
			Post	17.12	4.42		
		Rural (n=25)	Pre	22.68	3.19	2.266*	0.027
			Post	20.96	5.74		
	Girls (n=50)	Urban (n=25)	Pre	25.96	3.27	2.583*	0.012
			Post	23.36	4.69		
		Rural (n=25)	Pre	25.40	3.62	2.817*	0.006
			Post	22.36	4.60		
Lower socio economic group (n=100)	Boys (n=50)	Urban (n=25)	Pre	19.24	2.99	0.721NS	0.787
			Post	18.32	4.84		
		Rural (n=25)	Pre	21.96	4.55	1.194NS	0.238
			Post	20.08	7.14		
	Girls (n=50)	Urban (n=25)	Pre	24.26	2.74	5.949*	0.000
			Post	18.25	4.58		
		Rural (n=25)	Pre	25.00	3.42	5.164*	0.000
			Post	19.24	4.81		

*Significant,

NS=Non-Significant,

n=Total

The above **table 4.54** highlights the comparison of financial stress among the respondents before and after intervention. The table clearly indicates that financial stress in reduces after the implementation of intervention program. Among the upper socio economic respondents it was seen that in case of urban boys the t calculated was 4.542 and p value 0.000 and among the rural boys the calculated is 3.664 and p value is 0.00 signifying that financial stress was significantly reduced after the implementation of the intervention program. Among girls also it is seen that those belonging to urban as well as rural cultural setting there is a marked reduction in their financial stress levels as the t calculated was 2.201, p was 0.032 and t calculated was 2.967 and p was 0.004 respectively which clearly indicated the efficacy of the intervention program in reducing the stress among girls belonging to upper socio economic status.

As far as respondents from middle socio economic groups were concerned it was seen that the intervention had a significant impact in reducing financial stress among both boys and girls from urban as well as rural cultural setting. The t calculated for urban boys was 2.259 ($p=0.028$) and for rural boys was 2.266 ($p=0.027$), the means values indicated a drop in the financial stress after intervention. In case of urban girls it was seen that the t calculated was 2.583 ($p=0.012$) and for rural girls was 2.817 ($p=0.006$), the means values indicated a drop in the financial stress after intervention proving the effectiveness of the intervention planned and implemented on the respondents.

Among the respondents belonging to lower socio economic group it was seen that among the boys of urban as well rural cultural background a non-significant difference in pre and post intervention existed with regard to level of financial stress, t calculated was 0.721 ($p=0.787$) for urban boys and t calculated was 1.194 ($p=0.238$) for rural boys. The mean values further indicated a decline in the level of stress among both the group although the difference was not significant. Among girls also a significant difference in the stress levels pre and post intervention was noticed wherein in case of urban girls it was seen that the t calculated was 5.949 ($p=0.000$) and for rural girls was 5.164 ($p=0.000$), the means values indicated a drop in the financial stress after intervention proving the effectiveness of the intervention planned and implemented on the respondents.

Most of the youngsters are overambitious they set up unrealistic goals for their own self. They want to attain those things in their life, which are not possible through their present financial status. Youngsters compare them self with their friends whose parents are financially well and feel inferior. If their friends carry cell phone then they also want to use cell phone even if they cannot afford it. When the parents show disapproval on this front then youngsters become aggressive. **Joo *et al.*, (2011)** reported that college students who have sought financial counseling from a university based service typically report high levels of financial stress as their reason for seeking services.

Students experience financial stress for a variety of reasons. As students generally have few savings, they do not have extra money to pay for extra expenses. Mostly parents do not give extra money for unexpected expenses. These are the main reason by which boys as well as girl respondents frequently experience financial stress. Financial worries affect their academic performance. Financially stressed students feel difficulties in buying new dress according to trend, canteen expenses, transport expenses, buying stationary, and expenses of cultural programme. Most of the students agree that financial stress affect negatively on their academic achievement and their friendship also. Same as **Eisenberg *et al.* (2007)** examined that students under financial stress are more likely to also suffer from depression, anxiety or suicidal thoughts. **Crocker & Luhtanen (2003)** also mentioned that financial difficulties among college students affect their self-esteem and even their physical appearance. Financial stress may also lead to lower academic performance.

Table 4.55 Comparison of urban and rural boys and girls belonging to different socio economic groups based on family stress before and after intervention

Socio economic group	Gender	Socio cultural setting	Intervention	Mean	SD	t-cal	p-value
Upper socio economic group (n=100)	Boys (n=50)	Urban (n=25)	Pre	40.60	7.44	5.621*	0.000
			Post	29.64	4.54		
		Rural (n=25)	Pre	34.32	9.28	2.470*	0.017
			Post	28.60	7.17		
	Girls (n=50)	Urban (n=25)	Pre	45.28	6.32	6.026*	0.000
			Post	32.76	8.99		
		Rural (n=25)	Pre	32.40	9.42	0.646NS	0.521
			Post	31.00	7.55		
Middle socio economic group (n=100)	Boys (n=50)	Urban (n=25)	Pre	39.76	8.53	6.794*	0.000
			Post	26.88	4.47		
		Rural (n=25)	Pre	41.64	6.80	4.730*	0.000
			Post	32.16	5.72		
	Girls (n=50)	Urban (n=25)	Pre	43.28	4.94	4.111*	0.000
			Post	35.16	7.66		
		Rural (n=25)	Pre	41.48	6.44	4.832*	0.000
			Post	31.84	8.63		
Lower socio economic group (n=100)	Boys (n=50)	Urban (n=25)	Pre	36.20	6.75	3.724*	0.000
			Post	29.76	4.81		
		Rural (n=25)	Pre	30.24	9.51	1.374NS	0.175
			Post	27.28	3.62		
	Girls (n=50)	Urban (n=25)	Pre	36.92	8.89	2.524*	0.014
			Post	31.00	7.21		
		Rural (n=25)	Pre	37.00	7.56	2.125*	0.038
			Post	33.12	3.59		

*Significant,

NS=Non-Significant,

n=Total

Table 4.55 highlights the family stress among respondents before and after intervention. The table shows that in case of respondents from the upper socio economic group a significant difference in family stress before and after intervention is evident among the boys belonging to urban as well as rural cultural setting as the t calculated for urban boys was 5.621 and p value was 0.000 and that for rural boys the calculated t was 2.470 and p value was 0.017 indicating a significant impact of intervention in reducing the family stress among the boys from upper socio economic strata of the society. Among girls also it is seen that those belonging to urban cultural setting there was a marked reduction in their family stress levels as the t calculated was 6.026, p was 0.000 which clearly indicated the efficacy of the intervention program in reducing the stress among urban girls belonging to upper socio economic status. In case of girls from rural families a non-significant difference was seen in family stress before and after intervention as the t calculated was 0.646 and p was 0.521, however, the mean values before intervention was 32.40 and after intervention was 31.00 indicating a slight, although non-significant reduction in family stress of the respondents of this group.

In case of respondents from middle socio economic groups it was seen that the intervention had a highly significant impact in reducing the family stress among both boys and girls from urban as well as rural cultural setting. The t calculated for urban boys was 6.794 (p=0.000) and for rural boys was 4.730 (p=0.000), the means values indicated a drop in the family stress after intervention. In case of urban girls it was seen that the t calculated was 4.111 (p=0.000) and for rural girls was 4.832 (p=0.000), the means values indicated a highly significant reduction in the family stress after intervention proving the effectiveness of the intervention.

Among the respondents belonging to lower socio economic group it was seen that among the boys of urban cultural background a significant difference in pre and post intervention existed with regard to level of family stress as the t calculated was 0.721 (p=0.787) and there existed a non-significant difference in the family stress levels before and after intervention among the rural boys from lower socio economic strata as the t calculated was 1.374 (p=0.175). The mean values further indicated a decline in the level of stress among both the group although the difference was not significant. Among girls also a significant difference in the stress levels pre and post intervention was noticed wherein in case of urban girls it was seen that the t calculated was 2.524 (p=0.014) and for rural girls was 2.125 (p=0.038), the means values indicated a drop in the family stress after intervention proving the effectiveness of the intervention program implemented on the respondents.

Anything that impacts family can affect adolescents like unrealistic expectations, marital problems among parents, strained sibling relationship, illness in the family and even financial stress in the family can spike up family stress among the growing children. The primary intervention for stress management includes preventing stress, removing the source of stress and enhancing a sense of well- being among the target group. The findings of the current research are consistent with the study conducted by **Regehr *et al.* (2013)** who reported that an eclectic approach can be used, as it seems that various lengths, components and strategies can be successful in reducing stress in students. Mindful training was also found to be an effective component of wellness and stress management.

Table 4.56 Comparison of urban and rural boys and girls belonging to different socio economic groups based on social stress before and after intervention

Socio economic group	Gender	Socio cultural setting	Intervention	Mean	SD	t-cal	p-value
Upper socio economic group (n=100)	Boys (n=50)	Urban (n=25)	Pre	24.40	2.94	5.354*	0.000
			Post	19.44	3.66		
		Rural (n=25)	Pre	18.40	4.76	2.900*	0.005
			Post	14.84	4.89		
	Girls (n=50)	Urban (n=25)	Pre	22.36	3.49	2.757*	0.008
			Post	19.48	4.19		
		Rural (n=25)	Pre	21.64	3.20	4.926*	0.000
			Post	17.40	4.41		
Middle socio economic group (n=100)	Boys (n=50)	Urban (n=25)	Pre	20.72	4.98	3.154*	0.002
			Post	16.44	4.63		
		Rural (n=25)	Pre	18.60	5.73	2.102*	0.040
			Post	15.88	4.79		
	Girls (n=50)	Urban (n=25)	Pre	21.08	3.36	2.064*	0.044
			Post	18.20	6.23		
		Rural (n=25)	Pre	20.32	3.03	3.310*	0.001
			Post	16.76	4.38		
Lower socio economic group (n=100)	Boys (n=50)	Urban (n=25)	Pre	21.80	3.90	2.427*	0.018
			Post	18.92	4.37		
		Rural (n=25)	Pre	23.04	4.23	5.912*	0.000
			Post	16.28	4.28		
	Girls (n=50)	Urban (n=25)	Pre	19.68	3.66	3.258*	0.002
			Post	15.24	5.07		
		Rural (n=25)	Pre	20.76	2.52	4.973*	0.000
			Post	15.80	4.52		

*Significant,

n=Total

Table 4.56 shows the social stress among respondents before and after intervention. The table depicts a significant difference in social stress before and after intervention in case of boys from the upper socio economic group among those belonging to urban as well as rural cultural setting, the t calculated for urban boys was 5.354 and p value was 0.000 and that for rural boys the calculated t was 2.900 and p value was 0.005 indicating a significant impact of intervention in reducing the social stress among the boys from upper socio economic strata. Among the girls also it was seen that those belonging to urban cultural setting there was a marked reduction in their social stress levels as the t calculated was 2.757, p value was 0.008 which clearly indicated the efficacy of the intervention program in reducing their stress. In case of girls from rural families also a significant difference was seen in the social stress before and after intervention as the t calculated was 4.926 and p was 0.000, however, the mean values before intervention of social stress was 21.64 and after intervention the stress levels were reduced showing the mean as 17.40 indicating a marked reduction in the social stress of the respondents of this group.

In case of respondents from middle socio economic groups it was seen that the intervention had a highly significant impact in reducing the social stress among both boys and girls from urban as well as rural cultural setting. The t calculated for urban boys was 3.154 (p=0.002) and for rural boys was 2.102 (p=0.040), the means values indicated a fall in the social stress after intervention. In case of urban girls it was seen that the t calculated was 2.064 (p=0.044) and for rural girls was 3.310 (p=0.001), the means values also indicated a drop in the social stress after intervention proving the effectiveness of the intervention.

Among the respondents belonging to lower socio economic group it was seen that the intervention had a significant impact in reducing the social stress among both boys and girls from urban as well as rural cultural background as a significant difference in pre and post intervention existed with regard to their level of social stress. The t calculated for urban boys from lower socio economic group was 2.427 (p=0.018) and among rural boys the t calculated was 5.912 (p=0.000) indicating that there existed a significant difference in the social stress levels before and after intervention depicting a decline in the level of stress among both the groups. Among girls also a significant difference in the stress levels pre and post intervention was noticed wherein in case of urban girls it was seen that the t calculated was 3.258 (p=0.002) and for rural girls was 4.973 (p=0.000) which indicated that social stress was drastically reduced after the implementation of the intervention program. Home and school are the centers of social problems. Most of the conflicting issues arise because of the fear of loss of friends, parents. They become entangled in the grip of insecurity. Most of the time they have this fear that if they are not able to meet expectations of their near and dear ones then he or she will lose them. The additional burden of general expectations of parents, friend's teachers etc. stress the youngster and when confronted with failure hurts their self-esteem.

Table 4.57 Comparison of urban and rural boys and girls belonging to different socio economic groups based on educational stress before and after intervention

Socio economic group	Gender	Socio cultural setting	Intervention	Mean	SD	t-cal	p-value
Upper socio economic group (n=100)	Boys (n=50)	Urban (n=25)	Pre	105.28	17.084	2.565*	0.013
			Post	92.76	15.619		
		Rural (n=25)	Pre	103.88	12.498	3.657*	0.000
			Post	86.64	20.108		
	Girls (n=50)	Urban (n=25)	Pre	116.20	14.216	2.951*	0.004
			Post	104.92	9.296		
		Rural (n=25)	Pre	113.92	11.669	3.996*	0.000
			Post	101.08	13.045		
Middle socio economic group (n=100)	Boys (n=50)	Urban (n=25)	Pre	107.16	18.402	3.114*	0.003
			Post	87.52	23.146		
		Rural (n=25)	Pre	97.08	20.339	0.177NS	0.860
			Post	96.120	13.448		
	Girls (n=50)	Urban (n=25)	Pre	113.16	12.351	2.156*	0.036
			Post	104.40	15.368		
		Rural (n=25)	Pre	109.36	10.165	3.347*	0.001
			Post	100.00	9.274		
Lower socio economic group (n=100)	Boys (n=50)	Urban (n=25)	Pre	91.72	16.841	2.666*	0.010
			Post	82.80	22.794		
		Rural (n=25)	Pre	104.76	25.115	3.283*	0.001
			Post	85.20	15.403		
	Girls (n=50)	Urban (n=25)	Pre	107.84	8.572	4.498*	0.000
			Post	91.440	17.640		
		Rural (n=25)	Pre	106.48	12.176	3.306*	0.001
			Post	92.64	21.099		

*Significant,

NS=Non-Significant,

n=Total

Table 4.57 highlights the comparison of educational stress among the respondents before and after intervention. The table clearly indicates that the prepared intervention package was able to reduce the educational stress among the respondents belonging to upper socio economic group. Among the urban boys from upper socio economic strata it was seen that the t calculated was 2.565 and p value was 0.013 and among the rural boys the calculated value of t was 3.657 and p value was 0.000 signifying that educational stress was significantly reduced after the implementation of the intervention program. In case of girls also it was seen that among those belonging to urban as well as rural cultural setting there was a marked reduction in their educational stress levels as the t calculated value before and after intervention was 2.951, p was 0.004 and t calculated was 3.996 and p was 0.000 respectively which clearly indicated a fall in the educational stress among the group after the implementation of the intervention thus proving its efficacy in lowering stress levels of the respondents.

As far as respondents from middle socio economic groups were concerned it was seen that the intervention had a significant impact in reducing the educational stress among urban boys as the t calculated value before and after intervention was 3.114 and p value was 0.003 symbolizing that educational stress is significantly reduced as the result of implementation of the intervention package. The t calculated for rural boys was 0.177 (p=0.860) which indicated a non-significant difference in the level of educational stress pre and post intervention, however the mean values were 97.08 before intervention and 96.12 after intervention which indicated a reduction in the educational stress level of rural boys from middle socio economic group although the change was not statistically significant. . In case of urban girls it was seen that the t calculated was 2.156 (p=0.036) and for rural girls was 3.347 (p=0.001) which clearly depicted a significant difference in the educational stress after intervention proving the effectiveness of the intervention planned and implemented on the respondents.

Among the respondents belonging to lower socio economic group it was seen that among the boys of urban as well rural cultural background a significant difference in pre and post intervention existed with regard to their level of educational stress as the t calculated was 2.666 (p=0.010) for urban boys and t calculated was 3.283 (p=0.001) for rural boys clearly showing the efficacy of the intervention program in lowering the educational stress among both the group of boys. Among girls also a significant difference in the stress levels pre and post intervention was noticed wherein in case of urban girls it was seen that the t calculated was 4.498 ($p=0.000$) and for rural girls was 3.306 ($p=0.001$), the means values indicated a drop in the education stress after intervention proving the effectiveness of the intervention implemented on the respondents.

Educational stress is the anxiety and stress that comes as a result of issues and practices related to education. There is often a lot of pressure that comes with pursuing a degree and student's education. There are homework, tests, labs, reading, and quizzes which increase educational stress. There is the stress of doing assignments, balancing the time and finding time for extra-curricular activities. Educational stress is especially hard on college students who are often living away from home for the first time. Most of the time students may underestimate the amount of time it takes to complete reading and writing assignments, to print out copies of their work. Similarly **Marwan (2013)** clarified that academic overloads, insufficient time to practice, workload, tests, low motivation levels and high family expectations among participants can cause high levels of stress. Low self-esteem was also investigated as the main source of stress among college going students. **Deb *et al.* (2014)** also explained a high level of educational stress for all students, although those with lower scores showed higher stress levels than those with top grades. Students who participated in extra-curricular activities were more likely than those who did not participate in extra-curricular activities to experience exam anxiety.

Table 4.58 Comparison of urban and rural boys and girls belonging to different socio economic groups based on ego threat before and after intervention

Socio economic group	Gender	Socio cultural setting	Intervention	Mean	SD	t-cal	p-value
Upper socio economic group (n=100)	Boys (n=50)	Urban (n=25)	Pre	44.04	10.052	4.204*	0.000
			Post	33.68	7.186		
		Rural (n=25)	Pre	44.40	8.251	5.966*	0.000
			Post	33.68	6.414		
	Girls (n=50)	Urban (n=25)	Pre	53.20	5.93	10.279*	0.000
			Post	36.84	7.17		
		Rural (n=25)	Pre	39.24	9.68	1.128NS	0.246
			Post	38.96	8.60		
Middle socio economic group (n=100)	Boys (n=50)	Urban (n=25)	Pre	51.84	5.289	10.814*	0.000
			Post	33.72	8.634		
		Rural (n=25)	Pre	41.52	4.908	3.076*	0.003
			Post	35.68	7.888		
	Girls (n=50)	Urban (n=25)	Pre	47.40	7.38	4.269*	0.000
			Post	32.56	14.20		
		Rural (n=25)	Pre	47.04	10.37	3.609*	0.000
			Post	37.40	6.40		
Lower socio economic group (n=100)	Boys (n=50)	Urban (n=25)	Pre	45.60	5.874	7.042*	0.000
			Post	32.44	6.813		
		Rural (n=25)	Pre	35.80	5.416	2.690*	0.009
			Post	31.08	13.38		
	Girls (n=50)	Urban (n=25)	Pre	42.44	5.62	5.077*	0.000
			Post	33.52	9.11		
		Rural (n=25)	Pre	39.00	6.14	2.871*	0.006
			Post	33.20	7.56		

*Significant,

NS=Non-Significant,

n=Total

Table 4.58 reveals the pre and post comparison of stress related to ego threat among the respondents. The table clearly marks a significant difference in the level of ego threat after the implementation of the intervention among almost all the respondents from upper, middle and lower socio economic group. Among the urban boys from upper socio economic strata a significant difference in ego threat stress, before and after implementation of intervention was evident as the t calculated was 4.204 and p value was 0.000 and in case of rural boys from the same strata the t calculated was 5.966 and p value was 0.000 depicting a significant impact of intervention in lowering the ego threat among the respondents. As far as girls of upper socio economic group belonging to urban cultural background were concerned a significant difference in ego threat stress, before and after implementation of intervention was evident as the t calculated was 10.279 and p value was 0.000 showing a significant influence of intervention in bringing about reduction in the ego threat stress. A non-significant difference in the ego threat stress before and after intervention was seen among rural girls (t=1.128, p=0.246) belonging to upper socio economic group; although the means values pre intervention was 39.24 which was reduced to 38.96 post intervention which shows that ego threat stress was slightly reduced after the intervention which was statistically non-significant. Anything that tends to diminish a person's opinion about himself or herself can be termed as an ego threat. Ego threat can be a threat to the self- esteem of a person which refers to the degree to which one feels acknowledged and appreciated by significant others.

The table also revealed a significant difference in the level of ego threat experienced before and after intervention among both boys and girls belonging to middle socio economic group irrespective of their socio cultural background. The t values for both urban (t=10.814, p=0.000) and rural boys (t= 3.076, p=0.003) from middle socio economic status revealed a significant difference in the ego threat before and after intervention, the mean values indicated de-escalated ego threat after the implementation of intervention package proving the efficacy of the intervention. Similarly among both rural (t=4.269, p=0.000) and urban girls (t=3.609, p=0.000) also a significant difference in the ego threat before and after intervention was noted wherein a significant drop in the ego threat was seen after the implementation of the intervention package.

The table also reports a significant difference in the level of ego threat experienced before and after intervention among both boys and girls belonging to lower socio economic status irrespective of their socio cultural background. The t values for both urban (t=7.042, p=0.000) and rural boys (t= 2.690, p=0.009) from lower socio economic status revealed a significant difference in the ego threat before and after intervention, the mean values indicated a drop in the ego threat after the implementation of intervention package proving the efficacy of the intervention. Similarly among the both rural (t=5.077, p=0.000) and urban girls (t=2.871, p=0.006) also a significant difference in the ego threat before and after intervention was noted wherein a significantly lowered ego threat was seen after the implementation of the intervention package.

Most contemporary research conceptualizes ego threat as a threat to a person's self-image or self-esteem, but experimental operationalization of ego threat usually confound threats to self-esteem with threats to public image or decreased control over negative events, leading to an inability to distinguish the effects of threats to people's personal egos from threats to public image or threats to feelings of control. Forgiving oneself may be assumed to culminate in enhanced self-esteem and this, in turn, may play a significant role in shaping and predicting various dimensions of a person's wellbeing. It has been argued that individuals with a threat to self-esteem have a higher need for self-protection that can be compensated through increased self-forgiveness. **Elzohary *et al.* (2017)** also revealed that ego threats develop the negative relationship between academic stress and anxiety. Increased level of Ego threats increases the degree of perceived stress among college students and it was negatively associated with their life satisfaction.

Table 4.59 Comparison of urban and rural boys and girls belonging to different socio economic groups based on stress bereavement stress before and after intervention

Socio economic group	Gender	Socio cultural setting	Intervention	Mean	SD	t-cal	p-value
Upper socio economic group (n=100)	Boys (n=50)	Urban (n=25)	Pre	22.80	3.59	5.139*	0.000
			Post	18.28	4.00		
		Rural (n=25)	Pre	22.08	3.08	2.121*	0.039
			Post	20.60	2.53		
	Girls (n=50)	Urban (n=25)	Pre	22.92	3.05	5.705*	0.000
			Post	16.56	4.83		
		Rural (n=25)	Pre	25.12	19.80	2.414*	0.019
			Post	15.00	4.17		
Middle socio economic group (n=100)	Boys (n=50)	Urban (n=25)	Pre	20.80	5.13	3.715*	0.000
			Post	15.24	5.10		
		Rural (n=25)	Pre	20.96	4.72	3.503*	0.000
			Post	17.00	3.18		
	Girls (n=50)	Urban (n=25)	Pre	20.24	2.84	2.675*	0.010
			Post	17.48	4.18		
		Rural (n=25)	Pre	21.36	3.29	2.974*	0.004
			Post	18.48	4.19		
Lower socio economic group (n=100)	Boys (n=50)	Urban (n=25)	Pre	21.56	3.39	2.186*	0.033
			Post	18.84	4.10		
		Rural (n=25)	Pre	21.24	5.07	2.876*	0.005
			Post	17.64	2.66		
	Girls (n=50)	Urban (n=25)	Pre	19.24	2.81	3.708*	0.000
			Post	15.12	4.21		
		Rural (n=25)	Pre	20.68	2.81	4.184*	0.000
			Post	15.04	3.76		

*Significant,

n=Total

Table 4.59 highlights the comparative analysis of bereavement stress among rural and urban boys and girls belonging to different socio economic status. Among the urban boys from upper socio economic strata a significant difference in bereavement stress, before and after implementation of intervention was evident as the t calculated was 5.139 and p value was 0.000 and in case of rural boys from the same strata the t calculated was 2.121 and p value was 0.039 depicting a significant impact of intervention in lowering the bereavement stress among the respondents. As far as girls of upper socio economic group belonging to urban cultural background were concerned a significant difference in bereavement stress, before and after implementation of intervention was evident as the t calculated was 5.705 and p value was 0.000 and in case of rural girls the t calculated was 2.414 and p value was 0.019 showing a significant influence of intervention in reducing the bereavement stress among the female respondents belonging to upper socio economic group.

The table also revealed a significant difference in the level bereavement stress experienced before and after intervention among both boys and girls belonging to middle socio economic group irrespective of their socio cultural background. The t values for both urban (t=3.715, p=0.000) and rural boys (t= 3.503, p=0.000) from middle socio economic status revealed a significant difference in the bereavement stress before and after intervention, the mean values indicated de-escalated bereavement stress after the implementation of intervention package proving the efficacy of the intervention. Similarly among both rural (t=2.675, p=0.010) and urban girls (t=2.974, p=0.004) also a significant difference in the bereavement stress before and after intervention was noted wherein a significant drop in the bereavement stress was seen after the implementation of the intervention package.

Among the respondents belonging to lower socio economic group it was seen that among the boys of urban as well as rural cultural background a significant difference in pre and post intervention existed with regard to their level of bereavement stress as the t calculated was 2.186 (p=0.033) for urban boys and t calculated was 2.876 (p=0.005) for rural boys, clearly showing the efficacy of the intervention program in lowering the bereavement stress among both the group of boys. Among girls also a significant difference in the stress levels pre and post intervention was noticed wherein in case of urban girls it was seen that the t calculated was 3.708 (p=0.000) and for rural girls was 4.184 (p=0.000), the means values indicated a drop in the bereavement stress after intervention, proving the effectiveness of the intervention implemented on the respondents.

Bereavement stress is experienced after the death of a loved one. Many people will find that after the death of their loved one they have to adjust to a life that looks nothing like it used to. Experiences like trauma, loss, and grief can evoke new and intense emotions that people often feel ill-equipped to deal with. Part of what makes something stressful is an individual's belief that they lack the resources to cope with it. Internal conflict is also a common source of stress. Research shows that most people can recover from loss on their own through the passage of time if they have social support and healthy habits. Human beings are naturally resilient, considering most of us can endure loss and then continue on with our own lives. But some people may struggle with grief for longer periods of time and feel unable to carry out daily activities. Those with severe grief may be experiencing complicated grief. Researches prove that these individuals could benefit from the help of a psychologist or another licensed mental health professional with a specialization in grief.

Bereavement stress affect the social relationships, academic performance, productivity, emotional responses, psychosomatic responses, persistent thoughts of the deceased, affects the self-image, confidence, and maturity. Thoughtful intervention can be successful in reducing the bereavement stress. **Stroebe (1998)** indicated that women are more distressed by bereavement than men. Distressed rates of women compared to men were high. **Shear (2011)** also analyzed that bereavement is a severe stressor that typically incites painful and debilitating symptoms of acute grief. The stress caused by bereavement, like other stressors, can increase the likelihood of onset or worsening of other physical or mental disorders.

Table 4.60 Comparison of urban and rural boys and girls belonging to different socio economic groups based on separation stress before and after intervention

Socio economic group	Gender	Socio cultural setting	Intervention	Mean	SD	t-cal	p-value
Upper socio economic group (n=100)	Boys (n=50)	Urban (n=25)	Pre	15.00	4.23	0.728NS	0.470
			Post	12.12	20.76		
		Rural (n=25)	Pre	16.56	4.83	2.414*	0.019
			Post	14.00	3.76		
	Girls (n=50)	Urban (n=25)	Pre	17.90	3.97	2.672*	0.010
			Post	13.89	4.93		
		Rural (n=25)	Pre	16.47	4.46	3.901*	0.000
			Post	12.79	3.90		
Middle socio economic group (n=100)	Boys (n=50)	Urban (n=25)	Pre	17.04	2.16	7.119*	0.000
			Post	12.48	3.15		
		Rural (n=25)	Pre	17.24	3.81	2.675*	0.010
			Post	15.12	4.21		
	Girls (n=50)	Urban (n=25)	Pre	15.21	4.41	5.367*	0.000
			Post	11.56	2.89		
		Rural (n=25)	Pre	16.45	3.98	2.781*	0.007
			Post	14.78	3.01		
Lower socio economic group (n=100)	Boys (n=50)	Urban (n=25)	Pre	15.72	3.19	2.436*	0.018
			Post	12.60	4.23		
		Rural (n=25)	Pre	14.81	2.90	3.458*	0.001
			Post	11.76	4.73		
	Girls (n=50)	Urban (n=25)	Pre	15.23	4.91	3.048*	0.000
			Post	12.90	2.98		
		Rural (n=25)	Pre	16.40	5.91	2.891*	0.005
			Post	13.81	3.98		

*Significant,

NS=Non Significant,

n=Total

Table 4.60 shows the comparison of separation stress experienced by the respondents before and after intervention. Among the urban boys belonging to upper socio economic group a non-significant difference in the separation stress pre and post intervention was observed signifying that the intervention did not bring significant reduction in separation stress as the t calculated was 0.728 and p value was 0.470. the mean value further depicted a reduction in the separation stress post intervention as the mean values for stress before intervention was 15.00 and after intervention it was reduced to 12.12, however the difference was not statistically significant. Among the rural boys from upper socio economic strata a significant difference in separation stress, before and after implementation of intervention was evident as the t calculated was 2.414 and p value was 0.019 depicting a significant impact of intervention in lowering the separation stress among the respondents. As far as girls of upper socio economic group belonging to urban cultural background were concerned a significant difference in the separation stress, before and after implementation of intervention was evident as the t calculated was 2.672 and p value was 0.010 and in case of rural girls the t calculated was 3.901 and p value was 0.010 showing a significant influence of intervention in reducing the separation stress among the female respondents belonging to the upper socio economic group.

In case of respondents from middle socio economic groups it was seen that the intervention had a highly significant impact in reducing the separation stress among both boys and girls from urban as well as rural cultural setting. The t calculated for urban boys was 7.119 (p=0.000) and for rural boys was 2.675 (p=0.010), the means values indicated a drop in the separation stress after intervention. In case of urban girls it was seen that the t calculated was 5.367 (p=0.000) and for rural girls was 2.781 (p=0.007) which indicated a highly significant difference in the separation stress after intervention proving the effectiveness of the intervention.

Among the respondents belonging to lower socio economic group it was seen that among the boys of urban cultural background a significant difference in pre and post intervention existed with regard to level of separation stress as the t calculated was 2.46 (p=0.018) and there also existed significant difference in the separation stress levels before and after intervention among the rural boys from lower socio economic strata as the t calculated was 3.458 (p=0.001). The mean values further indicated a decline in the level of stress among both the group. Among girls also a significant difference in the stress levels pre and post intervention was noticed wherein in case of urban girls it was seen that the t calculated was 3.048 (p=0.000) and for rural girls was 2.891 (p=0.005), the means values indicated a drop in the separation stress after intervention proving the effectiveness of the intervention program implemented on the respondents.

College life can be stressful as separation from home is a source of stress **Rai (2016).** A significant relationship is seen between separation and academic performance among students. Separation was associated with a decrease in student's levels of motivation, their cognitive development, and academic achievement, social and emotional development. It was recommended that teachers, counselors, psychologist, social workers should identify students from divorced families and provide them counseling and the separated parents should also counsel regarding family and social needs of their children so that their academic performance will not suffer at college. **Amato *et al.* (2010)** also found that separation is associated with poor psychological well-being, student achievements and social relationships.

Table 4.61 Comparison of urban and rural boys and girls belonging to different socio economic groups based on personal setback stress before and after intervention

Socio economic group	Gender	Socio cultural setting	Intervention	Mean	SD	t-cal	p-value
Upper socio economic group (n=100)	Boys (n=50)	Urban (n=25)	Pre	40.20	5.20	7.900*	0.000
			Post	28.96	6.30		
		Rural (n=25)	Pre	39.41	9.69	3.871*	0.000
			Post	30.21	7.76		
	Girls (n=50)	Urban (n=25)	Pre	37.04	6.17	4.901*	0.000
			Post	33.45	4.90		
		Rural (n=25)	Pre	34.44	3.92	4.201*	0.000
			Post	28.56	3.10		
Middle socio economic group (n=100)	Boys (n=50)	Urban (n=25)	Pre	32.32	11.23	4.735*	0.000
			Post	19.68	7.39		
		Rural (n=25)	Pre	33.52	5.10	4.321*	0.000
			Post	23.81	4.98		
	Girls (n=50)	Urban (n=25)	Pre	37.64	2.79	3.321*	0.001
			Post	23.78	4.89		
		Rural (n=25)	Pre	33.88	3.80	3.001*	0.004
			Post	27.49	2.97		
Lower socio economic group (n=100)	Boys (n=50)	Urban (n=25)	Pre	33.64	5.42	4.937*	0.000
			Post	25.89	5.89		
		Rural (n=25)	Pre	37.40	6.40	5.659*	0.000
			Post	33.84	5.90		
	Girls (n=50)	Urban (n=25)	Pre	35.40	3.76	3.839*	0.000
			Post	22.38	2.82		
		Rural (n=25)	Pre	33.51	3.90	1.980NS	0.533
			Post	31.32	4.05		

*Significant,

NS=Non Significant,

n=Total

Table 4.61 depicts the comparison of personal setback stress experienced by the respondents before and after intervention. Table clearly highlights that among the respondents belonging to upper as well as middle socio economic group the personal set back stress is significantly reduced after the implementation of the intervention package. Among the rural as well as urban boys from upper socio economic strata a significant difference in pre and post intervention it was observed as the t calculated for urban boys was 7.900 and p value was 0.000, for rural boys the t calculated was 3.871 and p value was 0.000 showing a significant difference in the stress levels after intervention. As far as girls of upper socio economic group belonging to urban cultural background were concerned a significant difference in the person set back stress, before and after implementation of intervention was evident as the t calculated was 4.901 and p value was 0.010 and in case of rural girls the t calculated was 4.201 and p value was 0.010 showing a significant influence of intervention in reducing the personal set back stress among the female respondents as well belonging to the upper socio economic group.

Among the respondents belonging to middle socio economic group it was seen that among the boys of urban cultural background a significant difference in pre and post intervention existed with regard to level of personal set back stress as the t calculated was 4.735 (p=0.000) and there also existed significant difference in the personal set back stress levels before and after intervention among the rural boys from lower socio economic strata as the t calculated was 4.321 (p=0.000). The mean values further indicated a decline in the level of stress among both the groups. Among girls also a significant difference in the stress levels pre and post intervention was noticed wherein in case of urban girls it was seen that the t calculated was 3.321 (p=0.001) and for rural girls was 3.001 (p=0.004), the means values indicated a drop in the personal set back stress after intervention proving the effectiveness of the intervention program implemented on the respondents.

In case of respondents from lower socio economic groups it was seen that the intervention had a highly significant impact in reducing the personal set back stress among boys from urban as well as rural cultural setting. The t calculated for urban boys was 4.937 (p=0.000) and for rural boys was 5.659 (p=0.010), the means values indicated a drop in the personal set back stress after intervention. In case of urban girls it was seen that the t calculated was 3.839 (p=0.000) which indicated a significant difference in pre and post intervention. Among the rural girls from the lower socio economic strata a non-significant difference in the person set back stress was observed before and after intervention as the t calculated was 1.980 and p value was 0.533 indicating that the intervention was not able to lower the personal set back stress significantly among the rural girls belong to lower socio economic strata.

Table identified that the intervention positively reduce the stress level among all respondents from both socio cultural settings. Personal setback stress among college students can be due to diverse reasons like modernization, different educational system, transformation in societal actions, roommate disagreement, relationship with opposite gender, thinking about future plans, fear of failure, struggle to create uniqueness, sleeping habits, eating practice, speaking in public, financial problems, demise of family member, inferiority, injury, disagreement with parents, working with new set of people, understanding new friends and adoption of a new environment. **Vidya *et al.*, (2018)** also examined that stress was associated with personal problems, sleep disturbance and difficulty in time management among college going students.

Much of the ability to succeed comes from the way one deals with life and manages stress. One needs to recognize the inevitability of temporary disappointments and defeats and accept them as normal and a natural part of life. When one faces problems in life he needs to act with a positive attitude, learn from set-backs and keep moving forward in the direction of his goals. These aspects of stress management were dealt with in the prepared intervention package which proved to be beneficial in reducing the personal set back stress among the respondents.

Table 4.62 Comparison of urban and rural boys and girls belonging to different socio economic groups based on stress regarding health of others before and after intervention

Socio economic group	Gender	Socio cultural setting	Intervention	Mean	SD	t-cal	p-value
Upper socio economic group (n=100)	Boys (n=50)	Urban (n=25)	Pre	24.16	4.23	2.312*	0.025
			Post	20.08	3.12		
		Rural (n=25)	Pre	19.72	3.02	1.989NS	0.052
			Post	18.90	3.00		
	Girls (n=50)	Urban (n=25)	Pre	26.96	4.15	3.890*	0.000
			Post	21.96	4.55		
		Rural (n=25)	Pre	23.52	3.80	3.664*	0.000
			Post	18.88	5.28		
Middle socio economic group (n=100)	Boys (n=50)	Urban (n=25)	Pre	19.36	5.88	2.266*	0.027
			Post	17.12	4.42		
		Rural (n=25)	Pre	20.04	3.08	3.664*	0.000
			Post	18.33	4.85		
	Girls (n=50)	Urban (n=25)	Pre	22.48	3.25	2.259*	0.028
			Post	19.93	4.21		
		Rural (n=25)	Pre	20.76	2.00	2.903*	0.005
			Post	17.98	3.92		
Lower socio economic group (n=100)	Boys (n=50)	Urban (n=25)	Pre	23.64	2.73	2.259*	0.028
			Post	17.12	4.42		
		Rural (n=25)	Pre	20.64	4.47	5.673*	0.000
			Post	15.89	2.89		
	Girls (n=50)	Urban (n=25)	Pre	22.04	3.72	4.872*	0.000
			Post	15.67	4.93		
		Rural (n=25)	Pre	17.88	4.83	3.334*	0.001
			Post	14.36	5.63		

Significant,
NS=Non Significant,
n=Total

Table 4.62 highlights the comparison of stress regarding health of others among respondents before and after intervention. Among the urban boys belonging to upper socio economic group a significant difference in the pre and post intervention regarding health of other was evident as the t calculated was 2.312 and the p value was 0.025, the mean values showed a reduction in the stress regarding health of others which proved the efficacy of the intervention program. A non-significant difference in the stress was seen before and after intervention in case of rural boys belonging to upper socio economic strata. The t calculated was 1.989 and p value was 0.052 indicating that the implemented intervention did not significantly reduce the level of stress regarding health of others among the rural boys. Among girls it is seen that those belonging to urban as well as rural cultural setting there was a marked reduction in their stress regarding health of others as the t calculated was 3.890 and p value was 0.000 and t calculated was 3.664 and p was 0.000 respectively which clearly indicated the efficacy of the intervention program in reducing the stress among girls belonging to upper socio economic status.

As far as respondents from middle socio economic groups were concerned it was seen that the intervention had a significant impact in reducing stress regarding health of other among both boys and girls from urban as well as rural cultural setting. The t calculated for urban boys was 2.266 (p=0.027) and for rural boys was 3.664 (p=0.000), the means values indicated a drop in the stress after intervention. In case of urban girls it was seen that the t calculated was 2.259 (p=0.028) and for rural girls was 2.903 (p=0.005), the means values indicated a drop in the stress regarding health of others after intervention proving the effectiveness of the intervention planned and implemented on the respondents.

Among the respondents belonging to lower socio economic group it was seen that among the boys of urban as well rural cultural background a significant difference in pre and post intervention existed with regard to level of stress regarding health of others, t calculated was 2.259 (p=0.028) for urban boys and t calculated was 5.673 (p=0.000) for rural boys. The mean values further indicated a decline in the level of stress among both the group after the implementation of the intervention. Among girls also a significant difference in the stress levels pre and post intervention was noticed wherein in case of urban girls it was seen that the t calculated was 4.872 (p=0.000) and for rural girls was 3.334 (p=0.001), the means values indicated a drop in the stress regarding health of others after intervention proving the effectiveness of the intervention planned and implemented on the respondents.

It's common to experience anxiety over a loved one's health. When a loved one is facing health problems, most people experience some degree of worry and fear about whether a loved one will be okay. Concerns regarding health can be stressful. When anxious thoughts run amok, they feed on each other and grow large. It's natural to play the "what-if" game, wondering what will happen to our loved ones. Anxiety is a weed in our garden choking out all other thoughts and feelings and taking over what we think, what we feel, and what we do. Rather than being fully present with the loved one who needs us, we're lost in anxiety. Some anxiety naturally occurs because we care about someone. Letting it take over our physical and mental wellbeing isn't helpful to anyone. Intervention took care of counselling the respondents so as to lower their stress and anxiety in the aspect of health which proved to be beneficial in lowering the stress among the respondents. **Bernstein *et al.* (2008)** found that a negative social, emotional, cognitive, behavioural and physiological process that occurs with health stressors.

Kaur (2014) revealed significant differences among adolescents for the reason of health which increasing their academic stress. Girl students with high level of academic stress had poor health status than their counter part.

Table 4.63 Comparison of stress among boys and girls in various socio-economic classes before and after intervention

Socio economic group	Gender	Intervention	n=300		t-cal	p-value
			Mean	SD		
Upper socio economic group (n=100)	Boys (n=50)	Pre	328.22	26.46	6.982*	0.000
		Post	289.98	20.34		
	Girls (n=50)	Pre	346.10	28.27	7.328*	0.000
		Post	319.67	25.20		
Middle socio economic group (n=100)	Boys (n=50)	Pre	314.10	28.43	5.421*	0.000
		Post	267.29	30.59		
	Girls (n=50)	Pre	332.20	21.12	7.278*	0.000
		Post	281.65	16.97		
Lower socio economic group (n=100)	Boys (n=50)	Pre	302.54	27.60	5.891*	0.000
		Post	231.78	19.76		
	Girls (n=50)	Pre	310.08	16.50	5.980*	0.000
		Post	249.62	17.42		

*Significant,

n=Total

Table 4.63 indicates the comparison of stress among total boys and girls before and after intervention. The table highlights a significant difference in the stress level among both boys and girls belonging to upper socio economic group. The t calculated for boys from upper socio economic group before and after intervention was 2.982 and p value was 0.000 and for girls the t calculated was 7.328 and p value was 0.000 indicating a significant difference in the stress levels of respondents after the implementation of intervention program.

Among the respondents from middle socio economic group also a significant difference in the level of stress was observed after intervention both among the boys as well as girls. The calculated value of t for boys from middle socio economic group was 5.421 and p value was 0.000 and for girls from the same socio economic background was 7.278 indicating a significant difference in the stress level before and after intervention which proved the efficacy of the intervention program.

In case of respondents from lower socio economic group also a similar trend was observed as with the case of respondents from upper and middle socio economic group. A significant difference in the stress levels of both boys and girls was brought about with the help of intervention program. In case of boys the t calculated was 5.891 and p value was 0.000 and for girls the t was 5.980 and p value was 0.000 which indicated a significantly high difference in the stress before and after attending the intervention program. The mean values further clarified that stress level were drastically reduced as a result of intervention.

Majority of the adolescent undergo stress, whatever the sources may be internal or external it hampers the major functioning of the body. Most of the youngsters face multiple problems in their life. Each individual has to cope with different kinds of pressure laid down by the society and family. On the verge of coping with these pressures, an individual himself unconsciously frames a net and is caught in the same. Most of the youngsters confront parent's expectation, sibling's rivalry, status issues and financial issues in which some problems are actually genuine and some are self-created. Youngsters need to reduce their level of expectations. These people build unreasonable expectation from their life. Most of the students are pseudo they keep their own self in a rosy world and when they are confronted with the actual situation, they are unable to handle and thus it throws them to a stressful situation. Mindful counselling, engaging in fruitful activities, practicing yoga and meditation and understanding that problems and challenges are a part of growing up will help in lower the stress levels and increase the efficiency and coping mechanism of the adolescents. **Recabarren *et al.* (2019)** studied the short term effects of a multidimensional stress prevention program and the results indicated a significant reduction of psychological symptoms, including anxiety, interpersonal problems and symptoms of pain; a significant increase in quality of life, sense of coherence, and self-compassion in students who participated in the intervention program compared to the control group ($p<0.05$).

Table 4.64 Socio cultural differences among boys and girls with regarding to stress before and after intervention

Socio cultural setting	Gender	Intervention	Mean	SD	t-cal	p-value
Urban (n=150)	Boys (n=75)	Pre	326.45	27.46	8.903*	0.000
		Post	261.80	19.36		
	Girls (n=75)	Pre	342.24	30.06	9.328*	0.000
		Post	271.78	28.90		
Rural (n=150)	Boys (n=75)	Pre	303.45	26.54	7.569*	0.000
		Post	229.39	20.83		
	Girls (n=75)	Pre	319.21	18.20	8.438	0.000
		Post	245.70	23.49		

*Significant,

n=Total

Table 4.64 depicts the stress level of rural and urban boys and girls before and after intervention. A glance at the table reveals that there was a significant difference in the stress levels of both urban boy and girls before and after intervention as the calculated value of t for urban boys was 8.903 and p value was 0.000 and for urban girls the t value was 9.328 and p value was 0.000 indicating a significant difference in the pre and post level stress of the respondents. The mean values clarified that the intervention successfully lowered the stress levels of the urban respondents.

Among the rural respondents also similar results were obtained wherein stress levels were significantly reduced after the implementation of intervention program the calculated value of t for rural boys was 7.569 and p value was 0.000 whereas for rural girls the t calculated was 8.438 and p value was 0.000 indicating a significant difference in the stress level of respondents before and after intervention. The means values depicted a drastic reduction in the stress level of respondents after intervention proving the efficacy of the intervention. Various relaxation techniques, development of hobbies, group and individual counseling can play an important role in lowering the stress levels of people. Relaxation techniques are based on the assumption that states of relaxation and stress (i.e., highly aroused negative states of well-being such as anxiety, tension and anger) are antithetical **(Russell, 1979)**. In other words, you cannot be both relaxed and stressed at the same time, such that increasing levels of relaxation will necessarily entail lower levels of stress. Meditation is another relaxation technique but one that focuses on a mental rather than physical process. Techniques typically involve sitting in a quiet place and repeating a word or sound while maintaining a passive mental state that excludes intrusive thoughts. Although meditation has its roots in religious practice, secular and standardized methods appropriate for clinical trials have been developed **(Carrington *et al.*, 1980)** thus indicating that Stress management interventions can improve subjective psychological well-being.

CPSIA information can be obtained
at www.ICGtesting.com
Printed in the USA
LVHW021430011222
734355LV00016B/881

9 781805 459811